T0243456

The Art of
SMALL
BUSINESS
SOCIAL
MEDIA

The Art of SMALL BUSINESS SOCIAL MEDIA

A Blueprint for Marketing Success

PEG FITZPATRICK
Foreword by Guy Kawasaki

ROWMAN & LITTLEFIELD
Lanham • Boulder • New York • London

Published by Rowman & Littlefield
An imprint of The Rowman & Littlefield Publishing Group, Inc.
4501 Forbes Boulevard, Suite 200, Lanham, Maryland 20706
www.rowman.com

86-90 Paul Street, London EC2A 4NE

Distributed by NATIONAL BOOK NETWORK

British Library Cataloguing in Publication Information Available

Library of Congress Cataloging-in-Publication Data Available

ISBN 978-1-5381-9299-3 (cloth)
ISBN 978-1-5381 9300 6 (electronic)

♾️™ The paper used in this publication meets the minimum requirements of
American National Standard for Information Sciences—Permanence of Paper
for Printed Library Materials, ANSI/NISO Z39.48-1992.

This is dedicated to small business owners everywhere.
You're the heart of our communities.

Contents

An idea, like a ghost, must be spoken to a little before it will explain itself.

—*Charles Dickens*

Acknowledgements

I want to express my deepest gratitude to a few people without whom this book would not have been possible.

First and foremost, I am immensely thankful to my agent, Cole Lanahan, and the Seymour Agency for their unwavering support, encouragement, and belief in me throughout this journey.

I am indebted to Rowman & Littlefield and my editor, Jacquie Flynn, for their generous assistance and belief in the book, which have helped bring this project to fruition. Victoria Shi for your attention to details. To Linda Kessler for handling production details and Christy Phillippe for polishing her to a gem; Amanda Wilson for an eye-catching cover—although we may not have met in person it meant so much to me. Thank you to all the people behind the scenes at Rowman & Littlefield—we accomplished this together!

Thank you to my first editor, Mikaela Pederson, and my second editor, Jonathan Sperling, who was at McGraw Hill Business, where this book first had a home. I appreciated both of your thoughtful edits.

A special appreciation to Michelle Glogovac and the MLG Collective for their PR support and for being great listeners.

I am grateful to Jeff Sieh and Guy Kawasaki for their feedback and constructive criticism, which have greatly enriched the content of this book. Guy, thank you for showing me the writing and publishing ropes on *The Art of Social Media.*

Thank you to my family and friends for their patience, understanding, and encouragement during the countless hours spent writing and revising. Especially my dear friend Sandra Sallin and my favorite (and only) sister, Janet Beyo. Tricia Hurley at Cup of Life Healing for your listening and care. Your support means the world to me.

The biggest thank-you goes to my husband, Richard, who listened to me talk about this project for years and made me dinner every night. I am profoundly grateful for you. xo

To all the readers and social media friends who have inspired me, thank you for your years of ongoing support and encouragement. If you've been reading my blog for years, pinning my pins on Pinterest, or chatting with me in Instagram DMs, thank you! If you bought this book, *thank you*! Thank you in advance for you book reviews—they mean so much.

To librarians, I love you! Where would we be without great book recommendations and library resources?

Lastly, I acknowledge the countless authors and creators whose work influenced and inspired me.

Thank you to everyone who has contributed to making this book a reality. Your contributions have not gone unnoticed, and I sincerely appreciate your kindness and generosity.

Foreword

Hey, Entrepreneurs and Small Business Owners!

Maybe you've heard of a book called *The Art of Social Media: Power Tips for Power Users*, which the remarkable Peg Fitzpatrick and I wrote.

In its time, it was the required reading for anyone who wanted to rock social media.

Working with Peg over the past decade has been an incredible journey. We've done massive social campaigns for my Remarkable People podcast, and she even worked with me at Canva to help it rocket to the top.

With her firsthand social media experience, Peg's insights are game-changing, and now she's back with a tactical and practical book to enable you succeed in these wild and crazy times. Instead of power tips for power users, it's got down-and-dirty ways for you to increase $ales.

Remember: sales fixes everything.

Take it from me, if you're an entrepreneur or small business owner and want to master digital marketing, you need this book.

Guy Kawasaki

Preface

To be conscious that you are ignorant of the facts is a great step to knowledge.

—*Benjamin Disraeli*

After completing *The Art of Social Media: Power Tips for Power Users*, I began working on promoting the book through interviews and had hundreds of conversations about how to use social media with readers best. What I found was that although people learned a lot from *The Art of Social Media*, small business owners and entrepreneurs needed more hands-on help. I'm writing to help you, the small business owner, master the art of social media marketing for your business and jump into the changing sea of digital marketing.

For years, small business owners have been watching from the sidelines as big brands like Coca-Cola and Starbucks dominate social media while they waited to see if it was a good idea. Marketing has been moving from traditional marketing with flyers and mailers to tweets on X and Facebook posts. It's time to stop waiting to see if Facebook will work out—six billion people say yes, Facebook is a thing.

My goal with *The Art of Small Business Social Media* is for you to implement social media marketing for your small business and learn to communicate in the modern language of the online world to reach more people and make more money. It won't be nearly as painful or scary as you've imagined that it might be. I've tested every single tool and recommendation in this book to bring you solid social media advice for your small business.

Are you ready to get started?

READ THIS FIRST

The golden age is before us, not behind us.

—*William Shakespeare*

Welcome to the beginning of a journey that will unfold layer by layer, equipping you with the knowledge you need to harness the full potential of social media for your small business. Don't let the breadth of information overwhelm you; we will tackle this one piece at a time, building your understanding and skills progressively as you turn each page.

I wrote this book to guide you from the ground up, starting with the foundations of social media and building up to the strategies to make your business shine online. Here's some tough love, though: marketing is not optional. It's the pulse of your business's visibility and sales. And in today's world, social media marketing could be the linchpin of your success.

Sure, you might know how to post holiday photos on Facebook or share updates with friends, but what *The Art of Small Business Social Media* will teach you is far more valuable. You'll learn how to craft a brand identity, engage with your audience meaningfully, and use the power of social media to grow your business.

Let's embark on this path together. Step by step, we'll navigate the vibrant world of social media marketing. Ready to start? Let's turn the page and begin our adventure into the art of social media for small businesses.

1
THE SOCIAL MEDIA REVOLUTION FOR SMALL BUSINESS

Unleashing Social Media's Potential for Small Business

I am not afraid of storms, for I am learning how to sail my ship.

—*Louisa May Alcott*

*I*t's time to make the leap!

If you've been waiting for the right time to get started with social media, this is it. Larger social media platforms (Facebook, X [formerly known as Twitter], and Instagram) have existed for years, even decades. It's no longer a fad or just for teenagers.

Social media combines sales, marketing, public relations, and advertising for your company. Using online communication methods for your small business can help you grow locally and globally, depending on your goals. According to the Pew Research Center, "Today, around seven-in-ten Americans use social media to connect, engage with news content, share information, and entertain themselves."

At its most basic level, social media is people creating a post (a photo, video, or graphic) accompanied by text that may or may not have a link to elsewhere on the internet. Or it could just be a photo or video alone. Or just text. People create posts to share with their friends or people who are connected with them, or to share their thoughts on a current topic or event. Other people see these posts and might act by commenting, liking, or sharing the post. This is how ideas on social media spread.

I want to start with an overview of the different social media platforms and their demographics; later in the book, I'll walk you through finding out who your ideal customer and demographic is so you will know where to start social media marketing for your business. Don't get overwhelmed with choices; you do not need to be on all social media networks. The key is to find what's best for your small business and which will help you meet your marketing goals. Chapter 6 will cover them in more detail.

One thing to know is that social media platforms will come and go, but you want to create social media marketing that is platform-agnostic. This means that you won't be relying on the social platform or building one audience somewhere but instead shifting to what is working and current. I will teach you how to market your business; social platforms are just a tiny piece of the puzzle. The end goal isn't to be good at Instagram or TikTok; you want to *learn how to use marketing best to reach your business goals.*

Just a heads-up: we're about to zip through a snapshot of all the big-name social media platforms. It's totally okay if you're new to this—think of it as a mini-tour to get your feet wet. Have a look now to get a taste of what's out there, and remember, there's no need to commit everything to memory on the first go. You can always circle back later when you're ready to dive deeper. So, take a deep breath, and let's ease into it together, one step at a time.

Here's an overview of the social platforms:

FACEBOOK
The giant in the social media space is Facebook. Facebook is a social networking service launched by Mark Zuckerberg on February 4, 2004.[1]

People connect with friends and family by posting their activities in conversations with photos and videos.

Demographics:
Seventy percent of adult internet users/58 percent of the entire adult population use it daily.[2]

Facebook is now part of the Meta Platforms, Inc. parent company. The change to "Meta," a prefix indicating "beyond," downplayed the Facebook brand and foreshadowed its new mission beyond newsfeeds. The idea of the metaverse remains to be seen today, but it amounts to a world of online, virtual environments where users can work, hang out with friends, exercise, and communicate.

Facebook continues to be one of the world's most widely used social media platforms. While its overall usage has remained relatively consistent over the past few years, there have been notable changes in how people use the platform and what it offers.

Here are some key aspects of Facebook:

1. *Social Connections*: Facebook continues to be used to stay connected with friends and family. Users can share updates, photos, and videos, as well as comment on and react to posts from their connections. Facebook Messenger is a popular app for communicating with people and brands.

2. *News and Information*: In recent years, Facebook has tried to combat fake news and misinformation on its platform.

3. *E-commerce*: Facebook has continued to expand its e-commerce capabilities, allowing businesses to set up shops on the platform and sell products directly to consumers. Many users also use Facebook Marketplace to buy and sell items locally.

4. *Entertainment*: Facebook has also expanded its entertainment offerings with features such as Facebook Watch, which allows users to watch original shows and videos on the platform.

5. *Virtual Reality*: Facebook has invested heavily in virtual reality technology in recent years, with the launch of the Oculus VR headset. While still a niche market, many users use virtual reality experiences on Facebook to socialize, play games, and explore virtual worlds.

How people use Facebook varies greatly depending on the individual user. Some users may primarily use it to keep in touch with friends and family, while others may use it for news, entertainment, or e-commerce. Facebook Groups is a place where like-minded people connect and create small communities. These are social groups, not necessarily the place to conduct business. Many users also use Facebook and other social media platforms like Instagram and X to stay connected and informed.

X

X is a microblogging platform where you share short messages called tweets. Tweets were 280 [doubled from the original 140] characters or less, which kept things moving quickly. For all you chatty folks out there, they've expanded their text count. The once-concise 280-character tweet limit has now ballooned to a whopping 4,000 characters. But hold your tweets—there's a twist.

This luxury of lengthy musings is exclusive to subscribers of X Premium, the platform's paid monthly service. So, if you're ready to part with some of your hard-earned cash, you can enjoy the freedom of expressing yourself in mini-essays instead of bite-sized snippets.

People network globally on X or connect with people one-on-one by mentioning them directly. Hashtags are a word or phrase with a pound or number sign (#) in front of them with no spaces. For example, #hashtag or #breakingnews. Hashtags are clickable links that tie all the content together. More on hashtags later in the book. Trending topics and breaking news dominate the conversation on X.

Demographics:
Forty-six percent of adult Internet users[3]

X remains a popular social media platform for its real-time, concise, and public nature. Elon Musk purchased X in 2022, and since that time, there have been significant changes, not all positive. X has evolved to offer new features, enhance user experiences, and serve different purposes. X removed legacy-verified accounts marked by blue checks and replaced them with the subscription-based X Premium,[4] which includes verification and extra features, such as being able to edit a tweet, longer tweets up to 10,000 characters, and the ability to format text with bold and italics.

X Premium is a paid subscription service designed to enhance your online experience with additional features. It's structured into three levels: Basic, Premium, and Premium+, each offering a progressive range of tools and benefits.

With the Basic tier, you can access foundational enhancements such as editing your posts, expanding post-length and video-upload capacity, and prioritizing your replies to increase visibility. It also includes options for text formatting, creating bookmark folders for organization, and customizing your app's appearance.

The Premium tier builds upon the Basic offering by adding a verification checkmark next to your name for increased trustworthiness, fewer ads to streamline browsing, and opportunities to share ad revenue and create subscription-based content. This tier also gives your replies greater prominence and includes ID verification and Media Studio access for more advanced content management.

At the top, Premium+ incorporates all the features of the previous tiers and eliminates ads from your primary viewing areas for a cleaner interface. It also guarantees the most significant level of reply prioritization and provides access to Grok, an exclusive feature with limited availability based on region.

Here are some key aspects of X:

1. *News and Information*: X has returned to its roots and is now a go-to source for breaking news, real-time updates, and curated content. It offers its users a unique platform to stay informed with diverse voices, ranging from individual reporters to major media outlets and public figures.

2. *Engagement and Community*: X offers users a platform to participate in public conversation, discuss trending topics, share their opinions, and engage with other users worldwide. It provides a sense of belonging and allows users to join and create communities with people who share similar interests.
3. *Entertainment*: X is also known for being a source of entertainment, with many celebrities, influencers, and content creators using the platform to promote their work, share their personal lives, and connect with their fans.
4. *Advertising*: X offers advertisers a platform to promote their products and services to a wide range of audiences, with various targeting options, ad formats, and analytics.

Like Facebook, the way people use X varies greatly depending on the individual user. Some users may primarily use it to follow breaking news, while others may use it to engage with their favorite celebrities or content creators. Many users also use X to stay informed and engaged. X has maintained its position as a powerful tool for connecting people, sharing ideas, and staying informed in real-time.

INSTAGRAM

A visual platform owned by Meta Platforms, Inc., like Facebook, Instagram was once a photo-only platform but now hosts both live and published videos. Every Instagram post must have a photo, graphic, or video, with text being optional.

People connect based on things they like, such as beauty, fashion, travel, or being inspired. Big brands have mastered the art of Instagram. We'll dig into examples later, but a few brands crushing it are Dry Bar, Tarte Cosmetics, and the National Park Service. Successful Instagrammers and brands build vibrant communities based on hashtags.

Demographics:
Fifty-nine percent of adult Internet users[5]

Instagram remains one of the most popular social media platforms in the world. It has continued to evolve over the years, with new features and tools to enhance the user experience and meet the changing needs of its users. It gets some flak for copying TikTok and Snapchat features. Instagram features include:

1. *Visual Content*: Instagram is known for its emphasis on visual content, including photos, videos, and stories. Users can share their content, like, comment, and share content from others.
2. *Influencers and Brands*: Instagram has become a powerful tool for influencers and brands to promote their products and services, with sponsored posts, influencer marketing, and e-commerce features playing a role.
3. *Stories and Reels*: Instagram has continued to expand its Stories features, allowing users to create short-form, vertical video content that disappears after twenty-four hours. Disappearing content has made Instagram popular for sharing behind-the-scenes glimpses and creating more informal, authentic content. Reels[6] are another way to create and share videos. You can create captivating, multi-clip videos that can be up to a whopping ninety seconds in length! Unleash your creativity with a delightful array of user-friendly features like text overlays, enchanting AR filters, and immersive audio options. You're not limited to just recording within the app; you can also upload videos from your gallery to make your Reels even more captivating and personal. Reels live on a special tab on your profile.
4. *Messaging and Communication*: Instagram's messaging features have continued to evolve, with more options for direct messaging (DMs), including voice and video calls. DMs made Instagram a popular platform for communication and connection with friends and family.
5. *Augmented Reality*: Instagram has invested in augmented reality (AR) technology, with features such as AR filters and effects. AR has allowed users to create more engaging and interactive content and

has opened new possibilities for brands and influencers to showcase their products and services.

Instagram usage varies greatly depending on the individual user. Some users may primarily use it to share their content and connect with friends and family, while others may follow their favorite influencers and discover new products and services.

Overall, Instagram has maintained its position as a powerful platform for visual storytelling and connection, with new features and tools that continue to evolve the user experience.

Threads

Threads from Instagram is a text-based conversation app that brings a focused chat experience to your business. Here are the top-three features for small business owners:

- *Seamless Integration*: Use your Instagram credentials to connect with your existing followers and discover new ones instantly. Your business's identity remains consistent across both platforms.
- *Expressive Conversations*: Easily start discussions about your products or services and control who engages with your content, ensuring a space that's true to your brand's voice.
- *Engage with Your Community*: Quickly respond to and interact with customers and fellow entrepreneurs, fostering a community that's engaged with your brand's message.

With Threads, you can maintain meaningful dialogue, network effectively, and stay on top of trends that matter to your small business.

PINTEREST

Pinterest isn't a social platform but rather a discovery engine and bookmarking website where people gather inspiration and ideas. And shop! If you have a product or service, your small business needs Pinterest.

Every Pin must have a photo, graphic, or video. People save or "Pin" photos that they love to "boards" or repin Pins from other people.

From Pinterest: "On Pinterest, we tune our AI to prioritize explicit signals, not just views alone. We use a unique set of metrics that we call *inspired actions.*"[7] Pinterest strives to build a more positive place on the internet, and they encourage people not just to Pin, but to do the things they Pin. Do a craft, bake a cake, or decorate your home.

Demographics:
Thirty-one percent of adult Internet users[8]

Pinterest remains a popular bookmarking platform focusing on visual discovery and inspiration. It has continued to evolve but has yet to crack the social code or viral aspects of Instagram or Tiktok. One huge bonus is that Pinterest added the ability to link from any Pins, including video pins. This gives Pinterest a big advantage over other video sharing spots like TikTok and Snapchat. It means that you can create a video or graphic and add a link to your website or sales platform to sell products directly.

Pinterest key features include:

1. *Visual Discovery*: Pinterest is known for its emphasis on visual discovery, allowing users to discover and save images and videos related to their interests, hobbies, and aspirations. Users can search for content using keywords or explore curated content based on their interests.
2. *Inspiration and Planning*: Pinterest has become a popular tool for users to find inspiration and plan for future projects, events, and purchases. Users can save content to boards organized by topic to keep track of ideas and inspiration.
3. *E-commerce*: Pinterest has continued to expand its e-commerce capabilities with features such as shopping Pins and catalogs. Boosted shopping experiences have allowed businesses to reach new audiences and sell their products directly to consumers.

4. *Community*: Pinterest has also fostered community among its users with features such as group boards and following. Pinterest allows users to connect with others with similar interests and collaborate on shared boards.

5. *Advertising*: Pinterest offers advertisers a platform to promote their products and services to a highly engaged and targeted audience, with various targeting options, ad formats, and analytics.

Pinners may primarily use Pinterest to find inspiration and plan for future projects, while others may use it to discover new products and make purchases.

Overall, Pinterest has maintained its position as a powerful visual discovery and inspiration tool, with new features and tools that continue to evolve the user experience.

LINKEDIN

Many small business owners overlook LinkedIn, but it's the best social channel for professional networking. A solid LinkedIn profile is a must. LinkedIn is part of Microsoft, with the likes of Xbox, Minecraft, and Skype. LinkedIn doubled its user base after being acquired by Microsoft in 2016.

Demographics:
Twenty-eight percent of adult Internet users[9]

LinkedIn remains the world's largest professional networking platform, focusing on connecting professionals and businesses. It has continued to evolve over the years, with new features and tools being added to enhance the user experience and meet the changing needs of its users.

LinkedIn features:

1. *Professional Networking*: LinkedIn is known for its emphasis on professional networking, allowing users to connect with other pro-

fessionals, build relationships, and expand their network. Users can search for other users based on various criteria, including job title, company, and location.

2. *Job Search*: LinkedIn has become a popular tool for job seekers, with features such as job listings, job search tools, and company pages. LinkedIn allows users to search for jobs, research companies, and apply for positions directly on the platform.

3. *Personal Branding*: LinkedIn has become a powerful tool for personal branding, with users able to create a professional profile that showcases their skills, experience, and accomplishments. Building a personal brand has allowed users to build their professional reputations and establish themselves as thought leaders in their industry.

4. *Content Sharing*: LinkedIn has continued to expand its content-sharing capabilities, allowing users to publish articles, videos, and other types of content on the platform. This has allowed users to share their expertise and insights with others in their industry and to expand their reach and influence.

5. *Advertising*: LinkedIn offers advertisers a platform to promote their products and services to a highly targeted professional audience, with various targeting options, ad formats, and analytics.

LinkedIn users may primarily use it to connect with other professionals and build their network, while others may search for jobs and build their brand.

LinkedIn has maintained its position as a powerful platform for professional networking and personal branding, with new features and tools that continue to evolve the user experience.

YOUTUBE

Alphabet Inc., the same parent company as Google, owns the video search monster YouTube. Built on an algorithm, YouTube is the place to learn how to do anything or be entertained. You can find cat videos (and videos on how to make cat videos), but also serious marketing potential depending on your business.

YouTube remains the world's largest video-sharing platform, with a diverse range of content and a massive user base.

Key aspects of YouTube include:

1. *Video Content*: YouTube is known for its emphasis on video content, with users able to upload, watch, and share videos related to a wide range of topics and interests. The platform offers diverse content, from educational videos and tutorials to music videos and vlogs.
2. *Personalization*: YouTube has continued to improve its recommendation algorithm, which uses machine learning to suggest videos that users are likely to be interested in. This has allowed users to discover new content and creators that align with their interests.
3. *Livestreaming*: YouTube has continued to expand its livestreaming capabilities, allowing users to stream video content in real-time. Being able to livestream has made it a popular platform for live events, such as concerts, sports, and gaming.
4. *Advertising*: YouTube offers advertisers a platform to promote their products and services to a highly engaged and targeted audience, with various targeting options, ad formats, and analytics. It also allows YouTubers to make money from their videos based on how many people watch them.
5. *Community*: YouTube has also fostered a sense of community among its users with features such as comments, likes, and subscriptions. Building a community has allowed users to connect with others with similar interests and support their favorite creators.

YouTube usage varies greatly depending on the individual user. Some users may primarily use it to watch and discover new content, while others may upload videos and build a following. Many users also use YouTube and other social media platforms like Instagram and X to promote content and connect with their audience. Overall, YouTube has maintained its position as a powerful platform for video content, with new features and tools that continue to evolve the user experience.

TIKTOK

TikTok is a short-form social media platform used to make various videos ranging from dance and comedy to entertainment and education. Each vertical video can have a duration from fifteen seconds to ten minutes.

This is where viral content is born and trickles out into the world.

TikTok remains among the most popular social media platforms globally, especially among younger generations. It has continued to evolve over the years, growing to include filters, trending audio, and livestreaming.

There is some controversy around TikTok. As the *New York Times* reported, "Lawmakers and regulators in the West have increasingly expressed concern that TikTok and its parent company, Byte Dance, may put sensitive user data, like location information, into the hands of the Chinese government. They have pointed to laws that allow the Chinese government to secretly demand data from Chinese companies and citizens for intelligence-gathering operations. They also worry that China could use TikTok's content recommendations for misinformation."[10]

Because of these concerns, TikTok may eventually be banned in the United States, and several states have enacted partial bans on government employees using the app.

Key aspects of TikTok include:

1. *Short-Form Video*: TikTok is known for its emphasis on short-form, vertical-video content, with users able to create, watch, and share videos that are typically fifteen to sixty seconds long and now up to ten minutes for some users. The platform offers diverse content, from dance videos and lip-sync to comedy sketches and educational content.

2. *Personalization*: TikTok has a sophisticated recommendation algorithm, which uses machine learning to suggest videos that users are likely to be interested in. The For You Page has allowed users to discover new content and creators that align with their interests.

3. *Music Integration*: TikTok strongly focuses on music, with many videos incorporating popular songs and sounds. Users can also create their sounds and music tracks in their videos.
4. *Influencers and Brands*: TikTok has become a powerful tool for influencers and brands to promote their products and services, with sponsored content and influencer marketing playing a significant role. Influencer partnerships have allowed businesses to reach new audiences and sell their products directly to consumers.
5. *Community*: TikTok has also fostered a sense of community among its users with features such as comments, likes, and followings. Communities based on hashtags and topics have allowed users to connect with others with similar interests and support their favorite creators.

People may use TikTok to watch and discover new content, while others may use it to create and share their videos

SNAPCHAT
In Snapchat, photos and videos pop up and disappear after you view them. Mysterious and inspired, Snapchat is personal and fun.

Snapchat remains a popular social media platform focusing on short-form, interactive content. It has continued to evolve but is primarily used for personal communication.

Snapchat includes the following key aspects:

1. *Ephemeral Content*: Snapchat is known for its emphasis on disappearing content, with users able to share photos and videos that disappear after they are viewed. This has made Snapchat a popular platform for informal communication and spontaneous sharing.
2. *Interactive Features*: Snapchat has continued to expand its interactive features, such as lenses and filters, which allow users to add special effects and animations to their photos and videos. This has made Snapchat a popular platform for creative expression and playful communication.

3. *Messaging*: Snapchat's messaging features have also continued to evolve, with more options for direct messaging, including voice and video calls. This has made Snapchat a popular platform for communication and connection with friends and family.
4. *Discover*: Snapchat's Discover feature allows users to discover and explore content from various publishers and media outlets.
5. *Advertising*: Snapchat offers advertisers a platform to promote their products and services to a highly engaged and targeted audience, with various targeting options, ad formats, and analytics.

Most Snapchatters primarily use it for informal communication and spontaneous sharing, while others may use it to discover and explore content from media outlets and publishers.

TUMBLR

Automattic owns Tumblr, and they haven't changed it too much since making the purchase, which keeps Tumblr fans happy.[11] Tumblr is a great option for people who don't have time to manage an entire blog. Tumblr has a very active community, and sharing content here is straightforward.

Tumblr remains a popular website focusing on blogging, creativity, and community.

What is Tumblr? It is made up of the following features:

1. *Blogging*: Tumblr is known for its emphasis on blogging, allowing users to create and share content in various formats, including text, photos, and videos. The platform offers multiple themes and customization options, allowing users to create unique and personalized blogs.
2. *Creativity*: Tumblr strongly focuses on creativity, with many users using the platform to share their artwork, photography, and writing. The platform also offers a range of creative tools, such as photo editing and design features, to help users create and share their work.

3. *Community*: Tumblr has fostered a strong community among its users with features such as re-blogging, comments, and likes. This has allowed users to connect with others with similar interests and discover new content and creators.
4. *Privacy and Safety*: Tumblr has enhanced its users' privacy and safety with features such as two-factor authentication, abuse reporting, and more control over what users see in their feeds.
5. *Advertising*: Tumblr offers advertisers a platform to promote their products and services to a highly engaged and creative audience, with various targeting options, ad formats, and analytics.

Tumblrs may primarily use the platform to create and share their content and connect with others in their creative community, while others may use it to discover new artists and writers and engage with their work.

The bottom line is that people are on social media.

It would be best to reach people where they spend their time. Social media can help small businesses with marketing, PR, communications, and customer service.

Yelp reviews have scared the heck out of small business owners, and in response, they often take an ostrich approach to the whole online world by hiding their heads in the sand. If people discuss your business online, you must be there to respond, help, and thank them.

By the end of the book, I promise you'll have a plan for your business and feel confident to move forward with social media marketing.

2

What Types of Small Businesses Can Grow with Social Media?

The question is not what you look at, but what you see.

—Henry David Thoreau

*B*ut my business is unique . . .

One of the first things I hear from "small business owners is that they don't feel like their business will work on social media. As I've already mentioned, 71 percent of all adults on the internet are on Facebook. People are spending much of their time online for entertainment and work. Social media can work for your business; you must simply learn how to translate what you do to the digital world.

A few decades ago, people consumed news from the three big networks (ABC, NBC, or CBS) at 6:30 or 11 p.m. each night. There were two times a day that you could get the news. You chose a network you trusted and felt a bond with Walter Cronkite, who was the host of the first thirty-minute news show on CBS in 1962,[1] or the news anchor your family watched every night. Walter Cronkite broke some of the most gripping stories of the 1960s through the 1980s, including when President Kennedy was shot in 1963. If there was breaking news, it was a big deal, and the current television show was interrupted for the breaking news.

Newspapers also broke big news stories, but if you pick up a paper today, you've read many of the stories the day before online. Now you can open your smartphone to access news or weather anytime.

These changes have greatly affected the ability to reach people for marketing and sales opportunities. This is excellent news for small business owners and entrepreneurs like you!

There are basically two different types of companies:

- *B2B*: A B2B company is business to business. This means that your business services other businesses rather than the general population.
- *B2C*: B2C means business to consumer. If you're B2C, you'll be reaching out directly to the end user of your products or services.

While some people like to focus on how to use social media for B2B or B2C, as a small business owner, your main goal is to create great social media marketing for people. People are behind all decisions, whether B2B or B2C. Therefore, as a small business, you will focus on your products and services and how to market them.

Businessman and PureMatter CEO Bryan Kramer calls this H2H, or human-to-human. Bryan says, "Human beings are innately complex yet strive for simplicity. Our challenge as humans is finding, understanding, and explaining the complex in its most simplistic form. This means you, marketers. Find the commonality in our humanity and speak the language we've all been waiting for."[2]

Small businesses can reach their customers on social media by using a variety of different methods:

1. Paid search
2. Native advertising
3. Branded content
4. Content marketing

Paid search is paying for advertisements on search engines like Google or Bing. The biggest problem for small businesses, however, is expense. It takes time and money for paid search to be successful. You see examples of paid search each time you search on Google, and the top results say "AD."

What is *native advertising*? Native ads appear in social media searches with text like "paid promotion" or "sponsored content." They follow the natural flow of social media in context and feel, compared to advertisements that disrupt social media. Guess what? People don't mind native ads. Native ads get 20 to 60 percent higher engagement rates than display banner ads, according to *Marketing Land.*

The key is to be honest and transparent with native advertising. You never want to try to "trick" people into thinking they won't know something is sponsored. There is a "know, like, and trust factor" you want to build on social media—we'll talk about this in more detail in chapter 16.

And, of course, the Federal Trade Commission (FTC) has guidelines for sponsored content. There are rules for posting and disclosing your relationship to a brand if they sent you products or you were paid. The FTC Endorsement Guide covers all the details, but the main gist is that you need to practice truth in advertising. This means endorsements must be disclosed and clear to anyone seeing the post.

Branded content tells stories and entertains your audience. It doesn't focus on your products, but highlights your brand's causes and core values. Stories stick in people's minds and connect on an emotional level.

From *Adweek,*[3] "Branded content bests other online advertising in multiple ways, per a new joint study from IPG MediaLab, and Syracuse University's Newhouse School." The study[4] says brand recall is 59 percent higher for branded content than for display and native ads.

Content marketing is one of my favorite ways for small businesses to reach people. It unlocks the power to address your audience's burning questions effectively. By embracing the art of content marketing, you have the remarkable ability to foster unwavering trust with your treasured audience, amplify conversions, establish profound connections with customers, and nurture a flourishing stream of leads. In this modern era, customers expect nothing less than exceptional, unparalleled content that is not only consistent but also crafted with the utmost quality, radiating from their most beloved brands. With content marketing, you create helpful, relevant content that will educate or entertain your potential customers. For small businesses, content marketing can be a game-changer. It involves creating things like engaging newsletters, informative podcasts, dynamic social media posts, and captivating videos. The goal? To offer valuable content that not only pleases your audience, but also draws them toward what your business has to offer. We'll discuss content marketing and how you can reach your audience with your content.

Since we've established that most of the population is on social media, it's clear to me (and I hope to you) that any small business can reach people with social media. As we move through the chapters of this book, you'll see different pieces of the puzzle, but I promise I'll show you how to put them together as well.

Social Media versus Traditional Marketing

The New Frontier

I attribute my success to this: I never gave or took any excuse.

—*Florence Nightingale*

---

*D*oes social media replace traditional media? Short answer, no.

Currently, social media hasn't replaced traditional marketing or advertising. If your methods of reaching customers are working for you and show an acceptable return on investment (ROI), continue using them. But the great news is that social media marketing and traditional marketing can work in tandem.

The phone book was an extensive traditional marketing push for small businesses. Remember when you could look up the local pizza parlor and find their phone number? Well, that's been replaced by an app or Google search. You can place a standing order for your favorite pizza with Domino's Easy Order system[1] and order it by tweeting a pizza emoji, using their Zero Click app, or Google Home. Phone books have gone the way of dinosaurs, but people are still ordering pizza. You might use postcards or flyers for coupons and sales if you have a small business, and that's fine, but you'll want to add modern ways for people to reach you as well.

As everything moves into the digital world, you may find great success with traditional campaigns that are snail mailed to customers. A well-designed piece that people can put on their fridge is old-school, it but keeps your business top-of-mind.

You can work your traditional marketing with social media by gathering more names and addresses with social campaigns. I'll go into more detail later when we talk about email marketing.

Small giveaways like magnets or key chains can also be valuable in helping people remember your name and contact information. I recently had some work done at an auto body shop, and they returned my keys with a branded key chain. Super-smart!

My dog groomer creates a very low-budget appointment reminder card with dog stickers on white paper, and they're handwritten, but they're adorable, and I put them on my fridge to remind me of my dog's next appointment. I appreciate that they're a small, local business and don't have fancy print materials. The stickers are cute. Your marketing doesn't always have to be expensive or slick to be effective. It needs to meet your customers where they are and keep them returning to your business.

When you create traditional marketing pieces, include social media icons and a user name to let people know you're online and where they can find you. You can't assume people will search for you on social networks, so being precise is essential. QR codes are handy if you want to add one to your printed piece so people can scan it with their phone and go to the landing page of your choice. Here's an example of a QR code I created that includes the company logo and "scan me" so people know what to do.

Another brilliant idea is to place tent cards on your counters or tables that say, "Find us on Instagram," or "Follow us on Facebook now and get a 10% discount from this order." Enticing people to check in at your location is a great idea because then all the people they're friends with on Facebook will see the Facebook check-in on their timeline and newsfeed.

FIGURE 3.1. QR Code on social post.

Source: Kreussler Inc.

To create your marketing pieces on a shoestring budget, you can use Canva—found at canva.com. We'll go into creating graphics and branding later in the book, but remember that today we have multiple options for creating marketing. You don't always have to hire an agency and spend a lot of money. Armed with your smartphone and a computer, it is possible to create a valuable, professional-looking marketing piece. You could make the entire thing in the Canva mobile app, but I like to see something on the bigger screen to proof the text. For example, if you run a small boutique, you could create some flat-lay photos of your products or showcase a window display that you've created and turn this into a postcard for an upcoming weekend special.

Local businesses still rely on local ad placements in shopper magazines and newspapers. If you see a return on your investment (ROI) with such ad placements, keep doing them. However, make sure that you have some way of tracking the ads. We'll look into this in chapter 35.

To calculate ROI, take the revenue from your ads and listings, subtract your overall costs, then divide by your overall costs:

ROI = (Revenue – Cost of goods sold) / Cost of goods sold.

Example

Let's say you have a product that costs $50 to produce and sells for $125. If you sell five of these products for $625 and your shopper ad costs $100, your ROI is:

($625 – ($250 + $100)) / ($250 + $100) = 79% ROI for your ad placement

There are many ways to calculate ROI; make sure you create your formula and stick to it.

One crucial point is that marketing is an expense, not an investment. It should be a line item on your profit-and-loss statement. You're not investing in marketing; it's part of the cost of doing business.

FINAL THOUGHTS

Social media may replace traditional marketing in the future, but for now, we're in a transitional stage where both hold value for your small business. When starting your social media marketing, you'll want to keep your traditional marketing in place if it works to some extent. If you haven't been doing any other marketing, move forward with your social media efforts.

This is where your business is unique—you don't have to follow what other people do. Your small business will be moving toward modern marketing, but that doesn't mean the old ways—a.k.a. traditional marketing—isn't practical. There isn't one marketing plan to fit all companies; your company will need a custom plan to reach your marketing goals. You'll have the tools to make decisions and create a plan once you've finished this book.

Navigating Social Media Management

DIY or Pro?

Many hands make light work.

—John Heyword

*I*t is a complicated and straightforward matter. Do you have the budget to hire someone to manage your social media? Your business may need you to focus on your core functions to make money. Or you may be an entrepreneur like me, and you're the whole team.

If you don't have money pinned for marketing, you'll want to add this to your profit-and-loss statement as a line item. From three to five percent of your sales should be earmarked for all of your marketing expenses.

According to the Small Business Association (SBA),[1] many businesses allocate a percentage of actual or projected gross revenues—usually between two to three percent of their budget—for marketing. But the allocation depends on several factors: the *industry* you're in, the *size of your business*, and its *growth stage*. For example, during the early, brand-building years, retail businesses spend much more than other businesses on marketing—up to twenty to percent of sales.

As a rule, *small businesses (with less than five million dollars) should allocate seven to eight percent of their revenues to marketing.* This budget should be split between 1) *brand development costs* (which include all the channels you use to promote your brand, such as your website, blogs, sales collateral, etc.), and 2) *the costs of promoting your business* (campaigns, advertising, events, etc.).

This percentage also *assumes you have margins of ten to twelve percent* (after you've covered your other expenses, including marketing).

If your margins are lower than this, consider eating more business costs by lowering your overall margins and allocating additional spending to marketing. It's a tough call, but your marketing budget should never be based on just what's left over once all your other business expenses are covered.

Knowing your strengths and where to hire help is a superpower.

You don't have to hire someone to manage your social media immediately. Here are a few options to grow your social media to help you make a choice:

1. You can do everything yourself. Create social media posts, post things, and respond to all your comments. This is an excellent place to start. But know that doing it yourself also costs your time, which is precious as a small business owner. It might be wise to start doing your social media yourself to find out what you like and what works for your business. If you pay someone else, you will need to know what you're asking them to do.
2. You could work with a virtual assistant. This can be less expensive than hiring a regular employee. A virtual assistant will work remotely, and you may never meet this person face-to-face, but they can become an integral part of your business. You can find virtual assistants via Google search or on LinkedIn.
3. One of your current employees might love social media and be a great choice. Running social media for a business and doing it for one's own personal accounts are different, so if your employee loves Instagram for her personal use, she might need some training before you hand out the password to your business account. Meta Blueprint[2]

is a free, fantastic training platform for Instagram and Facebook. I recommended that you or your employee take advantage of this free tool.

4. You could work with a local professional or someone online who specializes in social media and has a proven track record with your type of business and social media. You'll want to ask for past social media work references and look at their accounts to see if they work well. Do their tweets have likes and retweets? Are people responding to their posts on Facebook?

5. You could contract pieces of your social media through places like Upwork or Fiverr, which are marketplaces for freelance work. It is a great place to see how someone works before hiring them for a more extensive project or to farm out smaller pieces of your social media that you don't have the time or talent to complete.

6. You could have a social media professional create a social media plan for you that you implement, or you could outright hire someone to manage your social media.

There's a way to work with someone to suit your budget and style. You simply need to figure out what will work best for you.

Take a few minutes to calculate your budget and your needs so you can figure out your plan. If you don't have money to pay someone right now, that's a quick answer to your question. And you've already picked up this book, which is going to be your own personal guide to figuring out what and how to manage your social media marketing.

Crafting a Social Media Brand Identity

No two leaves were alike, and yet there is no antagonism between them or between the branches on which they grow.

—*Mahatma Gandhi*

Why do I need a brand? I'm not Coca-Cola!

I hear you! This concept needs to be clarified. Does a small business need a brand? Yes. Can one person be a brand? Yes. You may already have a logo for your sign or marketing materials, and that's great. But if not, I'll explain what an online brand is and how to create one for your business. If you already have a business and you're not online yet, you'll be creating a mirror of your offline world for the internet.

The branding process can be overwhelming. This is a place in the social media process where you can and should hire someone to help you create and design your brand. However, it's one of the areas where many small businesses get online stage fright and don't get started, so I don't want this to happen to you.

Worse, some small businesses don't have any plan for their brand, but they just throw out a bunch of crap. I call these *random acts of marketing*—they will do nothing to build their brand or reach people.

31

Respect your brand and get all your pieces in place before you get started online. If you have already started, let's get you in shape.

An online brand is born by creating the assets you need to create social media posts and designs for your brand; sometimes this includes building a website. Building a website means having your own piece of real estate online. *It is essential and helps you become—and stay— platform agnostic.* Depending on YouTube or TikTok to be there forever is a risk. Remember MySpace, Vine, Google+, and Meerkat? All failed, and any social presence you built there is gone unless you moved them to your email list or hooked them on your website. It's a good time to note that I created a significant presence on Google+, over—1.4 million people, and it disappeared. While building it took a long time, I don't regret it because I made great connections by networking. It also helped me connect with Guy Kawasaki while he was writing *What the Plus!: Google+ for the Rest of Us*, his guide to Google+. I researched Google+ on the platform, read all of Google's Google+ Help section, and linked it in the text. It was a massive deep dive into the platform.

First, we'll need to find the essence of your brand and home in on three main topics you'll cover on social media. I like to call these three things the *three seeds of your brand.* Some people call these "content buckets" or "pillars"; these are a crucial part of your brand, not simply a piece of your content creation process. This is where you boil down the essence of your brand into three important seeds that will grow your brand story.

Let's start by distilling your brand into its purest form—it's all about getting to the heart of what you stand for and what sets you apart. Imagine we're nurturing a garden for your brand. Before we can see growth, we need to plant three seeds, each representing a core topic that you'll consistently explore on social media. These aren't just random subjects; they're the *three seeds of your brand,* fundamental themes that encapsulate your brand's identity, values, and message. They're the DNA of your brand's story, the starting point from which all your content will sprout. By focusing on these seeds, you'll cultivate a narrative that resonates with your audience and allows your brand to flourish organically in the social media landscape.

It's safe to assume that every business naturally develops its own brand identity, whether intentionally crafted or not. The key is to uncover what your brand truly represents and articulate it clearly—think of it as setting it in stone. Once you have that foundation, you can create a social media presence that genuinely reflects your business' unique character and values.

Examples of three seeds for different small businesses:

Everglow Wellness (small-town, independent fitness studio):

1. Wellness
2. Fitness classes
3. Community

Mike's Mobile Marine (boat repair small business):

1. Location/lake
2. Boats and boat lovers
3. Maintenance tips

Bloom by Camille (Small town, independent florist)

1. Holidays
2. Location
3. Seasonal flowers and their meaning

Working on these three core conversation pieces will inform everything you create and communicate. They're essential!

You must boil down your brand into three ideas you'll share consistently. Mine are: author, social media, and inspiration. Every piece of content I create or share covers one of these areas. If you follow me, you'll learn social media tips, follow along on my journey as an author, or gather some inspiration.

From three main topics of conversation and visuals, your brand will grow to be followed and loved by your social media community. It's finding that personality to fit who you and your small business are offline and translating it to everything online.

Some of the elements to examine are:

- *Logo.* This is part of your brand, but not everything. Having a professional create your logo is worth the investment, but there are also more inexpensive options.
- What will the *voice of your business* sound like online? Upbeat? Funny? Serious?
- What *types of photos and visuals* do you use? Corporate shots? Lifestyle photos? Product shots?
- *Color palette.* Do you have the primary color for your brand and one or two accent colors? It's essential to have the exact color codes for all your online work in the form of a hex code.
- *Fonts* are also necessary. Script? Playful? Serif or sans serif?

One way I use to figure out a brand is to create a mood board on a secret Pinterest board and Pin things that inspire the feeling and style that will help make the mood and style of a brand. Pinterest and Instagram are fantastic for seeking visuals. You could use magazines, scissors, a glue stick, and a poster board if you're old-school. How you build your mood board is optional, but it's crucial that you start searching for inspirations and ideas. The bonus of using Pinterest is that you can share your secret board with team members or graphic designers so that they can weigh in and work with you on this process.

The brand you build will be your unique footprint, and it should go without saying that you shouldn't copy someone else's work. I've seen this happen many times when people are new, and they confuse inspiration with cutting and pasting identical elements from successful brands. Imitation isn't the sincerest form of flattery. Your goal isn't to be a second-rate copy of something that works for someone else. When you've put some time into searching for visuals, you'll see a common thread or theme in your choices, and you can edit out the pieces that no longer fit.

When redesigning my website, I hired someone to create a logo. I researched independently and knew what I wanted for my primary brand color and style. But this was the place for me to hire a professional. Again, know your strengths. It was worth it to me to spend a few thousand dollars for a gorgeous custom logo. I use it on my website and social media graphics; it always looks great.

I found a perfect match for a professional branding expert on Instagram by searching through hashtags for branding professionals and graphic designers and checking out their portfolios on their websites. If you're looking for someone to help you develop your brand, this is what you should look for:

- Designs that draw you in, are attractive, and show what the brand does
- A portfolio that showcases the work that they created
- Testimonials from happy customers
- Consultation options so you can have a call with someone and see if they're a good fit
- Packages that outline what they'll do for you. Examples: consultation call, questionnaire, mood board, the first round of designs, call to discuss, the second round of changes, and the final design package and what that will include. One thing to note is that you don't get unlimited changes and requests. Two rounds of changes are hours and hours of work for a designer and are standard. Having an idea of what you want going into the process will help. This is where your earlier Pinterest inspiration will help you.

Price is a consideration—you must be able to afford them—but it's not the first objective. Creating a brand is an emotional process; getting it right is crucial. Your business will grow and be loved depending on the brand you craft, so reaching the right people—those perfect customers who will throw down their credit card for your products or services—is critical to your success. Does that sound overly dramatic? It's not. Your brand is that important, and this process will take time. Patience and focus are needed to make sure you get it right. Your mood board will help make the process flow better and help you communicate your wishes and dreams to your branding expert. At this stage, if you haven't started posting on social media, wait until your brand is completed. If you're already posting, you can make an announcement of your new brand identity when it's ready.

If you can't afford a full-blown branding package and are on your own for this process, I get it and have you covered. It is hard to invest money in your business before you've made any money or don't have any margin. To get started on your own, assess your three seeds, then work on a mood board to get your brand's colors, feel, style, etc. It's super easy to make a mood board in Canva.[1] Using Pinterest and Canva together, you can find images and colors that speak to you and become the pieces you need to create your brand. You can create a full Brand Kit within a Canva Pro account.

Here's where you can get inspiration:

- Design Seeds website—this website is a platform dedicated to color inspiration and color palettes, where a color palette is created from a beautiful photograph.
- Instagram
- Pinterest
- Magazines and websites
- Your favorite outfit or shirt

Interior designers use a tray or mood boards to combine design elements. Maybe there's a feather, a rock chosen from a walk, multiple fabric swatches, and a piece of tile. These elements will pull together to become the full-room design. Creating your brand is similar because you'll choose different parts (font, colors, style) that will inform your design choices.

Coordinating your elements to get the right mood and style is a process; when it comes together, it will feel right. Once you have a few logo options or color palettes, this is an excellent place to ask friends and family for opinions or even crowdsource it on your social media when you get down to two or three choices.

Using Fiverr or Upwork, you could hire someone to design your logo. They're not as expensive as branding and design professionals, but you must move forward from where you are with your process. Search for "logo design" on Fiverr, and you'll find people who create hand-drawn logos, graphic designs, and anything you could think of. The prices typically start at $50 and go up to hundreds.

Building your brand will take time, and working within your budget is a significant consideration. You can put aside money for a professional rebrand as your business grows. Everything won't happen overnight because communicating your brand takes time and thought. You're building your business, and your branding will help bring brand awareness and recognition.

Dry cleaners are exceptionally well branded, and I'm sure you recognize your local dry cleaner from their custom-wrapped vans, logos on their packaging, and front counters when you walk in. Crouse's Cleaners in Grand Prairie, Alberta, Canada, is an example of a dry-cleaning business that does exceptionally well with its online brand. They have a beautiful, helpful website and have translated their brand online on Instagram, Facebook, and LinkedIn. You know they're a family business, where they're located, and how to contact them.

CRAFT YOUR SOCIAL VOICE

Using all the information you've gathered, create your brand's social media voice and give it the characteristics that match your ideal customers. If you have a younger audience, hit up the hip audiences on Snapchat and Instagram with natural language and informal photos. If your brand is more corporate, use Facebook and LinkedIn to build your network with more serious language and branded images. The key is to create a unique brand voice and translate it to the content to match the format of the social platform.

Your brand voice is like the personality of your business expressed through words. Just like people, businesses have their own way of speaking and interacting with others. Your brand voice could be friendly, professional, quirky, or authoritative—it's all about how you want your customers to perceive your business and remember you when they read your content, whether it's a tweet, a blog post, or an ad. It's the consistent tone and style of your communication that makes your brand recognizable and relatable to your audience.

Wendy's has a notoriously sassy social media presence, and people love it. Aviation Gin, Ryan Reynolds's gin company,[2] regularly cranks out sarcastic videos and content that build brand awareness. People love and share the videos because they're timely, hysterical, or sometimes both. Grabbing ideas for how big brands create their social media presence will help you brainstorm your own small business' social voice. Think about your product or services and how you talk to customers when they enter the door.

The elements you'll need to define are:

- Logo
- Secondary logo or watermark
- Main font [for headers]
- Accent font [for subheaders]
- Accent font [for text]
- Color palette [one or two primary colors and accent colors]
- Photo filter [could be for Lightroom CC, Canva, or VSCO]
- Three seeds to describe your brand, which define its tone, style, and content.
- Social Voice

Recommended book: How to Style Your Brand: Everything You Need to Know to Create a Distinctive Brand Identity by Fiona Humberstone

Once you put in the work, you'll have the makings of your brand: the digital elements, social voice, and social persona you've created for your dream customers. I hope you're starting to feel more confident in your brand and your ability to translate it online. Let's keep moving forward by looking at who your ideal customer is and how you will reach them.

Discovering Your Social Media Soul Mate

Your Ideal Customer

To speak without thinking is to shoot without aiming.

—Margaret Cavendish, Duchess of Newcastle

---

*Y*our ideal customer isn't "everyone."

As social media has evolved, it's become clear that you need to reach the right people, not just lots of people. Every social channel is swamped with images, videos, and text. You need to hone in on who your ideal customer is and create content that will speak directly to their problems and needs.

The biggest question to answer for crafting a social media persona: Why should your ideal customer follow you on social media?

Being a brand on social media can be challenging because people want to connect with people rather than a logo or brand. So, how does a brand get into the mix in a practical way? They create a persona that fits their brand, helps them communicate their message, and works on social media.

No one is on social media to be sold to or talked to. You must *solve problems, entertain, inform, or be helpful to your community.* Gear your social media marketing toward these questions using the social media voice that fits your brand, and you will have your social media brand persona.

You will create a brand persona for your company on social media before you start tweeting, posting, and sharing. Will you have one person tweeting and posting or a team for your social media? This will be decided by what resources you have available for your business. Most times, it will just be one person posting for their small business. Be transparent and consistent if you have multiple people posting. Zappos' tweets include the initials of the poster on each tweet—like ^PF—while also saying "hello" at the beginning of each shift and "goodbye" at the end. By doing so, Zappos makes it clear that it's listening to its X followers and connects as a brand with the person behind it. Zappos' followers know whom they're talking to and who is representing Zappos at any given time. If you're a one-person show, you don't need to tell people who is behind the brand with every post, but it would be helpful to occasionally let your followers know. You want to avoid having people randomly post if they do not know the brand voice and style.

For example, Suzy at the front counter is in charge of posting for the dry-cleaning business she works for. She follows the brand voice and guidelines consistently. Her boss, the owner, randomly hijacks the Facebook page to complain about a city council vote. This is bad for the brand and a challenge for the person posting. Having discussions early and often can help alleviate these situations. If you're the person working for the small business, you might have some conversations about how the brand's Facebook page is different from their personal social media accounts.

WHO IS YOUR IDEAL CUSTOMER?

It would be best to decide who your ideal customer is and how to help them by *creating your perfect customer persona.*

Broad ideas like "I just want customers" aren't going to make it easy for them to find you. You don't want to try to be everything to everyone—*creating your dream customer persona will help attract the right customers to you.* Taking the time to attract your ideal customers will save you time and effort.

First, let's take a moment to make sure you know who your dream customer is. This is *super*-important.

If you're a small business owner just stepping into the customer insight game without using social media data, fear not. You'll use real-world interactions and available data points to understand clearly whom your business should target. You can still sculpt detailed customer personas with a few strategic moves:

Start with Sales Insights: Reflect on any direct customer interactions you've had, whether in-store or during service calls. Consider the types of customers interested in your products or services. Are there common threads in their concerns or what they delight in? These interactions are a gold mine for shaping your customer personas.

Evaluate Your Sales Materials: What messages in your marketing materials resonate with your audience? Notice when customers respond positively to certain aspects of your pitch—this reaction can guide you in identifying different customer segments.

Utilize Website Analytics: If you have a website, it's a potent observational tool. Use analytics to see where your visitors come from and their interest. Even basic metrics like the most-read pages or the number of contact-form submissions can shed light on who your potential customers might be.

Engage at Community Events: Whether it's a local market, a business conference, or a community event, these are fantastic opportunities to meet potential customers. Take note of who shows interest in your business, ask questions, and gather feedback. People's needs and interests can guide the attributes of your customer personas.

Customer Feedback Forms: Implement feedback forms at your business location or through direct customer interactions. The information collected here can offer insights into who your customers are and what they value.

Using these direct and indirect data sources, you can build a set of customer personas that will serve as the north star for your marketing and product development strategies, ensuring you're always on target with meeting your ideal customer's needs.

Here are some questions to help you out if you have data to work with. The goal of these questions is to help you understand your ideal customer better so you can create more-effective marketing strategies.

1. What are the key demographic characteristics of your ideal customer? (e.g., age, gender, location, etc.). See the "Use your analytics" section later in the chapter.
2. What are the key psychographic characteristics of your ideal customer? (e.g., interests, attitudes, behaviors, etc.).
3. What social media platforms does your ideal customer use most frequently?
4. What type of content does your ideal customer engage with the most on social media? (e.g., images, videos, blog posts, etc.).
5. What are the key problems or challenges that your ideal customer is facing?
6. What are the goals and aspirations of your ideal customer?
7. How does your product or service fit into your ideal customer's lifestyle?
8. What are the key values and beliefs of your ideal customer?
9. How does your ideal customer make purchasing decisions?
10. Are your customers local or online?

You can create a persona for your dream customer with a secret Pinterest board. Think about who they are, what they like to do, where they shop, what's attractive to them, etc. Pick a name for your dream customer and consider how your services speak to them.

For example, if you want to be a beauty influencer hoping to connect with beauty brands, your ideal customer could be MAC Cosmetics, Ulta, or Sephora. There are many different beauty brands, so consider price, quality, style, product, etc. You'll want to create content that people who love makeup will be interested in, such as tutorials, new product reveals, or other how-to's.

If you are a virtual assistant, your dream customer could be authors or busy professionals who don't have the time or skills to manage their social media. You'll want to showcase your expertise and knowledge with processes and planning.

If you're a dry cleaner, you might have multiple customer personas: Greta Greene, who wants wet cleaning and eco-friendly processes; Mikaela Millennial, who wants convenience and fluff and fold; and Karen, who wants weekly pickup and drop-off.

If you're a dog walker, you would want to create a persona for a dog lover who lives in your area.

Stating the obvious: *a brand isn't a human on social media.* A brand needs a "humanized brand" that speaks to its community. It would be best if you nailed down who your community is by age group and other demographics to help build your brand persona and find the correct language, images, and overall tone to reach people effectively. While your brand isn't a living, breathing individual, on social media, it needs to resonate as one. People crave connection, not just with each other, but with the brands they choose to welcome into their lives. To craft a "humanized brand" that truly speaks to your community, it's essential to dig deep and really get to know your audience. What are their ages, interests, lifestyles? This isn't just about numbers and data; it's about understanding the heartbeat of your community.

Pin down these details to forge a brand persona that can communicate with nuance and empathy. It's like building a bridge with your words, visuals, and the very ethos of your brand to reach across the digital space and connect. The right language, the most resonant images, and that perfect tone—when these elements align, they create a voice that doesn't just speak to your audience; it speaks for them. That's when your social media stops being a megaphone and starts being a conversation. And that's where true engagement begins.

USE YOUR ANALYTICS

I highly recommend you have a Facebook page and Pinterest for Business account or professional account on any platform you use. If you want to sell your products or services, you need to have professional accounts on social media as required by the Terms of Service for those social platforms. It's free to update from personal profiles, and you'll get various benefits with the upgraded platforms, including analytics.

Look at the following analytics to determine who your audience is:

- Facebook page insights
- Pinterest for Business analytics
- X card analytics
- Google analytics

How Can You Use This Data?

1. Determine the age range for your fan base.
2. Determine the gender ratio.
3. Factor in what your product is and how it's best to present your products.
4. Choose your social platform or platforms based on the above information using the popular content type and the medium's demographics.
5. Scope out popular accounts on these platforms and see what content works best. Video? Still images? Custom graphics? Text-only updates

Identifying your dream customer is the first step. Once you have a grasp on who they are, it's time to tailor your approach to engage them directly. The strategies outlined in this chapter are your starting blocks for building a connection with those ideal customers.

Remember, the key is to be proactive and intentional. Use the insights you've gained to inform your marketing efforts, and always be ready to adapt as you learn more about your customers' evolving needs and preferences. With each interaction, you'll refine your understanding and improve your outreach.

Now, armed with knowledge and strategies, you're set to take the next steps: reach out, engage, and grow your business with the confidence that comes from knowing you're speaking directly to those who will benefit most from what you offer. Let's turn these insights into actions and start making meaningful connections with your ideal customers.

TO DO NOTES

1. Who is your ideal customer?
2. What are their demographics?
3. Create a customer persona and speak to this person while creating your content.

Which Social Media Platforms Should You Choose?

It is never too late to be what you might have been.

—*George Eliot (Mary Ann Evans)*

*W*hile this decision may seem crucial, you can make changes later when needed. Don't panic.

Social media can be a powerful tool for publicizing your company and increasing your audience base, but it can also be overwhelming. Choosing the most advantageous social channels to use on your terms, especially as a small business, is essential, but don't let the decision-making process freeze your progress.

Overthinking comes into play here, and you might ask the wrong people or too many people what you should do. As a small business owner, you are the heart of your business. This gives you a unique insight into who would love your product or services. You will make an informed choice based on your past customers, your products or services, the current array of social media platforms you're using, and others available. Things change rapidly, new platforms pop up, and they make changes. All the while you must remain flexible, but stick with your plan six months at a time to ensure it works.

Here are the factors to consider when choosing social media channels:

- What are your goals?
- What are your competitors doing?
- What resources (including time and tools) do you have?
- What industry are you in?
- Who are your current customers?

Here is a small business example to show you how to choose where to start. A small stationery shop, The Feather Quill, is located in the Back Bay area of Boston. It's a new business that opened six months ago. Initial foot traffic was good, but they wanted to grow their business.

Goals: They want more foot traffic and sales and to open an online shop in the future.

Competitors: Other small shops on the street have Facebook pages that aren't doing well. Another stationery shop in Boston has a thriving Instagram account, and there are creators on TikTok who make video content using calligraphy pens and specialty papers.

Resources: The time commitment will be made by the owner, who is carving out time to create content for social posts and communicate online. Include the cost for your social media tools.

Industry: Stationery, Retail.

Current Customers: Based on foot traffic in the store, customers are generally women between the ages of eighteen and thirty-five, with a wide range of other customers.

The owner of The Feather Quill adds three jars on their sales counter with the logos of Instagram, Facebook, and TikTok, along with a fourth jar filled with beans and a sign saying, "Help us decide where to start on social media by voting for the social channels you use." She leaves this on this counter for two weeks and gets feedback from her current customers on where they like to spend their time online. Creating a method for customers to vote is a fantastic way to get low-key and no-spend information, and people standing at the register are happy to do so.

At the end of two weeks, it is clear that most of her customers are on TikTok and Instagram. She's spent time looking at competitor accounts and the platforms and decided that, while TikTok might be great for going viral, she'd like to try Instagram and get comfortable with its slower-paced environment. Her demographic fits Instagram, and she likes the feel of it best.

There are multiple reasons you can choose one platform over another. You might hear stories about someone's cousin who went viral on TikTok and how easy it was for them. But viral content shouldn't be your goal. It's too hard to reach and almost impossible to plan. When it does happen, it's mostly with funny content or something that happened to hit a trend just right. If you were a pop star, you'd start on TikTok. But you're a small business owner with different goals and marketing aspirations.

Choosing the platform that you like using the most could also be a valid reason. If there's a specific type of content you feel most comfortable creating, this could weigh in too. Your passion for the platform counts! There's almost no wrong answer unless your product or services aren't appropriate for the social channel.

One thing to avoid is starting too many social media channels at a time. I am going to recommend that if you are just getting started, you should choose one social channel and give yourself time to learn it before adding anything else. Building a social presence and learning how to use the platform takes time.

There are many places to learn step-by-step processes and keep up with updates. YouTube is a fantastic place to research "how to get started on" the platform of your choice.

When beginning your social channel, choose a username that's as close to your business name as possible. If you post there later, you might want to open accounts on each platform to grab your version of @TheFeatherQuill. Grab the name, so no one else does.

Each social platform has elements that users create and share in various sizes and lengths of photos, graphics, or videos. We'll call this content. You have likely heard of "content creators" (people who create content, such as beauty influencers making makeup tutorials) and content marketing.

Content marketing is the creation and sharing of content (blog posts, videos, images, and text) that doesn't promote your brand but builds interest and grows your community. It's about providing value without overt brand promotion, building relationships, and becoming a trusted resource. Through storytelling, visual appeal, and thoughtful writing, content marketing cultivates genuine interest and connections with your audience.

You will create content marketing for your business using photos, graphics, and video. Sounds easy enough, right?

Each social channel has its formula for content: how long text captions can be, photo sizes, etc. When you choose where to start your online journey, research the current specifics for posting content. The only constant with social media platforms is that things change, so expect to learn and catch up with the current guidelines.

What would content marketing look like for The Feather Quill? Here are a few examples:

- A photo of a holiday window display
- An unboxing video showing the latest Japanese pens arriving in the store
- A picture of the owner sharing a story about their day in the caption
- A "this or that" split graphic with two choices to vote on
- An inspirational quote that has been handwritten using supplies from the shop
- A meme about fonts

As you can see, the posts are related to the shop, but they're not all sales and promos. There's a place for those, but it's not in every post.

Putting "content" before "marketing" changes the focus from your business to your customer.

Look at CopyBlogger's[1] four A's of content marketing. (Check the resources at the end to find the website information.)

- *Attraction* content helps you reach a new audience and get your message in front of new people.
- *Authority* content builds trust and shows your expertise.
- *Affinity* content is how you build your community and get those people on board with your beliefs.
- *Action* content will help you take immediate action to be successful.

A piece of content should speak to one of these attributes, but it could be a combination of two or more. *You want to have a goal with each part of your content.* This will bring it purpose and help you build your business.

As you can see, I'm more interested in what you'll create than in which social channel you will use. Our goal is to market your business. Reaching your goals is what you do rather than where you post your content. We'll go into this more in chapter 27, when we talk about how to create posts for social media.

Here's how people use the most popular social media channels available today:

Facebook: Members post photos, text, or videos, which are heavily gated by algorithms and are mainly used to communicate with friends and family on personal profiles and messages.

Instagram: Users share Reels, Stories, and Posts with text captions. Growing here had been more accessible, but now it's also algorithmically controlled. Direct Messages are very popular for communication.

X: People use tweets to share their hot take on the latest political news, entertainment scandal, or whatever they like. Photos are shared, but it's mostly text. People want to stay on X to browse and look for conversations, but they don't click on links as much as they did in the past.

TikTok: Users post entertaining short videos. This is very shareable content and engages conversation in the comments. People can also be rude in the comments. Very rarely, TikToks can go viral and get a million views. Trends are significant here—trending sounds, dances, or snippets of music. Content can become repetitive when people create the same content. There are also some safety issues with the TikTok app.

On December 2, 2022, FBI director Christopher Wray warned about the potential risks of using TikTok.[2] He expressed concern that TikTok's privacy and data collection policies could result in collecting sensitive, personally identifiable information, which the Chinese government could access for purposes beyond user permissions. The FBI has deemed TikTok a national security risk and testified before the House Homeland Security Committee in November 2022. Small business owners must take this warning seriously and consider the potential risk before using TikTok for business purposes. As of March 2024, the U.S. House of Representatives passed a bill that could ban TikTok. It's still up in the air as to the fate of the platform, its users, and their content.

LinkedIn: A professional platform for posting opinions on news or updates on your career. Building a community here is possible if you provide services or products. Posts can be either text-only or have a photo with them.

Pinterest: People go to Pinterest for inspiration and aspiration. Vertical photos, graphics, or videos show steps for projects. Each post on Pinterest links that lead to your website or landing page. This is a huge advantage over Instagram where you can only link from Instagram Stories.

YouTube: A top-rated platform for learning new things. All videos explain something, show how to do something, or share opinions.

Take some time to check out each social platform that makes sense to you and your business. Where do you see that your business might have a home? Do you see companies similar to yours making a go of it?

For our example, the owner of The Feather Quill is choosing Instagram, but she has her eye on TikTok for later, when she's more comfortable with creating content.

Does one platform speak to you?

TO DO NOTES

1. Choose one or two social platforms.
2. Set your goals for social media.
3. Grab your account name on all social platforms. Make sure it matches everywhere.

8

Time Mastery in the Social Media World

Guard well your spare moments. They are like uncut diamonds. Discard them and their value will never be known. Improve them and they will become the brightest gems in a useful life.

—*Ralph Waldo Emerson*

*G*uarding your time and using it wisely is everything.

Small business owners wear many hats. I probably don't need to remind you that you're responsible for making everything happen in your business. If you're lucky, you'll have a partner invested in helping you.

Setting a budget for your social media time ensures that you will create content regularly without taking away crucial time for making your product or meeting potential customers. There's a balance between productivity and wasting time. Procrastinating on complex tasks because you're watching TikTok videos isn't going to put money in your bank account.

I am always asked how I manage everything I do with social media and blogging; the best answer is time management. People want to hear that you can hit one magic button to fast-track your to-do list and become successful, but there's none.

One trick that I love is to use Friday afternoons for planning. Before you shut down your business brain for the week, take the time to plan for the following week while projects are still fresh in your mind. Your weekend will be more relaxed when you have the next week organized.

Scheduling time to create content is essential. If it's not on your calendar, it won't happen. Add two hours (or however long you can spare) to your calendar each Friday. Add two fifteen-minute blocks daily to check your social posts and join the conversation on your chosen platform.

Once you determine how often you'll check social media, track your time using free tools like FocusBooster.

FocusBooster is an app based on the Pomodoro Technique, a time management system designed to improve productivity instantly. The Pomodoro Technique is a popular time management method that asks you to alternate between periods of focused work with frequent breaks. It's simple to learn, it's efficient, and it positively impacts your quality of work and prevents mental fatigue.

Here's how to use FocusBooster with social media:

1. Choose the social networks you will visit.
2. Determine your goals for the day and have content ready to share.
3. Set the timer for twenty-five minutes.
4. Focus on your task(s) for twenty-five minutes, then shut down your social networks.
5. Give yourself a five-minute break.
6. Move on to your next moneymaking activity.

TOP-NOTCH TOOLS TO BOOST YOUR PRODUCTIVITY

With the right tools, you can streamline your workflow and get more done in less time. Here are some popular productivity apps to consider:

- *Notion*: A versatile tool for project management, note-taking, and more. Notion has a Mac app for the desktop as well as smartphone apps.
- *Trello*: A visual tool for organizing tasks and projects. Trello has a Mac app for the desktop as well as smartphone apps.

- *RescueTime*: A time-tracking tool that helps you understand how you're spending your time.
- *Focus@Will*: A music app that provides background music designed to help you stay focused and productive.
- *Forest*: A productivity app that uses gamification to encourage you to focus on your tasks by growing a virtual tree. It also has a Chrome Extension Google Chrome extensions are little programs that you can install in your Chrome browser, allowing you to modify and enhance its functionality. These are found in the Chrome Web Store and live on your menu bar once you add them to Chrome.
- *Freedom*: A website and app blocker that helps you eliminate digital distractions and focus on your work.

Another idea is to set a limit within Instagram. Here's how to set a daily time limit reminder:

1. Tap the person icon or your profile picture in the bottom right to go to your profile.
2. Tap the three lines in the top right.
3. Below *How you use Instagram,* tap *Your activity.*
4. Below *How you use Instagram,* tap *Time spent.*
5. Tap *Daily limit.*
6. Choose an amount of time and tap *Done.*

Apps can't do everything for you, but they can help you focus if you use them correctly. Setting a schedule and a time budget will allow you to be focused and more successful with your marketing efforts.

TO-DO NOTES:

1. How will you focus?
2. How much time will you commit to social media daily? Weekly?
3. What will your schedule look like?

Your Social Launchpad

Kick-Starting Your Online Presence

Do not wait to strike till the iron is hot; but make it hot by striking.

—*William Butler Yeats*

---

*L*et's build some buzz for your brand-new brand!

Our goal with this chapter is to announce your arrival and start building buzz for your business. These ideas and examples should help you with your own business; of course, you'll use the overlay of your own brand voice and story. Stay on brand with your content using your brand colors and logo to create your cohesive brand which will become recognized over time.

For a small business launch on social media, consider this strategy:

1. Start with a teaser campaign to create anticipation.
2. Create a countdown to the launch day, adding excitement.
3. Regularly post content.
4. Use a unique hashtag for content organization and tracking.
5. Engage your audience with a contest to build excitement.
6. Ensure consistent messaging across all social media platforms.
7. Design an interactive quiz for a fun engagement tactic.

8. Incorporate strong calls to action in your posts to encourage interaction.
9. Actively participate in social media conversations to build relationships and showcase your brand's personality.

CRAFTING YOUR ANNOUNCEMENT POST
The key features of a persuasive announcement include:

1. A robust and attention-grabbing headline that clearly states the purpose.
2. A concise introduction that hooks the reader and outlines the announcement.
3. Detailed information essential for the audience, including what, when, where, and why.
4. Any calls to action, such as signing up, registering, or visiting a website for more information.
5. Contact information or next steps for readers who want to learn more or have questions.
6. A closing that reinforces the main message or offers thanks to the audience for their attention

Let's look at this template in action for two examples.
Example one: A small-town yoga studio is opening in downtown. They have a website link in their bio to find out class information, and they are hosting free classes for their opening week.

Downtown Serenity: Your New Yoga Haven Opens Next Week!
Exciting news, downtown dwellers! Serenity Yoga Studio is opening its doors to a world of tranquility and strength in the heart of our bustling town. Kick off your wellness journey with us during opening week—enjoy *complimentary yoga classes* for all levels. Whether you're a seasoned yogi or new to the mat, our doors are open to everyone seeking balance and peace.

🧘 *Opening Week Special:* Free yoga sessions for everyone!

📅 *Join Us:* [Insert opening week dates]

📍 *Find Us:* The heart of downtown at [Insert specific address]

👀 *Explore Classes & Schedules:* Website link in bio

Come flow with us and make our space your sanctuary. Bring a mat, bring a friend, and discover your inner zen. Don't forget to sign up on our website and dive into the details. Let's celebrate the start of something beautiful—your wellness path with Serenity Yoga Studio. #serenityyoga

Namaste, and see you on the mat! 🙏

Example two: A bake shop opening on Main Street, with specialties that include cookies and muffins.

Sweet Aromas Await on Main Street:
The Grand Opening of Main Street Bake Shop!
We're thrilled to announce that Main Street Bake Shop will open its doors this weekend! Get ready to indulge in the cozy comforts of fresh baked gourmet treats with our mouthwatering cookies and muffins, baked fresh daily with love.

🍪 *Specialties to Savor:* Gourmet Cookies and Muffins

📅 *Grand Opening Date:* [Insert date]

📍 *Visit Us:* Nestled in the heart of our community on Main Street

🎉 *Opening Treat:* Exclusive discounts and samples during our opening day!

Our oven is warming up to bring joy to your taste buds and hearts. Come by, say hello, and treat yourself to the sweet life at Main Street Bake Shop. #mainstreetbakes

For a sneak peek at our menu and to learn more, follow the sweet crumbs to our website [insert website link here].

These announcements can be posted on your business social media account and shared to your personal accounts as well to reach people and let them know that your business is now on social media. In your shared post to your personal account, you will craft a personal message sharing that your business is live, thanking people who've helped you get your business up and running, and inviting people to follow your brand-new or revamped social media accounts.

Here's a sample plan for a week of teaser posts and countdowns pre-launch for Main Street Bake Shop on various social media platforms:

Day 1 (7 Days to Launch)
- Instagram Post: Share a whimsical photo of ingredients with "Something sweet is coming in 7 days!"
- Facebook Page: Post a teaser image of the shop under construction with the caption, "Get ready to satisfy your sweet tooth. Stay tuned!"

Day 2 (6 Days to Launch)
- Instagram Story: A playful boomerang of the shop sign being painted.
- Facebook Page: Share a "Did you know?" fact about cookies, hinting at the upcoming offerings.

Day 3 (5 Days to Launch)
- Instagram Post: Share a close-up of baking tools with the caption, "Our ovens are preheating . . . 5 days to fresh-baked bliss!"

Day 4 (4 Days to Launch)
- Instagram Reel: A sneak peek into the recipe testing with a "4 days away" sticker.
- Facebook Page: A teaser post with a blurred image of the menu, "Our secret recipes will be revealed in 4 days!"

Day 5 (3 Days to Launch)
- Instagram Story: Countdown sticker feature with a background of muffins in the oven.
- Facebook Page: Share a story post with a countdown and a message, "Only 3 days left until we open the doors!"

Day 6 (2 Days to Launch)
- Instagram Post: Post a photo of the storefront with a "Coming Soon" overlay.
- Facebook Page: "2 days to go, and our bakers are busy! Can you guess what's baking?"

Day 7 (1 Day to Launch)
- Instagram Reel: A dynamic video of the final touches being put in place with an overlay, "Tomorrow's the big day!"
- Facebook Page: A final teaser post, "Join us tomorrow for our grand opening and free muffin samples!"

Be sure to engage with comments or questions to keep the momentum and anticipation high.

Here's a sample first-week social media content schedule for Main Street Bake Shop:

Day 1: Grand Opening Announcement
- Instagram Post: Share a photo of the storefront with a "Now Open" sign.
- Instagram Reel: Quick clips showing the first batch of cookies and muffins being made.
- Instagram Story: A welcome message with a swipe-up link to the menu.
- Facebook Page: Post about the grand opening with details of free classes.
- Share to Personal Facebook Profile: A personal note about the excitement of opening day.

- LinkedIn Announcement: A professional note introducing the bake shop to the professional network.

Day 2: Highlight Specialties
- Instagram Post: A carousel of cookie and muffin close-ups.
- Instagram Reel: Time-lapse video of cookies baking in the oven.
- Instagram Story: A poll on followers' favorite cookie flavors.
- Facebook Page: Share the Instagram post and invite followers to vote on their favorite product.

Day 3: Meet the Team
- Instagram Post: Profile of a team member with their favorite bake shop item.
- Instagram Reel: Fun Q&A with a baker.
- Instagram Story: A quiz about baking facts.
- Facebook Page: Introduce the team with a group photo.

Day 4: Customer Favorites
- Instagram Post: Showcase a popular muffin with a special offer mention.
- Instagram Reel: Customer testimonials about their favorite items.
- Instagram Story: Share user-generated content with a thank-you overlay.
- Facebook Page: Post about the customer favorite with an invitation to try it.

Day 5: Behind the Scenes
- Instagram Post: Photos of the baking process, from dough to finished cookies.
- Instagram Reel: A "day in the life" of a baker.
- Instagram Story: Sneak peeks into the kitchen prep.
- Facebook Page: Share a behind-the-scenes look at the bake shop.

Day 6: Community Engagement
- Instagram Post: Announcement of a weekend special or event.
- Instagram Reel: A baking tip or trick related to making cookies or muffins.
- Instagram Story: Countdown to the weekend event.
- Facebook Page: Details about the weekend community event with a call to action to join.

Day 7: Customer Appreciation
- Instagram Post: A collage thanking customers for a successful first week.
- Instagram Reel: Highlights from the week.
- Instagram Story: Customer shout-outs and reposts of tagged content.
- Facebook Page: A thank-you note to the community for the support.

Throughout the week, make sure to engage with comments and direct messages to build a strong online community. Use the location tools to tag your business on the social platforms so people posting or searching for your community can find you. Use location hashtags as well. You'll want to create content ahead of time whenever possible, but some items, like Instagram Stories, can be created the same day.

After the ribbon-cutting, the real fun begins with the community you're creating around your brand. Think of every comment as a conversation starter; reply with warmth and a dash of wit to transform customers into raving brand ambassadors. Get creative to encourage your customers to share their own snapshots featuring your products. Maybe it's a photo contest with the theme, "Morning Muffin Moments" or "Cookie Comforts," with the most delightful posts being celebrated on your feed.

It's all about crafting that cozy corner on the internet where everyone feels welcome, at home, and seen, just like in your shop.

⏸ SOCIAL MEDIA STRATEGIES FOR CAPTIVATING AUDIENCES

10

Building Your Tribe

Cultivating a Community

The ties that bind us to life are tougher than you imagine, or than anyone can who has not felt how roughly they may be pulled without breaking.

—*Anne Brontë*, Agnes Grey

---

*A*lthough you'll be online to market your business, you'll join the more extensive community on your chosen social channel. You'll create shareable pieces to reach new people.

Humans need connection and a sense of belonging—a community. The word *community is* derived from the Latin *communitas* (meaning the same), which is derived from *communis* which means "common, public, shared by all or many." We look for people who share the same beliefs, interests, and sense of humor in person and online. Building your community online is essential to growing your social media presence.

Communities can function as powerful multipliers for your business, but only when they're founded on momentum from an audience ready to engage. You'll start by sharing content and finding your like-minded community using keyword or hashtag searches.

Here are a few ways to grow your community:

- Ask questions to engage people who follow you.
- Use a live chat feature on your website.
- Create polls with thoughtful questions.
- Answer questions on social media and in your comments.
- Provide helpful resources.
- Listen to what your community is saying.
- Share what you're passionate about in your business.
- Engage in community conversations.

Communities offer a nurturing environment, providing essential support to individuals and businesses fostering a deep sense of loyalty and belonging. These shared qualities seamlessly intertwine, enriching the lives of everyone.

In 2014, I started working as the head of social strategy for a small, unknown Australian company. One of the first things I needed to do was to figure out how to build a community, sometimes called a "tribe" online, for the company. A competitor had a much larger social profile with a cute mascot that everyone was talking about. I created a *branded hashtag* and posted it online, mainly on X and Instagram. I stayed glued to Hootsuite (a social media scheduling platform), and when people shared something about the company or a design they created, I tweeted back with a cute, branded graphic and used the hashtag #*CanvaLove*. It caught on! Canva users (you've probably heard of Canva now, right?) started sharing their designs using #CanvaLove. A quick check on X and Instagram today shows that it's still being used by Canva and Canva fans alike. In fact, on Instagram, over 193,000 posts are using #CanvaLove and more with #CanvaLovers and other versions. It even snowballed to TikTok, which didn't exist until 2016, with thirty-one million views on videos using the #CanvaLove hashtag.

Why did this work? Most of all, it's because we started connecting with people using Canva and giving them positive feedback on their designs. The hashtag #CanvaLove was easy to remember and spell, and I could track it even if people didn't tag the Canva company account. Plus,

Canva ✔
@canva

Replying to @nowellie5

Aww, thanks for the shoutout, Noelle! 🖤 So happy to be a part of your learning experience. Sending you tons of #CanvaLove! 😊 ^nm

6:40 AM · 9/5/22 · Sprout Social

FIGURE 10.1. Canva Love Tweet.
Source: Canva.

Canva users loved working with the design tool, even in its early stages. #CanvaLove feeds the idea of loving the product. It goes a long way to thank and appreciate those using your product, especially when it's new.

At the latest valuation, Canva was valued at forty billion dollars and had millions of users worldwide. Canva's last Canva Create, in-person and online, hybrid event had 1.5 million people sign up to watch it online. They've come a long way from being a small company helping people with a more accessible design platform. Mission accomplished with #CanvaLove! (And, of course, the Canva team!)

To back it up, a branded hashtag like #CanvaLove was created by a company for community engagement. A branded hashtag can include company names like #TargetRun or ideals like REI's #OptOutside campaign.

#OptOutside started as a onetime campaign against Black Friday and a statement about capitalism. From Sprout Social's research,[1] "Brand awareness and perception were the initial goals for the 2015 launch of #OptOutside, driven primarily by media and social impressions and dependent on the boldness and novelty of REI's stand against consumerism in favor of spending time in nature. But as REI looked to extend the campaign, the clear link between supporting environmental causes and growing the reach and impact of the movement became clear."

HOW TO USE A BRANDED HASHTAG

Many brands include their community hashtags in their bios and social profiles so people can find them. They also use them on social posts for communication.

If you have an idea for a contest or a weekly challenge, you could use your branded hashtag in your campaign. Initially, you will have to share how to use your branded hashtag, but the online community is much more hashtag-savvy now than it was in 2014. It's a great start to growing your online fan base.

Farmgirl Flowers is an online florist that's gained a loyal following of customers who appreciate its commitment to sustainability and locally sourced flowers. It also has a solid social media presence, with over 501,000 followers on Instagram and a branded hashtag, #fgflove, with 16,488 posts.

The brand has built a community of engaged fans by encouraging customers to use the #fgflove hashtag when sharing photos of their Farmgirl Flowers arrangements. This branded hashtag has helped the brand increase its reach on Instagram and showcase its unique floral designs to a broader audience.

Through this hashtag, Farmgirl Flowers has also collected user-generated content (UGC) featuring their products, which they can use to showcase their offerings on their social media accounts. By reposting UGC, the brand can show its products in real-life settings and inspire its followers with new ways to use their flowers.

FIGURE 10.2. Farmgirl Flowers.
Source: Farmgirl Flowers.

#fgflove

16,490 posts

FIGURE 10.3. Farmgirl Flowers hashtag stream for #FGFlove.
Source: Farmgirl Flowers.

The above image shows the results for the #fgflove hashtag.

Overall, the #fgflove hashtag has been a valuable tool for Farmgirl Flowers to build brand awareness, increase their reach, and engage with their customers on social media. It's a great example of how a well-crafted branded hashtag can help businesses connect with their audience and build a community around their brand.

COMMUNICATION IS KEY

Social media is an essential online communication tool for businesses today. Communication is a critical aspect of marketing. It is reasonable to assume that after forming an online presence, your customers will reach out to you, whether actual or potential. Being active and helpful with your responses will only serve to grow your business in the best possible way. Proactive communication with your target audience is the perfect medium to obtain feedback and, more importantly, build the trust that your business relies upon to survive.

FIGURE 10.4. Author photo of Farmgirl Flower bouquet.
Source: Author.

Communication is a big part of the community and can't be a one-way street. You can't post and ghost and expect to grow a following. Responding to questions or comments on your posts is essential, but you should also go to people's profiles and add thoughtful comments to their posts. This isn't the time to promote your business unless you answer a question.

Whether you're using X, Instagram, TikTok, Pinterest, or LinkedIn, direct messages (or DMs) are a path to deeper connection and a chance to go beyond public comments. Direct messages can help you build a genuine relationship with real people. This, however, will take time and could become a sale in a week, a month, or maybe longer.

It does take skill to get the DM process down, but here are some ideas:

- Start with a question or prompt to open the conversation, such as, "What's your favorite XYZ?" Take a moment to look at their profile and find a common interest or something they love.
- Remember that you're building a relationship, so don't start by sending links to your website or a sale.
- Send a nice note thanking them for connecting and letting them know you're looking forward to learning more about what they do.
- Make sure to check your messages and respond to those that are sincere. If you're getting spam messages, delete and block them.
- Once you've established a relationship, reach out when you have a promotion or send an exclusive promo code for your sale.

This communication is part of your daily social media task schedule. Initially, it might feel like you're talking to yourself, but people will find your brand if you create meaningful content and join in by commenting on other posts and using hashtags.

Community-building on social media is essential for making a small business sustainable. By building a loyal following, small companies can foster a sense of belonging and engagement among their customers, creating a community that supports and advocates for the company. Social media allows small businesses to connect with their audiences personally and get real-time feedback on their products and services. Engaging with customers on social media helps to build trust and credibility, which are critical factors in creating a sustainable small business.

Social media can create a dialogue with customers, allowing small businesses to better understand their needs and preferences. By leveraging social media to build a community, small businesses can create a foundation for long-term success and growth.

TO DO NOTES

1. Do you have a branded hashtag? If not, create one.
2. Where will your community hub live?
3. Start DMing important community members.

11

Balancing Conversation and Customer Service

*Z*appos has legendary customer service. Selling shoes online was a radical idea that worked because it was backed by easy-to-find customer service and the company nurtured it. Zappos invested time, money, and resources in three key areas: its customer service team, its company culture, and its employee training and development.

Have you ever had a question about a product or service and tried to find the brand online? It's frustrating when you can't find contact information or reach them. Zappos includes its phone number on its website so people can quickly call them. "Customer Service" is at the top of their website with a drop-down menu with options to call, text, or connect with live help. You can also find them on X and Instagram. Zappos is an excellent example of a company that is present for its actual and potential customers.

You will be online to market your business, but customers are online because they have questions or are looking for information. You'll balance your regular communication ("we're having a sale" or "our hours this week are XX") with your customer service. It's great to share options for people to reach you on your website and social media accounts, but that doesn't mean people will see those options. They might tweet a rant about their last order or offer praise through a video showing them unboxing their purchase from your Etsy shop. At least some of your online communication might be customer service when you answer direct messages and questions, which is excellent!

The vast majority of Instagram users—90 percent to be exact—follow a brand on the platform. Also, a whopping 150 million people are conversing with brands on Instagram monthly according to the *2022 Sprout Social Index™*[1]: *"13% of US consumers expect brands to respond within the first hour of reaching out on social media, while 76% expect a response in the first 24 hours."*

In short, many customers expect a same-day response from brands on social media.

I know it's a lot to think about, but you'll be covered if you keep up with your daily check-ins. I have a few shortcuts I can share with you, too.

First, you can create a document of pre-written responses in Google Docs or the Apple Notes app. Include things you might often repeat, like:

- Thank you for asking! Here's a link to our website: smallbizshop.com.
- I'd love to help you with that! Please check your direct messages.
- We appreciate your support.

Having them in a handy spot from which you can cut and paste will make it easier and more efficient to provide a response. Add an emoji and their name to personalize each response in real-time.

You may have heard of the marketing adage: "surprise and delight" your customers. While this sounds lovely, it doesn't build brand loyalty. *Customer service does.* Gartner research[2] found that "customer loyalty depends on how easy you make it for your customers to do business with you, and that's when they'll return your service with their repeat business." They also found that "customers want to contact companies through newer, self-service channels."

AUTOMATIC RESPONSES WHILE YOU'RE OFFLINE

One newer customer service trick is to use chatbots. You can create a helpful and prompt customer experience with chatbot responses. Chatbots can be a nifty addition to your customer service tool kit, acting like helpful digital assistants while you're tending to other parts of your business. Designed to keep the conversation going, they can provide quick replies and guidance when you can't be there in person. Whether you choose a simple rule-based program or a more complex AI-driven chatbot, they can be set up on platforms like Facebook and Instagram to ensure your customers always have a way to reach out.

Think of chatbots as your business-friendly night-shift workers, there to direct customers to your email or provide a contact number when needed.

If the thought of setting up a chatbot feels like a tech leap, don't worry. Take your time, bookmark this page, and reconsider when you're ready. There's no rush, and plenty of resources are available— from YouTube tutorials to blog posts with easy-to-follow guides— perfect for a leisurely Friday afternoon learning session. Remember, chatbots are here to complement your customer service, not complicate it, so ease into it at your own pace.

A chatbot is a program that responds to a message. The two main types of chatbots are rule-based and AI-learning programs. You can create a chatbot to respond to in-bound messages and assist customers through text chats, voice commands, or both. You can set it up on social media platforms like Facebook, Instagram, and X so your chatbot is always available to your customers when you're offline.

Chatbots aim to reach customers quickly, particularly when you're offline. You can redirect people from your direct message to your email or give them a number to text if you're small enough to handle the volume. You might not frequently receive direct messages, but it could significantly impact getting a personal response.

With a Meta Business Suite account, you can create free, automated messages to communicate on Facebook or Instagram. These can be as simple as "we're busy making the pies and muffins, please call us at (000)-000-000 if you need something right away. We'll check messages later." Software companies like Manychat provide a more sophisticated system for responses. Manychat has the option for free accounts or paid plans starting at $15 per month.

Chatbots aren't meant to replace human interaction but to pick up the slack for offline times and help. The key is using simple language without sounding robotic. Starting your message with a greeting is helpful. There's great information about creating chatbots on YouTube and blogs with step-by-step guides. Research it in one of your Friday afternoon social sessions if you want to try it.

I like to have a chatbot message on a Facebook Page that I manage because, even though we service North America, I get questions from around the globe–which typically come in any time of the day or night. The automated message gives some information and email contact for more in-depth questions. You can set up instant replies and away messages for Facebook and Instagram in the Meta Business Suite at business.facebook.com/ or in Creator Studio.

Unfortunately, Meta scores your Pages on your response time and response rate if you don't respond to messages. In the world of social media, it's all about making connections that count. And when it comes to your Facebook Page, how swiftly and reliably you answer messages can make all the difference—it's your digital handshake, your promise of attentive service. Nail that, and you could earn the coveted "Very responsive to messages" badge, a shiny little signal to visitors that you're on the ball.

Think of your Page's response rate as your batting average for customer conversations—the higher, the better. It's all about the first messages after a day's silence between you and a customer. The aim? Keep that response rate sky-high over the last thirty days, and you're golden.

What if your Page is more like a boutique than a busy marketplace, with less than a handful of messages in recent days? Your response rate will use the last ten messages you've had. And if your Page is starting to make waves and hasn't yet hit the ten-message mark? Then every message counts, and your response rate will reflect your entire chat history. Every message is a chance to shine and show how much you value those reaching out.

Whether tapping out replies personally or setting your friendly chatbot to lend a hand, each response is a step toward that sparkling response rate and time. Just remember, quick hellos and "I'm out of the office" notes don't count toward this number—nor do those messages that slip into the spam folder. It's a juggling act of warmth and speed, so keep those replies thoughtful and timely, and watch as your Page becomes a beacon of superb service.

Using a chatbot isn't something you have to do—really, nothing in this book is a "have to." But I want to share options from which you can pick and choose. This might not be where you want to start, but you could include it in future processes.

Adding a little automation to your social media marketing is an intelligent way to use your time wisely and work at connecting with customers. It's just one step toward responding; the next step always requires a human.

Customer service and communication are essential to your business and can help you grow faster.

TO-DO NOTES

1. Create a list of customer questions/FAQs.
2. How will you monitor conversations?
3. Check out chatbots for messages.

Weaving Your Brand Story into the Social Tapestry

If history were taught in the form of stories, it would never be forgotten.

—*Rudyard Kipling*

Stories connect people.

Why is storytelling important in today's busy online world? We're all swamped with messages all day long from email, social media, television, and our smartphones—you get the picture! Storytelling has been around since we first started communicating with each other, and while the mediums may have changed, it's still a powerful way to communicate. These powerful storytelling ideas can help boost your social media marketing and reach more people.

Author and marketing expert Seth Godin said, "I would like to describe marketing as the art of telling a story that resonates with your audience and then spreads. That story better be true, which means that implicit in marketing is making something for which, or about which, you could tell a story that resonates."[1] *Storytelling can turn into story selling* as you incorporate your story into your marketing.

Stories have been passed down through many generations. Before we had written language, we had oral storytellers. They created and shared legends that were passed down from one generation to the next. These were our trusted communicators who kept the narrative of the culture alive and passed down valuable information about how to support the tribe and stay safe.

Today, stories are passed down to us from our grandparents, parents, and even siblings. I'm sure we all have advice we treasure from our grandparents and stories from our siblings that became part of our family heritage. My sister told me I was adopted (which wasn't true), but it is part of the sibling narrative in many families.

We also absorb stories from media such as television and movies, which become part of our cultural narrative. Our shared stories become cultural shorthand as we can retell them just from hearing a specific name or a tiny story snippet. "Once upon a time" may conjure the story of a girl with a red hood going to her grandmother's house. "A long time ago in a galaxy far, far away" zips us into the *Star Wars* saga. Millions of people know these familiar phrases.

As humans, we're inherently wired to connect with people through stories. This is how relationships and trust are developed. Trust is the currency of social marketing. Attention is given to trusted, authentic brands. Fluffy narratives, stories without substance, are a waste of time. Trust is built through the repeated sharing of stories, which is evident in social marketing. You must show up consistently and work on the relationships you're developing in your community. There are no shortcuts to building the foundation of trust, but storytelling can be a building block within your communications with your community.

Crafting a compelling story that resonates with an audience is crucial for building a solid brand identity and engaging with your target audience. In social media, your story acts as a bridge, connecting your brand's heart to the audience's pulse. It's a journey unfolding with each post and update, inviting your audience to enter your world. The narrative you craft should echo the beat of authenticity—stories that are true to you will resonate most. They'll feel the emotions you weave into your content, whether it's the warmth of joy or a surge of inspiration. And clarity? It's your North Star. Each message, clear and crisp, should illuminate the values that your brand embodies. By sharing these genuine snippets of your brand's life, you'll find that storytelling on social media isn't just about telling—it's about engaging, sharing, and connecting.

1. *Authenticity*: Your story should be genuine and authentic. Don't try to be someone you're not or tell a story that isn't true. People can sense when something is fake or disingenuous, and it can harm your brand's reputation. Be honest and transparent, and don't be afraid to show vulnerability. People will connect with your story more deeply when you share your authentic self and experiences.

2. *Emotional Resonance*: A compelling story should evoke emotions in your audience. Emotions make stories memorable—joy, sadness, anger, or hope. When crafting your story, consider what emotions you want to elicit in your audience and how you can do so effectively. Consider sharing personal anecdotes, using powerful imagery, or incorporating music or sound effects to enhance the emotional impact of your story.

3. *Clear Messaging*: Your story should have a clear, concise message that aligns with your brand values and resonates with your audience. It should be easy for your audience to understand what your brand stands for and what you are trying to communicate. Be more specific, and do not use industry jargon that your audience may not be familiar with. Keep your message simple and easy to remember.

Using an example of a small family law practice shows how the brand's story on social media can be both powerful and engaging. Here are some ideas:

Share the origin story of your practice: Talk about the moment or the experiences that inspired you to start your firm. Maybe it was a personal encounter with family law or a desire to fill a gap in your community's legal services.

Explain why you chose family law: Your followers will be interested to know why you're passionate about family law. Share stories that shaped your decision—perhaps it's about helping families find fair resolutions or protecting the interests of children.

Highlight your community involvement: Tell stories about your pro-bono work and how it impacts the community. You could share testimonials from those you've helped or discuss how offering pro-bono services aligns with your firm's core values.

Share your success stories: Without breaching client confidentiality, you can share anonymized success stories that illustrate how you've guided clients through challenging times to successful outcomes.

Remember, storytelling is not just about the narrative—it's about human connection. Your stories should reflect the empathy, expertise, and commitment your practice brings to the table daily.

In social storytelling for a small family law practice, three emotions that could be strategically woven into the narrative are:

1. *Compassion*: Demonstrating deep understanding and empathy for clients' situations.
2. *Trust*: Building a sense of reliability and integrity around the practice.
3. *Hope*: Conveying an optimistic outlook for resolutions and new beginnings.

These emotions can humanize the law firm, making it more relatable and approachable to potential clients.

Here are some practical tips and strategies for incorporating storytelling into your social media marketing strategy:

1. *Use visual content*: Visual content, such as images and videos, can be a powerful storytelling tool. Use it to bring your story to life and help your audience connect with your brand on a deeper level. Consider

creating short videos showcasing your brand's personality or using compelling images highlighting your brand's values.

2. *Be consistent*: Consistency is key when it comes to storytelling. Ensure that your brand's messaging and storytelling are consistent across all social media platforms. This will help to reinforce your brand's identity and make it easier for your audience to connect with your story.

3. *Engage with your audience*: Encourage them to share their stories and experiences related to your brand. This can foster a sense of community and further enhance the emotional resonance of your storytelling. Respond to comments and messages and show your audience that you value their input and appreciate their support.

Turn a creative eye on your brand and think of ways to share the people and pieces of your brand that make you unique and memorable. Telling your brand story will help customers know you better and love you for what you do.

Let's look at a few examples of storytelling on social media.

One of my favorite authors, Elizabeth Gilbert, shared her journey in her best-selling book *Eat, Pray, Love* and connect with millions of readers worldwide. Writing about her experience of self-discovery, love, and finding hope helped so many people realize that because she went through all that and came out okay, maybe they could go through hard things and be okay, too. Liz shares many tidbits of her life and works on social media, and I love seeing her kick-in-the-pants messages as part of my day.

One of my new favorite authors is best-selling romance author Katherine Center. She uses her social media to share her writing process, behind-the-scenes peeks at book events, and creative pursuits. She talks about why she writes about love, and you get to know her piece by piece as she shares about the characters she writes about or something in her past that inspired a location in a book. She's fully emersed in the art of writing and excels at connecting with social storytelling.

Dove is a well-established beauty brand that goes all-in on the stories. They've used their campaigns to talk about more than just their product. In 2004, they launched their successful Real Beauty campaign, one of the most successful campaigns in the history of advertising, according to the *New York Times.*[2] They are currently focusing on their film *Toxic Influence*, part of their Dove Self-Esteem campaign. Their description: "You wouldn't give your daughter toxic beauty advice, but she could hear it online. Every. Single. Day."

In the short film, they had mothers, and their preteen daughters, watch deep-fake AI videos of the mothers giving toxic beauty advice that teens see on Instagram and TikTok daily. Deep fakes are a technology that uses artificial intelligence to manipulate digital media, such as video, by swapping one person's likeness with another. The process is achieved through deep learning algorithms. The video doesn't reference Dove's products but inserts them into the beauty conversation online. The campaign touched many emotions as the mothers and daughters talked through the experience and how they felt about the toxic beauty advice.

What could storytelling look like for your small business? I'll use an example of a dry cleaner called Main Street Cleaners. This is a third-generation dry-cleaning business where Joe works with his parents, who inherited the business from his grandparents. Joe went to college and studied marketing. He wants to share his family's rich history and community connections on their new social media account. Here's what a week of social posts looks like for Main Street Cleaners:

- Monday: A short video shot in the front office showing their easy checkout process. They've added Apple Pay and Venmo to make it easy for people on the go.
- Tuesday: Band uniforms are in from the local high school, and they take some photos of them for a carousel post. Community spirit! They include a vintage photo of someone from their family in their band uniform and ask people what instrument they used to play in the text.

- Wednesday: A reminder to schedule free pickup and delivery by calling or using their app.
- Thursday: A "Throwback Thursday" photo of the original owners, Betty and Michael, in the first year of running the business. They share how long they've been downtown and in business.
- Friday: They share one of their best services with the text: "Have you heard about our white glove service? Let's show you exactly how it works and a few of our favorite things about it!" [They list the features and benefits of their service and remind people to book now].
- Saturday: An update on weekend hours.
- Sunday: A seasonal post with leaves changing or the first snow of the year. Something timely.

In addition, you could home in on these storytelling ideas:

- Share how your brand started.
- Create a visual brand that helps people understand who you are and what you do.
- Invite "super fans" to give testimonials about your product or service.
- Share social media posts made by other people that reference your brand. This is known as User Generated Content (or UGC). GoPro does a fantastic job with this. Your fans sharing what they love is part of your story.
- Use video to introduce your staff to the world.

Telling stories that resonate with your audience is essential for building a strong brand identity and engaging with your target audience. By emphasizing authenticity, emotional resonance, and clear messaging and using practical tips and strategies for incorporating storytelling into your social media marketing strategy, you can create a powerful and memorable brand story that connects with your audience and drives business success.

We'll go into more detail about how to create social media content later in the book. I hope these storytelling examples inspire you and help you weave your story into your social media messages. It might seem scary or challenging at first, but I think you'll find that the things that make you unique will also make you successful.

People online will connect with your brand through your stories. Done correctly, they'll build a connection and a sense of community.

I hope you see how all the pieces are fitting together!

TO DO NOTES

1. Research three brand origin stories.
2. Write out your brand's origin story.
3. Create a mood board in Canva for your origin story.

Crafting Impactful Content

Canva Essentials for
Small Businesses

Everything you can imagine is real.

—Pablo Picasso

---

*I*n this chapter, we'll explore a tool that has revolutionized how small businesses approach visual content creation: Canva. As entrepreneurs, we understand the power of effective branding and engaging social media presence. Canva offers many features and functionalities that can help elevate your brand's online presence and captivate your audience. Let's look at Canva and discover how it can empower you to create stunning visuals for your business. Full disclosure: I worked with Canva as the head of social strategy. And I still love them!

GETTING STARTED WITH CANVA

Getting started in Canva is a breeze for small business owners, even if you need to gain design experience. With its user-friendly interface and extensive library of templates, Canva offers a seamless introduction to graphic design. To begin, create a free account and explore the platform's design options. Whether you're crafting social media posts, presentations, or marketing materials, Canva provides intuitive tools for customizing your creations to suit your brand's aesthetic. With no prior design experience required, Canva empowers users to unleash their creativity and quickly bring their ideas to life.

DESIGNING EYE-CATCHING GRAPHICS

Designing eye-catching graphics is a pivotal aspect of establishing a compelling online presence. With Canva's extensive range of templates, users have a plethora of options to choose from to kick-start their design journey. Once a template is selected, customization becomes key in tailoring the design to align with specific branding and messaging. Canva's intuitive editing tools enable users to effortlessly tweak elements such as colors, fonts, and imagery, ensuring each graphic resonates with the intended audience. Moreover, incorporating brand elements such as logos and color palettes further reinforces brand identity and fosters brand recognition across various platforms. Through thoughtful selection and meticulous customization, Canva empowers users to craft visually stunning graphics that easily captivate and engage audiences.

ENGAGING SOCIAL MEDIA POSTS

Engaging social media posts are the lifeblood of any successful online presence, serving as the primary vehicle for capturing audience attention and driving interaction. With Canva's versatile tool kit, crafting attention-grabbing posts becomes an effortless endeavor. Users can tap in to an extensive array of design elements, from captivating visuals to dynamic typography, to create posts that stand out amidst the digital noise. Moreover, Canva's design tools and effects suite empower users to elevate their posts with stunning graphics, eye-catching animations, and polished finishes. Whether enhancing images with filters, adding stylish overlays, or incorporating striking text effects, Canva provides the flexibility and creativity to make every post shine.

However, engaging social media posts go beyond aesthetics and thrive on interactivity. Canva offers a range of interactive elements, such as poll templates, quizzes, and countdown-timer videos that users can seamlessly integrate into their posts to foster meaningful engagement and encourage audience participation. By leveraging these interactive features, users can spark conversations, gather feedback, and forge deeper connections with their followers, ultimately driving greater brand affinity and loyalty. With Canva as their creative ally, users can unleash their imagination and craft social media posts that captivate and compel audiences to take action, amplifying their online presence and fostering a vibrant and engaged community.

DESIGNING FOR DIFFERENT PLATFORMS

Designing for different platforms ensures that your content resonates effectively across various channels and devices. Canva's intuitive platform allows users to seamlessly tailor their designs to meet the unique specifications of each platform, from social media posts to website banners and beyond. Whether adjusting aspect ratios, cropping images, or fine-tuning layouts, Canva offers a range of tools to optimize designs for maximum impact.

One standout feature that simplifies the process of adapting designs for different platforms is Canva's "Magic Resize" tool. This powerful feature allows users to instantly resize their designs with a single click, saving valuable time by eliminating the need for manual adjustments. Whether repurposing a Facebook post for Instagram or resizing a banner for a website header, Magic Resize ensures that your content maintains its visual integrity across every platform.

In addition to resizing, Canva provides options for optimizing image sizes to ensure fast loading times and optimal display quality. Users can easily compress images, adjust resolutions, and optimize file formats to perfectly balance quality and performance. By tailoring designs and optimizing image sizes with Canva, users can confidently deliver engaging and visually compelling content that resonates with their audiences across every platform they use.

BRAND STORYTELLING

Brand storytelling with Canva offers businesses an exceptional opportunity to connect with their audiences on a deeper level and convey their unique brand identity. At its core, brand storytelling is about communicating a brand's values, mission, and essence in a compelling and authentic way. With Canva's versatile design platform, businesses can bring their brand stories to life through visually captivating content that resonates with their target audience.

Communicating brand values is a fundamental aspect of brand storytelling, and Canva provides the tools to convey these values through visuals effectively. Whether it's through striking imagery, impactful typography, or evocative color schemes, Canva empowers users to create designs that authentically reflect their brand's core beliefs and principles. Businesses can forge emotional connections and foster brand loyalty by infusing designs with elements that resonate with their audience.

In addition to communicating brand values, Canva enables businesses to design branded templates that visually represent their brand identity. These templates can encompass various marketing materials, including social media posts, presentations, and promotional materials, providing consistency and cohesion across all touchpoints. By incorporating brand logos, colors, and imagery into templates, Canva ensures that every piece of content reinforces the brand's visual identity and strengthens brand recognition. You can create a brand kit in Canva Pro that saves all your visual brand elements.

Through brand storytelling with Canva, businesses can craft compelling narratives that resonate with their audiences and leave lasting impressions. By effectively communicating brand values and designing branded templates, companies can establish a solid and cohesive brand identity that sets them apart in a crowded marketplace and fosters meaningful connections with their audience.

CANVA PRO: ADVANCED FEATURES

Canva Pro unlocks a treasure trove of advanced features tailored to elevate your design game and streamline your workflow. One of the standout benefits of Canva Pro is access to a vast library of premium templates and graphics. These professionally crafted assets are designed to help you stand out in a sea of content by offering polished and eye-catching designs across various categories. Whether you're creating social media posts, presentations, or marketing materials, Canva Pro's premium templates provide a solid foundation for your creative endeavors, saving you time and effort in the design process.

Furthermore, Canva Pro's collaboration tools revolutionize how teams work on design projects. With features like real-time collaboration and commenting, teams can seamlessly collaborate on designs, regardless of their location or time zone. Whether you're brainstorming ideas, providing feedback, or making edits, Canva Pro's collaboration tools ensure that everyone is on the same page and working toward a common goal. Additionally, Canva Pro allows you to create custom branding kits to maintain consistency across all your designs and streamline your brand management process.

By harnessing Canva Pro's advanced features, users can unlock new levels of creativity, efficiency, and collaboration in their design endeavors. Whether you're a solo entrepreneur looking to improve your visual content or a team striving to streamline your design workflow, Canva Pro provides the tools and resources you need to bring your creative vision to life and achieve your goals with confidence.

CANVA LIKE A PRO

Advanced techniques in Canva dig deeper into design with animation, video editing, and infographic creation, offering users the tools to elevate their designs to new heights of creativity and engagement. With Canva's intuitive platform, mastering animation and video editing becomes accessible, even for those with limited technical expertise. Users can effortlessly bring their designs to life with dynamic animations, transitions, and effects, transforming static content into captivating visual experiences. Whether adding subtle movement to text elements or creating eye-catching video presentations, Canva empowers users to captivate their audience with stunning animated content.

In addition to animation and video editing, Canva enables users to create compelling infographics that distill complex information into visually digestible graphics. With a wide range of customizable templates and design elements, users can seamlessly craft infographics that communicate data, statistics, and critical insights clearly and engagingly. From charts and graphs to icons and illustrations, Canva provides the building blocks needed to create visually striking infographics that resonate with audiences and convey information effectively.

By mastering advanced techniques in Canva, users can unlock the full potential of their designs and create visually compelling content that stands out in a crowded digital landscape. Whether breathing life into static designs with animation and video editing or simplifying complex information with captivating infographics, Canva empowers users to push the boundaries of creativity and craft impactful visual experiences that leave a lasting impression on their audiences.

Canva is constantly adding new features and elements to its platform. Be sure to check out the Canva Design School Courses, their blog, and their social channels for up-to-date tips and updates.

Whether you're a seasoned marketer looking to elevate your brand's visual identity or a small business owner striving to make a splash in the digital landscape, Canva provides the tools and resources you need to succeed. Remember, visual content is the heart and soul of social media, serving as a powerful tool for capturing attention, sparking engagement, and fostering meaningful connections with your audience.

Staying ahead of the curve in the ever-evolving world of social media requires a commitment to creativity, innovation, and authenticity. By embracing Canva's intuitive platform and harnessing the power of visual content, you can stand out from the crowd, make a lasting impression, and achieve your goals in the dynamic world of social media. Go forth and unleash your creativity with Canva and watch as your visual content transforms into a driving force for success for your business.

TO DO NOTES

1. Craft a visually engaging social media post for Instagram, Facebook, or Twitter using Canva. Choose a template, add your message, and customize with visuals and text.
2. Design a vibrant flyer to promote your event with Canva. Pick a template, insert event details, and personalize with eye-catching graphics.
3. Create a professional business card using Canva. Select a template, add your contact info, and customize with your branding elements for a polished look.

How to Grow Your Social Media Presence

Social media for business isn't the same as a personal brand or influencer trying to get a million followers on TikTok; you will want to grow your account to reach potential customers.

Everyone wants a shortcut to social media success, but sadly there is no "easy" button. I want to share some proven tricks for achieving the best results on social media. They're sure to give you a boost in your results.

BE HELPFUL

Being helpful is a great way to connect with people. Best-selling social media author Jay Baer says, "Youtility is marketing so useful, people would pay for it (if you asked them). It's marketing customers want, instead of marketing that companies think they need."[1] Providing free help can lead to paying customers down the road.

BE THOUGHTFUL

Leaving thoughtful comments on other people's posts goes a long way! Here are three ways you could comment thoughtfully.

1. *Acknowledge the content*: Start by expressing appreciation for the post's content or message. For example, "Wow, what an insightful perspective! Your post really got me thinking about [topic]."
2. *Share personal insights or experiences*: Relate the post to your own experiences or thoughts, adding depth to the conversation. For instance, "I can totally relate to this. I had a similar experience when [share your story]."
3. *Offer encouragement or support*: End with words of encouragement or support to the poster, fostering a positive and uplifting atmosphere. You could say something like, "Keep spreading positivity! Your posts always brighten my day."

BE A PROBLEM SOLVER
Try to solve problems daily and always put your best foot forward. Be a giver first. Give your knowledge, expertise, and experience.

BE A LISTENER
Social listening can help you find frustrated people needing solutions in your industry. Create hashtag or keyword searches to connect with people—who may turn into grateful customers down the road.

BE BRIEF
Brevity beats verbosity on social media. You compete with millions of posts daily, and people make snap judgments and move right along if you don't capture their interest quickly. BuzzSumo's tests determined that Facebook posts with 150 to 200 characters and tweets with only around 100 characters performed the best. The sweet spot for written content is 500 to 1,000 words.

Data from Orbit Media[2] says, "Blog posts vary in length from a few short paragraphs (Seth Godin style) to 40,000 words (Neil Patel style). If your goal is search engine traffic, longer is better." The ideal length for a search-optimized blog post is 1,500 words and up. The key is to make sure you're providing value.

BE BOLD

Success favors the bold and the interesting on social media, so don't hesitate to think outside the box. Guy Kawasaki's theory is that "if you're not pissing people off on social media, you're not using it right." At the same time, I don't take as bold a stance as Guy; I don't try to make people angry, but pushing boundaries can be good. If everyone loves what you're doing, you might be too bland.

BE CONSISTENT

Posting daily keeps your account top-of-mind and relevant. Creating a content creation calendar will help you stay consistent. (More on this in the chapter on creating an editorial calendar!)

BE SHAREABLE

Likes aren't the goal; you want to create sharable and saveable content. Shareable content can be funny, entertaining, helpful, or relevant.

BE VISUAL

Every post—literally every single one—should contain "eye candy" in the form of a picture, graphic, or video. According to a study by Skyword, total views of its customers' content increased by 94 percent if a published article contained a relevant photograph or infographic, compared to pieces in the same category without an image. An excellent graphic or embedded video is as essential for the success of a post as its text. ninety-five percent of B2B customers—B2B is business to business—evaluate a company based on visual content, according to Ziflow.[3]

BE FOUND

Hashtags are a beautiful thing. They connect posts from people worldwide and add structure to an otherwise-unstructured ecosystem. When you add a hashtag to a post, you tell others that the post is relevant to a shared topic. For example, #socialmediatips connects posts that are about social media. X, Instagram, and Facebook all support hashtags. I recommend adding two or three to all your posts. If you use more than that, however, you look like an #newb trying to #gamethesystem. The sweet spot for Instagram hashtags is currently three to four but it's also valuable to add important keywords into your caption contextually. The jury is still out on hashtags on Facebook. They do work, but they can look spammy. Hashtags on Facebook aren't wrong, but they aren't as effective or as widely used.

BE INTERESTED

Showing interest in other people helps you maintain your connection online. Remember their names and read their content. Follow people who are interesting and who engage with your account. Social media won't work for you if you treat it as a one-way form of communication.

Here are some specific examples of how businesses can apply the tips mentioned in this chapter to their social media strategy:

1. *Being helpful*: A pet store could create a series of posts or videos that provide helpful tips for new pet owners. Recommendations could include advice on training, grooming, or choosing the right pet food. By providing valuable information, the pet store builds trust with its audience and positions itself as an authority in the pet care space.
2. *Leaving thoughtful comments*: A local bakery could leave thoughtful comments on posts from other small businesses in the community. Comments help to build relationships and create opportunities for collaboration in the future.
3. *Solving problems*: A tech company could monitor social media for posts from users experiencing issues with their product. By responding quickly and offering solutions, the company shows that it cares about its customers and is committed to providing high support.

4. *Social listening*: A fashion brand could monitor social media for conversations about sustainable fashion. The brand can attract a passionate and engaged audience by joining the discussion and sharing information about its sustainable practices.

5. *Brevity*: A software company could share short, informative Threads posts highlighting new features or product updates. By keeping the message short and to the point, the company is more likely to capture the attention of busy professionals looking for quick, valuable information.

6. *Boldness*: A social media marketing agency could share controversial opinions on industry trends. The agency can generate conversation and establish itself as a thought leader by taking a solid stance.

7. *Consistency*: A fitness studio could create a content calendar with daily posts about upcoming classes, healthy recipes, and motivational quotes. By staying consistent and providing regular updates, the studio can keep its followers engaged and encourage them to visit the studio more frequently.

8. *Shareability:* A coffee shop could create visually stunning posts highlighting its latte art or unique brewing methods. By creating visually appealing and informative posts, the coffee shop can encourage its followers to share the content with their friends and followers.

9. *Visuals*: A real estate agent could create a video tour of a new property that it has listed. By showcasing the property in a visually engagingly way, the agency can attract potential buyers and differentiate itself from competitors who only share static images.

10. *Hashtags*: A nonprofit organization could create a campaign around a specific cause and encourage its followers to share posts with a designated hashtag. The nonprofit can mobilize its followers to act and support its cause by creating a sense of community and shared purpose.

Creating entertaining and relevant content is crucial for any success-ful social media strategy. Here are a few tips on how to achieve these qualities:

1. *Attention-grabbing headlines*: A great headline can mean the dif-ference between someone scrolling past your post or clicking to read more. Use catchy phrases, ask thought-provoking questions, or make a bold statement. Be sure to keep it short and to the point.
2. *Incorporating humor*: Humor can be a great way to make your content more engaging and memorable. Be bold and show off your brand's personality and sense of humor. Just keep it appropriate for your audience and avoid being offensive.
3. *Using storytelling*: As mentioned earlier in the chapter, storytelling is a powerful tool for engaging your audience. Use stories to connect with your audience personally and make your content more relat-able. Share success stories, customer testimonials, or even behind-the-scenes glimpses of your business.
4. *Being relevant: To* be relevant, you need to know your audience and stay current with your industry's current events and trends. Share timely content that addresses your followers' needs and interests. Use social listening tools to monitor conversations and stay ahead of the curve.
5. *Engaging with your audience*: Engagement is a two-way street. En-courage your audience to participate in conversations, ask questions, and share their opinions. Respond promptly and authentically to comments and direct messages. The discussion will help build trust and loyalty with your followers

Remember, being entertaining and relevant on social media takes time and effort. Be patient, experiment with different types of content, and continuously track your results to see what works best for your business.

Here are a few more tools for social media success:

1. Trello keeps my life organized, and you can use it to color-code! It's an essential item for people working on teams, saving ideas, and planning content.
2. Notion is a user-friendly organization app that syncs between devices. It's easy to customize to your preferred aesthetic.
3. Canva lets me create gorgeous graphics on the go. It's free and super-fun to use. Everything looks 100 percent professional, and they have free images you can use in your designs.
4. Plann is my favorite tool for Instagram and other social media management. It allows you to create posts and track and respond to comments.
5. SmarterQueue is a fantastic tool for managing multiple platforms.
6. Buzzsumo is a great place to find content to share on social media.

A shiny new toy or tool constantly pop up, but don't waste your time trying every new thing. Don't pull your focus from getting real work done. It's more important to be consistent and engaging on your social media than to spend too much time testing new tools, unless that's the focus of your job. Try one social planning tool and one organizational tool and test drive them for a while before trying something else. It takes time to get your accounts set up and get used to using them.

Take the time to work on what will make your social media unique and inviting, and then do the work.

TO-DO NOTES

1. Try three social media scheduling tools. Choose one.
2. List three growth ideas you will try.
3. List ten ways you can be helpful to your community.

Capturing Hearts and Minds

Engagement Essentials

My experience is what I agree to attend to. Only those items which I notice shape my mind.

—*William James,* The Principles of Psychology, Vol I

*T*he attention economy is the concept that attention has become scarce in today's digital age, with so much content vying for users' attention. In this economy, businesses and individuals compete for users' attention and time, and those who can capture and hold attention the longest are the most successful. Social media platforms have become major players in the attention economy. Algorithms, by design, are created to keep users engaged and on their platforms for as long as possible.

Herbert Alexander Simon, an American economist, political scientist, and cognitive psychologist, is recognized for formulating the notion of the *attention economy*.[1] In his 1971 article titled "Designing organizations for an information-rich world," Simon explained that information and attention operate under the laws of supply and demand. He wrote:

"In an information-rich world, the wealth of information means a poverty of attention."

Fast-forward to the current day, and we can see that Herbert was right. The University of California–San Diego has reported that the average American consumes approximately thirty-four gigabytes of data and information daily. This quantity is equivalent to reading or hearing about a hundred thousand words daily, approximately the same as the number of words in J.R.R. Tolkien's *The Hobbit* (95,356 words).

"In 2004, we measured the average attention on a screen to be two and a half minutes," Gloria Mark, author of *Attention Span: A Groundbreaking Way to Restore Balance, Happiness, and Productivity* said. "Some years later, we found attention spans about 75 seconds. Now we find people can only pay attention to one screen for an average of 47 seconds."[2]

More data and less attention span push humans and the attention economy to the brink. Why is this important to social media? Algorithms fuel the attention economy on social media.

ATTENTION DRIVES ALGORITHMS AND SOCIAL PLATFORMS

Algorithms are the mysterious forces behind social media platforms and search engines. An algorithm is a set of step-by-step instructions a computer program follows to perform a particular task or solve a problem. In general, algorithms automate repetitive or complex processes, making them more efficient and accurate.

In search engines, algorithms process and rank the results of a search query based on various factors such as relevance, popularity, and authority. The specific algorithms used by search engines like Google and Bing are closely guarded trade secrets. Still, they typically consider many factors, including keyword density, site structure, user behavior, and backlinks.

Algorithms are like a set of instructions or rules that search engines use to decide which websites should rank highest in the result pages. When you enter a search query, the algorithm processes all of the possible websites that could show up and analyzes different signals and metrics to calculate each site's relevance and authority. Specifically, some things the algorithm may look at include:

Keyword density: How often is the main search term used on the page compared to other words? Using the main keyword carefully and several times can signal relevance.

Site structure: Is the website well-organized with headings, titles, and relevant sections? A clear structure helps search engines parse the content.

User behavior: How long do visitors stay on that site? Fast bounce backs may indicate poor user experience.

Backlinks: Does the site have some websites linking back to it, signaling it's a quality authority on the topic? Lots of editors/sites referencing can equal endorsements.

There are many additional signals algorithms use, too. The exact mathematical formulas and weights given to each factor is top secret. But analyzing and optimizing based on known signals can help improve rankings over time. The key for creators is producing high-quality, useful sites and content that aligns with search intent.

On social media platforms, the content you encounter is tailored to your tastes through complex algorithms that curate your experience. You might assume your feed only displays posts from accounts you follow, but algorithms are at work. Take Instagram, for instance: if you spend time watching a Reel about gardening, don't be surprised if your feed suddenly blooms with similar, green-thumbed content. This is because social platforms analyze your interactions, behaviors, and even the freshness of the content to present you with posts they believe will captivate your attention and keep you scrolling. They're designed to deliver a stream of posts and videos that catch your eye and increase your engagement with the platform.

Pinterest's algorithm[3] works as a discovery engine by combining user data and content features to suggest personalized content to users. The platform uses several signals, such as search terms, user interests, and past engagement, to determine what types of content to show to each individual user.

One of the key features of Pinterest's algorithm is its use of visual search technology. When a user searches Pinterest, the platform uses image-recognition technology to identify the visual elements of the search query and suggest visually similar content. For example, if you search for a recipe on sugarplums, Pinterest will find you a Pin, and underneath this Pin will be other visually similar images and Christmas treat recipes. This means users can find new and interesting content simply by searching for an image they like.

Overall, Pinterest's algorithm works as a discovery engine by combining data and content features to suggest personalized content to users. The platform's focus on visual search and user engagement makes it a popular destination for users looking for inspiration and new ideas.

Attention plays a critical role in social media algorithms and the attention economy. Social media platforms rely on users' attention to generate revenue through advertising. They use algorithms to maximize user engagement and keep users on their platforms for as long as possible.

Social media algorithms prioritize the content that is capturing and holding users' attention. This means that users will likely be shown more visually appealing, emotionally engaging, or controversial content.

IMPORTANCE OF UNDERSTANDING THE ATTENTION ECONOMY FOR SMALL BUSINESSES

Understanding the attention economy is essential because it can help businesses create more effective marketing strategies better suited to the digital age. In today's digital landscape, attention has become a scarce and valuable resource, and small businesses that can capture and hold their target audience's attention are more likely to be successful.

One of the important ways in which small businesses can leverage the attention economy is by creating high-quality, engaging content that resonates with their target audience. This means creating visually appealing, emotionally engaging content tailored to their target customers' interests and preferences. Small businesses can increase their visibility, build brand awareness, and attract new customers by creating content that captures their audience's attention.

Small businesses can leverage the attention economy by using social media platforms and other digital marketing channels to reach their target audience. Proper planning allows you to create campaigns designed to capture your audience's attention and drive engagement using targeted advertising, influencer marketing, and other tactics.

Understanding the attention economy is crucial for small businesses that want to succeed in today's digital landscape. Small businesses can capture and hold their audience's attention by creating engaging content, leveraging digital marketing channels, building brand awareness, and attracting new customers.

The attention economy and algorithms are driving the online world. Using data and analytics, make the best choices possible to create content worthy of your audience's attention.

TO DO NOTES

1. Watch *The Social Dilemma* on Netflix. It's a documentary investigation and narrative drama filmed with Silicon Valley insiders that uncovers the hidden machinations behind everyone's favorite social media and search platforms.
2. Create a plan to make sure you're using your time wisely on social media. Try the Freedom app: https://freedom.to/.
3. Consider how you will respond to messages in a sustainable way?

The LKT Factor

Leveraging Like, Know, and Trust

Kindred spirits are not so scarce as true love but it is rarer than a blue moon.

—*L.M. Montgomery*

---

*W*hat is the LKT strategy (*like*, *know*, and *trust*), and how do you nurture this with your small business brand?

The LKT strategy is essential for small businesses because it establishes a strong relationship between the company and its audience, which can lead to increased customer loyalty and sales.

The "like" stage of the LKT strategy involves creating engaging, relatable, and relevant content for your target audience. This can include posting on social media, writing blog posts, creating videos or podcasts, or formulating other content that resonates with your audience. By creating content your audience likes, you can build a relationship and establish your brand as one that understands and cares about its customers.

The "know" stage of the LKT strategy involves building trust and credibility with your audience. This can be done by sharing your expertise, providing valuable information or advice, or showcasing the quality of your products or services. By establishing yourself as a knowledgeable source of information or a high-quality provider, you can build trust with your audience and increase their confidence in your brand.

The "trust" stage of the LKT strategy involves fostering a sense of loyalty and commitment from your audience. This can be achieved by delivering on your promises, providing exceptional customer service, and maintaining consistent and transparent communication. Building a solid relationship with your audience can increase loyalty and encourage repeat business.

Embracing the LKT approach—*like, know, trust*—for your small business means crafting content that strikes a chord with the folks you aim to serve. Give them something of value, not just through what you sell, but in how you sell it. Build a bond steeped in trust and loyalty. How? By showing up on social media, having honest conversations, listening, and acting on feedback—and maybe throwing in a cheeky little discount. Top-notch customer service is your golden ticket here. Keep your word, overdeliver where you can, and create those warm, fuzzy customer moments. Do this, and y*ou're* not just a brand, but a trusted friend in the digital marketplace.

While there is no single definitive source for the LKT strategy, it is a widely recognized and accepted approach to building customer relationships in the context of small business branding and marketing. The LKT strategy is based on the idea that customers are more likely to do business with brands they like, know, and trust, and building relationships with customers is vital to long-term success.

The LKT strategy has been widely discussed in marketing and business publications, including *Forbes*, Entrepreneur, and *Inc.* Magazine. It is also commonly taught in business and marketing courses. Small business experts and consultants often recommend it as an effective way to build brand awareness, generate leads, and increase customer loyalty.

While the specifics of the LKT strategy may vary depending on the context and industry, the underlying principles of building customer relationships through likability, knowledge, and trust are widely recognized as key to building a successful small business brand.

Here are five examples of social media content that could help a local surf shop grow its LKT factor:

1. *Behind-the-scenes*: Share glimpses of your surf shop, from how you make your surfboards to daily life at the store. This gives your audience an insight into your business and helps them get to know your brand better.
2. *Customer Testimonials*: Share customer testimonials, featuring photos of them surfing with your products or enjoying the overall experience at your store. This helps build trust and credibility with potential customers as they see others enjoying your products and services.
3. *Educational content*: Share educational content, such as tips on how to select the best surfboard for different types of waves, how to care for your wetsuit, or how to choose the right fins. This shows your audience you are knowledgeable about the surf industry and helps position your brand as a trusted source of information.
4. *Surfing lifestyle photos:* Share photos of people surfing, enjoying the beach, and participating in the lifestyle that comes with it. This helps create a sense of community around your brand and positions your business as more than just a retail shop, but as part of a larger surfing culture.
5. *Promotions and deals*: Share promotions and deals, such as discounts on surfboard rentals or free wax with any purchase. This can incentivize people to visit your store while showing that you value your customers and are willing to go above and beyond to create a great experience.

By sharing different content, such as behind-the-scenes glimpses, customer testimonials, educational content, lifestyle photos, and promotions, this surf shop can build its LKT factor and increase its visibility and credibility with its target audience.

Let's look at ways that you can show likeability, share your knowledge, and build trust with an online community:

Likeability:
1. Be nice.
2. Show your face.
3. Create conversations.

Knowledge:
1. Create at least one valuable resource for your audience.
2. Create value beyond your product.
3. Share a regular newsletter with industry news or relevant information about your company.

Trust:
1. Build and share your brand's values.
2. Show up consistently.
3. Be original.

Hitting the LTK factor will breed familiarity, connection, and authenticity, creating a company that people will support, want to be part of, and support with their purchases, sharing positive experiences, building word-of-mouth buzz, and bringing in new business.

TO DO NOTES

1. List three brands that you feel have the LTK factor.
2. What makes your brand likeable?
3. How will your brand build trust?

Navigating the Storms

How to Handle a Digital Crisis

Imperfection is in some sort essential to all that we know of life. It is the sign of life in a mortal body, that is to say, of a state of progress and change. Nothing that lives is, or can be, rigidly perfect.

—*John Ruskin*[1]

---

*M*istakes happen; how you handle them matters.

There are different kinds of crises that will arise. Some are societal crises, like the outbreak of a war, and sometimes your business has a crisis. We'll look at both of them.

Some mistakes are small, like a typo. Do you delete and repost or move on? If you can fix it, do. Let's look at what happens when something bigger and unexpected happens.

Creating a crisis plan for your business will help you handle events with as little stress as possible. Decide if you'll stop posting on social media during a local or worldwide crisis. Brands need to be aware that emotions will be high, and if you have your usual scheduled posts going out, they could hit wrong and make people angry.

Brands can sound tone-deaf if they post the wrong content or, in some cases, anything mundane during an event fraught with emotion.

Your first step should be to review any scheduled content. Pausing everything while you check is smart.

Here are your options for managing social media during a crisis:

1. Continue posting (risking a faux pax or being tone-deaf).
2. Pause all postings (a wise place to start).
3. Pause and post with empathy (stop regular content and post about the event).
4. Pause and post to help people (providing changes in your service, hours, or community resources).
5. Create a meaningful post and pin it to your profile. Here's an example: "In times like these, words often fall short. As we navigate these challenging moments together, we want you to know that our hearts are with each of you. We're here for support and to help where we can. Let's care for each other and come through this stronger, with hope and solidarity. #CommunityStrong"

SOCIETAL CRISIS

Should you post something for the event? Is it related to your brand, community, or country? While I was writing this book, Queen Elizabeth passed away after a historical seventy-year reign. A pause and post would be a good idea if you were in Great Britain or a Commonwealth.

Remember that people seek more than "thoughts and prayers" posts nowadays. Thoughts and prayers have been widely denounced as a platitude offered in place of meaningful action. There are even memes making fun of this type of post. If you post, have a solid thought behind your post. Posting for the sake of posting without meaning is unnecessary.

Barron's research[2] found that "nearly 60% of Americans want the companies they buy products from to have a position about issues such as racial discrimination and social justice." Brands must think carefully about when and how to make their stances known or if they do at all. Silence is no longer a reliable strategy, especially in political turmoil.

Weigh in on your values and what you feel is important to your small business and community. It is up to you if you want to stay out of all issues. If you can honestly support issues like women's rights or Black Lives Matter, know that some people might not agree, but others will support you because you're supporting their cause.

This is another place where brand voice and values are important; don't mistake your business social media accounts for your personal platform and jump into posting election posts randomly. People are following your business for their own reason, not for your personal opinions.

Remember, as well, that when you post things on your personal profiles, your community will most likely see them.

Authenticity matters greatly. Please don't jump on the bandwagon and use a hashtag simply because it's trending. Before posting that content or message, ask yourself if it adds value to your audience and company.

From Agorapulse,[3] "Does toning down your message make sense? In many cases, it's clear that your brand should either put everything on pause or lend a voice to a cause. But what happens when neither option seems quite right? Perhaps the situation isn't relevant to your brand's mission, but you know it's causing hardships for others. The situation may continue indefinitely, but you can't hold off on publishing social media content for months. Instead, consider toning down your message."

PAUSE ALL PUBLISHING

If you are using a social media scheduling tool, the system will most likely have a "pause all social media posts" option. Here's what it looks like in SmarterQueue. It's easy to hit the "pause all publishing" button and restart posting.

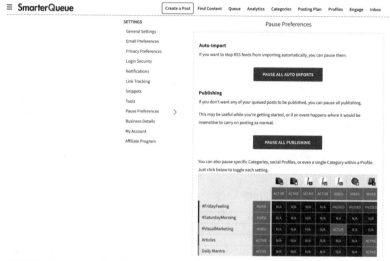

FIGURE 17.1 Example of how to pause all posts in SmarterQueue.
Source: SmarterQueue

BUSINESS CRISIS

Another type of crisis could be related directly to your business. For example, Amy's Bakery and Boutique had an infamous meltdown on Facebook. Buzzfeed [4]called it the most epic brand meltdown ever. Gordon Ramsey had the owners on his show, *Kitchen Nightmares,* and said they were too difficult to work with. The owners started posting angry messages on their Facebook page trying to defend themselves, and comments got heated. The Facebook posts went crazy, and they would not stop posting.

Ultimately, they claimed their social media pages were hacked, which no one believed, and they went out of business. Yelling at people online is never a good tactic; it gets ugly fast, and all the details are on Google forever. Remember that responding to comments is public, and even if you send a private message, it could be screenshotted and shared. The best business is good karma.

The situation with Amy's Bakery and Boutique serves as a critical lesson in crisis management and digital etiquette for small businesses.

Here's a solid recommendation for small businesses to consider:

Maintaining composure and professionalism on social media is paramount in the digital age, in which online interactions are as impactful as those in person. If your business faces a crisis or negative feedback, step back before responding. Craft your messages carefully and consider the long-term impact of your words. Address concerns with grace and seek to resolve issues privately when possible. Do this by commenting publicly and asking them to move the conversation to email or private messages.

It's wise to have a crisis management plan, including designated spokespeople and a strategy for various scenarios. Always remember, the internet has a long memory, and the goodwill of your business is one of its most valuable assets. Strive for resolution over conflict, and let kindness and patience guide your online engagements.

TO-DO NOTES

1. What will you do during a crisis?
2. Learn how to pause posts in your social media management tool.
3. When in doubt, respond publicly, then move to private conversation.

18

The Art of Online Reputation Management

It is not the strongest of the species that survives, nor the most intelligent that survives. It is the one that is most adaptable to change.

—*Charles Darwin*

---

*S*mall business owners have firm opinions about Yelp and online reviews. Many have received harsh reviews and don't know what to do about it. Ignoring them isn't the answer. Let's solve some of the issues with online reviews for small businesses and build positive momentum for your brand online.

People leave online reviews on various platforms, including popular review websites such as Yelp, Google My Business, TripAdvisor, and Facebook. Additionally, industry-specific review sites and directories provide avenues for customers to share their experiences. Social media platforms like Instagram and Facebook also serve as platforms for customers to leave feedback and reviews. It's important for businesses to monitor and engage with reviews on these platforms to maintain a positive online reputation.

Here's why Yelp packs a punch:

1. *Social Proof*: People trust other people. When they see a lot of glowing (or not-so-glowing) reviews, they're more likely to trust (or not trust) that business. It's like getting advice from a friend, except your friend is a bunch of strangers on the internet.
2. *Decision Making*: Choosing where to eat or which service to hire can take time and effort. Yelp swoops in with reviews, ratings, and photos to help make those decisions easier. It's like having a personal recommendation engine in your pocket.
3. *Transparency*: Yelp holds businesses accountable. If a restaurant serves up soggy fries or a mechanic tries to rip you off, you can bet someone's going to Yelp about it. That transparency keeps businesses on their toes.
4. *Community*: Yelp is not only reviews; it's a community. People share tips, photos, and experiences. You can follow reviewers whose tastes match yours or join discussions about your favorite spots.
5. *Business Impact*: For businesses, Yelp can make or break their reputation. Positive reviews can drive in droves of customers, while negative ones can send them running for the hills. It's like word-of-mouth on steroids.

According to a study by Nielsen,[1] a whopping 85 percent of consumers find local business information online, where reviews, store hours, deals, and maps are just a click away. Nielsen also observed that "more than half (51%) of Yelp users make their purchase decisions after visiting the site. The figure for mobile Yelpers is even higher. While Yelp visits don't always result in action, users report that 93 percent of the time, Yelp usage results in occasionally, frequently, or always purchasing a local business."

The biggest reason to be active on Yelp is to know what people say about your company. The same advice follows for Google and Facebook reviews. Since you're a local small business, being active on Yelp for your personal use will help you to understand how it works and what types of things people comment on.

Start by downloading the Yelp app to your smartphone: iOS or Android. Then use it occasionally to find a restaurant or service in your community. If you have a great meal or good service, leave a positive review and help another small business build its Yelp reviews.

Leaving positive reviews in your community can help build your relationships with other small business owners. Connecting with other business professionals might be counterintuitive to how you've done business offline, but in the online world, relationships are everything, including those with your peers. You're extending a friendly hand within your community by leaving reviews for other businesses. It's a way to show support and build relationships with local businesses. They might return the favor someday! Have you ever heard of the law of reciprocity? It's the idea that when you do something nice for someone, they're more likely to do something nice for you. By leaving positive reviews for other businesses, you increase the likelihood of receiving positive reviews yourself.

In addition to leaving positive reviews, there are several other ways in which building relationships can help small businesses grow:

1. *Collaboration and Partnerships*: You can explore collaboration opportunities and partnerships by establishing solid relationships with other businesses. This can include joint marketing campaigns, co-hosted events, cross-promotion, or even sharing resources. Such alliances can help expand your customer base and increase brand visibility.

2. *Referral Network*: Cultivating relationships with fellow business owners can lead to a strong referral network. When you have a positive connection with someone, they are more likely to refer customers to your business, and vice versa. Referrals are an effective method for acquiring new customers and fostering trust in your business.

3. *Knowledge Sharing and Learning*: Connecting with other business professionals allows you to tap in to a wealth of knowledge and expertise. You can exchange ideas; learn from each other's experiences

through discussions, networking events, or online communities; and stay updated on industry trends. This can help you adapt and innovate your business strategies.

4. *Social Media Engagement*: Engaging with other businesses and professionals on social media platforms can widen your reach and increase brand exposure. You can foster relationships, spark conversations, and enhance your online presence by commenting, sharing, and tagging. This engagement also demonstrates to your audience that you are an active participant in your industry.

5. *Support and Mentoring*: Building relationships with business owners who have achieved success can provide valuable mentorship and support. They can offer guidance, advice, and insights based on their own experiences, helping you avoid common pitfalls and navigate challenges. Having a mentor can accelerate your growth and provide a sounding board for new ideas.

Building relationships is an ongoing process that requires genuine effort, consistency, and mutual benefit. By investing time and resources into fostering connections with other small businesses, you nurture growth opportunities and contribute to a strong and supportive business community.

ALWAYS BE HONEST AND POSITIVE

I can't stress enough that Yelp reviews (and all online reviews) need to be organic, heartfelt comments. Don't ask your family members to leave reviews, and don't leave your own thoughts about your business. People are savvy—they will notice—and it's an unethical practice.

Also, definitely don't use Yelp to post negative reviews of your competition as posting fake negative reviews can be considered defamatory. In one case, according to *USA Today*, "A Massachusetts jewelry store employee was ordered to pay $34,500 to a competing jeweler after he posted a false negative review of the store on Yelp."[2]

There isn't a way to game or cheat the system that could beat authentic, real-life comments from customers who love your business. Focus on the positive aspects of your business to earn five-star reviews. Refrain from wasting your time with fake, automated reviews that could do more damage than good. You've probably spent years building a positive reputation for your business; learning to do the same online takes some practice.

If people show up to a restaurant after reading its great Yelp reviews and then have horrible service and bad food, they'll leave an even worse review, letting others know that the restaurant's existing reviews might have been fake.

RESPOND TO YELP REVIEWS WITHIN 24 HOURS

According to a blog post by Yelp, increasing your review count and improving your rating is simpler than you might expect. One strategy that can yield impressive results is responding to reviews with personalized messages promptly. Yelp's Data Science team discovered that users are 33 percent more likely to enhance their reviews when they receive a personalized response within twenty-four hours. Additionally, businesses that respond to reviews experience a 5 percent increase in review counts. As a bonus, this surge in review volume helps attract organic traffic to businesses' Yelp pages. It's time to start crafting those personalized responses and reaping the benefits!

Be positive and proactive in responding to reviews and comments online. To make sure you receive timely notifications for new messages or requests, enable email or push notifications. If you notice a recurring theme in the messages received regarding a specific topic, it's worth considering updating relevant sections of your Yelp page or your website to proactively address these questions. This proactive approach can save time and provide helpful information to potential customers.

In addition to the benefits mentioned, responding promptly to reviews demonstrates that your business cares and is actively engaged with the community. When customers see your timely and personalized responses, it shows them that their feedback is valued and taken seriously. This level of attentiveness can foster a positive perception of your brand, build trust, and encourage customer loyalty. It also gives you an opportunity to address any concerns or issues raised in the reviews, showcasing your commitment to providing excellent customer service. By actively participating in the online conversation and showing genuine care for your customers, you can strengthen relationships and enhance your reputation as a business that values its community.

CLAIM YOUR YELP PAGE

There's no one better suited than you for telling your company's story and helping people who have questions about your business. Being active on Yelp ensures you're the one to help customers and keep your fingers on the pulse of what's essential to them. An excellent place to start is by claiming your business's page on Yelp. Claiming your Yelp page gives you control over your business's online presence. It lets you update crucial information like hours, contact details, and photos, ensuring potential customers get accurate information. Additionally, claiming your page enables you to respond to positive and negative reviews, demonstrating your commitment to customer satisfaction and potentially resolving issues publicly. Claiming your Yelp page empowers you to manage your reputation and engage with your audience effectively and actively.

One way to welcome customers to your Yelp Page is a check-in offer. Check-in offers on Yelp reward customers when they "check in" at your business. Displayed on both mobile and desktop, apps they are a great way to differentiate yourself from your competitors. You have full control over the terms, ensuring that you offer only what you're comfortable with, be it a discount, percentage off, or a free item.

Not limited to physical businesses, service-based businesses can also benefit from check-ins. When customers use your service, they can check in upon your arrival. Creating check-in offers on Yelp is free, trackable, and flexible. How do these offers convert Yelp users into customers? They amplify your Yelp page, spreading the word about your business.

Add photos to your Yelp page—people like to see faces and get an idea of who runs the business, even while checking it out online. People want to do business with people they know and are comfortable with.

ADD PHOTOS AND BUSINESS INFORMATION

Upload photos of your business with your sign, add a link to your website, and ensure that your hours are up-to-date so consumers searching for your business can easily find it. Taiyaki Ice Cream in New York City has a fabulous Yelp presence with its location, website, hours of operation, and great reviews with customer photos. If you look them up, you'll see a blue check that says "Claimed" next to their name. The blue check means Yelp has verified them. This also shows they care about Yelp reviews and are engaged on the platform.

To date, 4,673 photos have been shared on Yelp. You know people are checking them out!

This example is Everglow Wellness; they've claimed their profile and added their hours. They've also added photos that show their space and their fun community.

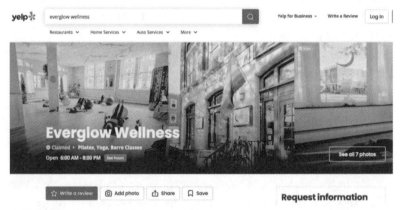

FIGURE 18.1. Everglow Wellness Yelp Page.
Source: Everglow Wellness.

REVIEW YOUR BUSINESS ANALYTICS

You can track visitor engagement and customer leads from your Yelp Business Page. Yelp page visits and leads are intended to help you understand the amount of exposure to and interest in your business from potential customers.

Yelp page visits measure how often your page is accessed or viewed on the Yelp website, mobile website, and mobile apps.

Leads include phone calls, website visits, and other actions potential customers take to engage with your business on the Yelp website, mobile website, and mobile apps.

GO MOBILE

Download the Yelp for Business Owners mobile app to get the power of Yelp's tools in your pocket.

ASK FOR REVIEWS

Asking for Yelp reviews is tricky and needs to be done correctly. Adding a "find us on Yelp" official window sticker is a great way to let people know you're there. While it's not a violation of the Yelp Terms of Service to ask for reviews, offering incentives to customers in exchange for reviews or asking them to remove reviews is considered a violation.

This is an open-and-shut case: *you can ask your customers for reviews*. When you know a customer is happy, you should ask them for a Yelp review.

You might wonder if a business can pay Yelp for better overall reviews . . .

- Do they get a higher rating?
- Do they get their negative reviews removed?
- Can they recommend more of their positive reviews?

The answers are no, no, and no! Money doesn't buy anything on Yelp but ads. Yelp ads can be effective for some businesses. They are placed at the top of the search results and marked as "sponsored" to help them stand out. They can be a great way to generate leads and increase bookings or sales from Yelp users.

ASK YOUR EMPLOYEES, "IS THAT FIVE-STAR TREATMENT?"

Create a *five-star mentality* within your business to create a *five-star rating* on Yelp. Is that package wrapped in a five-star manner? Is that piece of jewelry five-star quality? Bake the five-star thinking into everything you do, and look at your business from a customer's perspective. Do you have a place for customers to take cute photos for reviews and social postings?

FIGURE 18.2. Author selfie at Everglow Wellness creating UGC.
Source: Author.

FIVE-STAR LOCATION IN ACTION

I took this mirror selfie, which I never do, posted it on my Instagram Stories, and tagged @EverglowWellness and their location after attending a yoga class. I'm in yoga clothes with no makeup, so that's usually a no-photo zone for me, but I was inspired by their aesthetic. Posting online allows them to reshare it to their followers and for people looking for places in my central downtown square to find them.

Is there something you can do like Everglow Wellness did with their space? It doesn't have to be over-the-top, but you could make it fit your brand perfectly.

Yelp can be crucial in the growth of your brand. Starting from the top down and reaching every level of your business will help your employees learn how critical Yelp reviews are for the company. Share positive and negative thoughts in your staff meetings and use them as an opportunity for open communication.

Hopefully, this has given you a few ideas to help with your Yelp page and grow your brand online. The time it takes to manage will be worth it!

TO-DO NOTES

1. Claim your Yelp Page.
2. Post photos of your shop or office.
3. Turn on notifications for reviews so you can respond promptly.

What about the Elephant in the Room?

Google

Let me embrace thee, sour adversity, for wise men say it is
the wisest course.

—*William Shakespeare,* Henry VI, *Part 3*

$\mathcal{G}$oogle is the "elephant in the room" when it comes to thinking about anything online. Google search, Google maps, Google reviews, Google it! It's easy to see why Google can't be ignored in our conversation about how to be found online.

Google Search is the dominant search engine, used by billions of people worldwide to access information and find answers to their questions. It has become an essential tool for consumers, businesses, and organizations alike to navigate the vast amount of information available on the internet.

It may seem impossible to move the needle on Google, but there are many things small business owners can do to be found and float up higher in a Google search. No one knows precisely what it takes to get to the top of a Google search; they may change the algorithm daily. Play Media says that most experts estimate Google changes its search algorithm around five to six hundred times yearly. That's somewhere between once and twice each day. While most of these changes don't significantly change the SEO landscape, some updates are significant.

Imagine you're in a huge library filled with books on every topic you can think of. Now, you might feel overwhelmed if you're looking for a specific book in this vast sea of knowledge. Where do you start? That's where the librarian, or in our case, Google's search algorithm, comes in.

The SEO landscape is like trying to get that librarian to notice your book and recommend it to readers first. Just as a book must be interesting, well-written, and well-placed to catch the librarian's eye, your website must be optimized to catch Google's attention. This means having relevant and high-quality content, using the right "keywords" that people are likely to search for, and ensuring your website is easy to navigate and loads quickly.

However, Google is like a librarian constantly learning and changing their criteria for what makes a book—or, in this case, a website—worthy of recommendation. These are the algorithm updates mentioned. While most of these changes are minor tweaks, occasionally, a big shake-up changes the game—sort of like if the librarian suddenly decided that all books need to have blue covers to get a prime spot on the display.

For a small business, moving up in search rankings involves understanding what Google currently likes and dislikes, which can be like hitting a moving target. But by focusing on creating great content and a good user experience and staying informed about SEO best practices, business owners can improve their chances of getting noticed by Google's ever-evolving search criteria.

Information and attention are two of the most valuable commodities in today's fast-paced world. We're in the attention economy, which is the concept that attention is a scarce resource and, as such, is valuable. In this context, Google Search plays a crucial role in the attention economy because it helps users find the information they are looking for quickly and efficiently while enabling businesses and organizations to reach their target audience and compete for attention in a crowded online landscape.

Google is also important to social media for small businesses regarding search engine optimization (SEO). Having a strong presence on social media can help increase the visibility of your business on Google search results. When ranking search results, Google considers the relevance and popularity of social media profiles.

Furthermore, social media platforms often rank high on Google search results for brand names, often appearing higher than the business website. An active and optimized social media presence can help potential customers quickly find your business on Google.

Google also has an advertising platform that allows businesses to create and display ads on Google search results and other websites in the Google Display Network. Using Google Ads with social media advertising, small businesses can increase their online visibility and reach more potential customers.

One thing that hasn't changed with Google's algorithm is that it favors content created for people, not for SEO purposes. (You can read more about this in a recent Google update[1] called the "Helpful Content Update.") When creating content for your website, you should focus on answering fundamental questions that your customers may have or providing insights that they will find genuinely useful. Whether it's a step-by-step guide on how to use your products, insightful articles about the services you offer, or discussions on topics related to your industry that are currently trending, the key is to ensure that the content is engaging, informative, and above all, helpful to your audience.

What does this look like in practice? Let's say you sell culinary gadgets. Instead of just listing the specifications of a garlic press, you could create content that shows how to make a variety of dishes with it, the benefits of using it over other methods, and even user-generated content like customer recipes or hacks. This approach provides value to the reader and signals to Google that your website is a resourceful place for people interested in culinary tools.

By creating content for people, you're aligning your website with Google's "Helpful Content Update," designed to reward content that adds real value to users. When thinking about SEO, flip the script: don't just think about what might attract an algorithm; think about what will attract and benefit a human being. Because when your content resonates with people, the algorithms will follow.

As a small business, you can do the following things to help be found on Google:

- *Publish helpful content*: Create original blog content to educate or inform readers.
- *Keep your Google Business Profile up-to-date*: It's free and easy to create your profile at https://www.google.com/business/.
- *Manage your Yelp and other online reviews.*
- *Use local keywords*: Incorporate location-based keywords in your website content to increase visibility for local searches.
- *Utilize social media*: Regularly posting on social media platforms and linking to your website can help drive traffic and increase visibility.

Local keywords are phrases people are likely to use when searching for local services and businesses. The keywords for a small-town florist in Iowa could include the town or nearby towns and landmarks, plus terms related to the florist's offerings. Here are some examples:

1. "[Town Name] florist"—Replace [Town Name] with the actual name of the town.
2. "Flowers in [Town Name]"
3. "Wedding bouquets [Town Name]"
4. "Flower delivery [Town Name] Iowa"
5. "Best florist near [Town Name]"
6. "[Town Name] flower shop"
7. "Buy flowers [Town Name]"
8. "[Town Name] sympathy flowers"
9. "Mother's Day flowers [Town Name]"
10. "[Town Name] Valentine's Day flowers"

11. "Floral arrangements [County Name]"—Replace [County Name] with the name of the county the town is in.
12. "[Local Landmark] area florist"—Replace [Local Landmark] with a well-known local landmark.
13. "[Town Name] [Holiday] flowers"—Replace [Holiday] with relevant holidays like Easter, Christmas, etc.
14. "Gift baskets in [Town Name]"
15. "Florists that deliver in [Town Name]"
16. "[Nearby Town] florist"—Including nearby towns can also capture customers from surrounding areas.
17. "[Town Name] roses" or "[Town Name] orchids"—Specific types of flowers if the florist specializes.
18. "Custom flower arrangements [Town Name]"
19. "Florist on [Street Name in Town]"—If the florist is located on a well-known street, include it.
20. "[Town Name] event flowers"—For those looking for services for events.

Remember to replace the placeholders with actual names relevant your business's location. This will help your business appear in searches by locals and others looking for services in that particular area.

Google has an educational website for small businesses at https://smallbusiness.withgoogle.com/#!/. Learn about what Google offers and what you can do to help more people find you online.

FIND THOSE FAQS

One way to find out what potential customers want to know is to try a tool like Answer the Public—you can find this resource at https://answerthepublic.com/. You type in a topic related to your business, and it populates questions people are asking. Using this data, you can reverse-engineer some helpful content to provide value to your blog. Answer the Public used to be entirely free, but now you can run three searches free of charge daily; after this, you'd need to purchase a plan.

For example, I typed "flowers" into Answer the Public and got these questions that people were searching for:

- how flowers grow
- how flowers reproduce
- how flowers look to bees
- how flowers get their color
- how flowers changed the world
- can flowers mold
- can flowers stay in a cold car
- can flowers feel pain
- which flowers last the longest
- which flowers are toxic to cats

You could use these to create social media posts and blog content to answer questions that people are searching for that relate to your floral business.

Overall, Google plays a significant role in a small business's online presence and visibility. By optimizing their social media profiles and content for Google searches, small businesses can increase their chances of being found by potential customers and ultimately grow their business.

Google is the elephant in the room, but sticking to your social media plan, being helpful, and providing value to your followers will help you grow. As they say, "Cream rises to the top."

TO-DO NOTES

1. Claim your Google page.
2. Make a list of five Google search terms you want to dominate.
3. Create a keyword list to use on your social media and blog.

Social Listening

The Secret Ingredient for Brand Success

We have two ears and one mouth, so we should listen more than we say.

—*Zeno of Citium*

In life and business, listening is more important than talking.
When you use social media platforms to listen to the needs of your market and then cater to them by offering solutions, you bridge the gap by meeting their needs and gaining valuable insight into your industry.

Social media can allow you to reach people looking for help, customers complaining about your company, and even your competitor's frustrated customers. This helps you manage your online reputation and track your competition.

Social listening is tracking social media conversations, mentions, keywords, and hashtags to look for insights into your current and potential future customers and your competition.

It allows you to learn what people think about your brand. It's a good idea to track the following items in your social listening efforts:

- Your products
- Your services
- Your brand
- Your competition

There are a wide variety of tools you can use for social listening. These tools can be expensive, but you can devise a low-budget plan. Here's what I suggest:

- *Google alerts* are free to set up; you get an email notification when results match your search. Sign up for them at https://www.google .com/alerts.
- *Talkwalker* is a Google alternative where you can create alerts for search terms like your name, company name, or a topic: https://www .talkwalker.com/alerts.
- *Agorapulse* is excellent for managing your inbox, scheduling, and monitoring. They have a free plan for one user and three accounts. Paid plans start at $79 per month.
- *Sprout Social* is another all-in-one tool with robust social tools, including listening. Their plans start at $89 per month.

Let's consider a small café in Iowa as a different example for setting up Google Alerts. Here's how the café owner might use Google Alerts to their advantage:

1. *Café Name*: To monitor when and where the café is mentioned online, including reviews, social media posts, or in local news articles.
2. *Menu Items*: If the café has unique offerings or signature dishes, setting alerts for these items could provide insights into what's popular or being talked about.
3. *Local Food and Beverage News*: Keywords like "Iowa food scene" or "Des Moines café trends" to help keep tabs on the local gastronomy trends and what competitors might be doing.

4. *Local Events and Festivals*: Alerts for "food festivals in Iowa" or "Des Moines community events" can help the café find local events to participate in or cater.

5. *Competitors' Names*: This helps you to stay informed about what other local cafés and restaurants are doing, such as menu changes, renovations, or events they might be hosting.

6. *Industry Trends*: Use phrases like "specialty coffee trends" or "artisanal bakery" so the business can stay ahead of industry shifts and adapt their offerings accordingly.

7. *Health and Safety Regulations*: This is especially important for food businesses, so they should set alerts for terms like "food service health regulations Iowa" to remain compliant with health codes and safety practices.

8. *Food Suppliers*: Monitor the names of local suppliers or specific products they source, like "organic coffee beans" or "wholesale bakery supplies," to monitor any news that could affect their supply chain.

9. *Seasonal Ingredients*: Setting up alerts for "seasonal produce Iowa" or "local Iowa produce" could help plan menu changes based on what's fresh and available.

10. *Café Equipment and Technology*: Alerts for new café equipment, like "espresso machine innovations" or "café POS system updates," can help keep technology and appliances current.

11. *Sustainability and Eco-Friendly Practices*: If the café prides itself on sustainability, alerts for "eco-friendly café practices" or "sustainable food packaging" can help them stay aligned with those values and find new ways to implement them.

12. *Special Days and Observances*: Using alerts such as "National Coffee Day" or "World Baking Day" to leverage these days for marketing and promotional activities.

By setting up these alerts, the café owner is equipped to manage their online reputation effectively, keep a pulse on the café industry, adapt to customer preferences, find local opportunities for promotion, and stay ahead of operational aspects like supply chain and regulation.

Using Instagram's search feature, you can conduct social listening on a budget. Imagine a small-town yoga and wellness studio aiming to grow its customer base, engage with the community, and stay informed about competitors. They'll utilize Instagram to search for growth opportunities, community engagement tactics, and competitor analysis. This could involve searching relevant hashtags, exploring nearby businesses, and monitoring competitor profiles for insights and improvement ideas.

They will search for these things on Instagram:

1. Keyword search: *yoga, wellness.*
2. Hashtag search: their location, their city, and fitness terms like *wellness* and *yoga.*
3. Their competitors.
4. They will also track their mentions.
5. Location tags for their studio and town. The location tag can be added to any Instagram Post, Story, or Reel. It will show on the post, and you can click them to reveal a location page that shows a map at the top, as well as things tagged for this location.

Make sure to follow everyone who posts about your business and say thank you!

If I were the wellness studio owner, I would repost Instagram Stories from customers, follow them, and send them a thank-you message. I would also send them a coupon for a free class to go above and beyond. If you look at the value of this customer posting, the coupon for a free course is a worthwhile business expense, and it invites them to come back again. Happy customers bring in more people!

Scoping out your competition on social media is another way to listen. You would never want to copy a competitor, but seeing what they post and how often is good. What social posts are appealing to their customers and what kinds of comments they're getting can also help inform your future content. If they have a brand hashtag, check that out and follow it.

Your main goal with social listening is to connect with customers and help you with future content creation. Checking your customers' accounts will help you see what they post and what's important to them.

Through social media listening, you can gather interesting insights that may provide intelligence on how to market better to your customers. And yes, there's much noise in social media, but there's also gold waiting to help you stand out from your competition.

CASE STUDY FOR SOCIAL LISTENING: MCDONALD'S

When the earnings for McDonald's declined for seventeen quarters, they tried tweaking their menu to recapture their customers. With the help of Sprinklr, an enterprise social media tool, they listened to what customers were asking for and uncovered a demand for breakfast items beyond the traditional 10:30 a.m. cutoff. People weren't saying, "We want all-day breakfast," but they were saying, "Wow, I can't believe I got to McD's at 10:31 a.m. and can't get my Egg McMuffin!" Using the social listening data, McDonald's created a massive campaign for the All-Day Breakfast.[1]

McDonald's unlocked the secret to all-day-breakfast success with social listening, and all-day breakfast was a huge success. Interestingly, when I was researching this book, McDonald's no longer has all-day breakfast, and on X, people are screaming and begging for it to come back.

Social listening can also inform your future content creation by identifying what posts resonate with your audience. The McDonald's case study is a prime example of how social listening can lead to successful campaigns and increased revenue. Start listening to what your customers say on social media and use that information to improve your small business and stand out in front of the competition.

TO-DO NOTES

1. Set up Google alerts.
2. Consider where you will listen on social media.
3. Check your local locations to see what is trending and being posted.

21

How to Design a Brand to Leave Your Competition in the Dust

Simplicity is the ultimate sophistication.

—*Leonardo da Vinci*

*B*randing comprises design elements such as color schemes, font selections, logos, and other design choices.

Visual branding is the art of marrying imagery and design to convey the essence of your business at a glance. It's the careful selection of colors, typography, logos, and other visual elements that tell the story of your brand's personality, values, and promises to your audience.

Effective visual branding transcends mere aesthetics; it's a language that communicates to consumers, creating a memorable identity and differentiating your brand from the competition. It's not about being seen—it's about being recognized and remembered, forging an emotional connection that resonates with your customers every time they encounter your brand.

We covered visual elements earlier, but here we'll look at what to do with these pieces to create visual marketing for your social media. Learning to communicate visually is a skill worth learning. In fact, research from Canva found that 85 percent of global business leaders agree that communicating visually carries more authority. "This is the era of the *visual economy*. Thriving in it requires organizations and their employees to think and work differently," says Zach Kitschke, chief marketing officer of Canva (from Canva's Visual Economy Report[1]).

Consistency is essential for brand recognition and awareness. This is another place where Canva hops in. In the paid version, Canva Pro, you can create a brand kit that locks your brand elements (font, color palette, logo, etc.) into place and creates a foolproof way to maintain consistency.

A cohesive style for your brand creates a memorable visual experience and helps your audience connect with you across the web. Creating your brand elements and locking them into place makes it easy to stay on brand and easily communicate your visuals. If you have a team, using the brand kit allows everyone to stay on-brand with the same color palette, fonts, etc., locked down.

If you need help with this process, hiring a professional designer to create your logo and a brand style guide would be a great way to invest in your business.

It's essential to create something unique and not copy the style of another brand, including a social media personal brand, you love.

A solid visual brand ties your content across social media platforms and helps people recognize your posts. One of my highest compliments on social media is when people say, "I saw a beautiful graphic and immediately knew it was yours, so I had to check out your post." People recognize my style of graphics and my signature pink circle logo in the corner, and they know that when they click through, they can trust my content to be worthy of their time.

That's WHY you spend the time to create a visual style.

It took me a long time to nail down the pieces of my current visual style. I started with a Pinterest board and pinned elements as I saw them, knowing I'd want to find them later to include in my branding. I kept adding tiny pieces until I was ready to work on a total rebranding for my blog and social media. I created a mood board with photos that spoke to me and helped convey what I wanted my brand to look like.

This process can also be helpful if you're working with a designer to create a brand, logo, and style guide for you. Working with a pro is great, but your brand needs to capture your essence.

Don't let someone else dictate your style and force a final design on you that you don't like. It won't grow on you—trust me on that one. Sharing what you do love with them will help the design process. When the time came, I shared my Pinterest board with the designer, and she could immediately see what I wanted for my brand.

You should also have the option to get several rounds of designs in your creative process while working with a designer. This doesn't mean you get unlimited changes; you may get two or three rounds total, so having an idea of what you'd like up-front helps ensure you'll get a final design you love.

This new design is one hundred percent me and what I love. It makes me happy to create designs that coordinate with it; people get a great sense of who I am. This is something you can absolutely do with your brand.

Collect visual pieces you enjoy, and combine them to create something you love!

CREATING GRAPHIC DESIGNS

Customize each graphic or design using your brand elements to inspire and delight your social media followers. While your graphic might not be the *Mona Lisa*, it can be branded with your signature look and feel.

You should also ask yourself how you can make your image funny, inspirational, or informative. Let your brand voice and visual style connect with your overall message. Your goal is to create something that's not just visually appealing, but also meaningful and purposeful.

Here are the questions you must answer when creating a graphic:

- What is it? Why are you making this?
- How does it work?
- Whom will it help?
- How does it feel?
- What problem does it solve? Get to the heart of its reason for being.
- What do you want the viewer to do next? Think about the action you're prompting.

- How does it align with the brand or message? Ensure it fits with the overall style and communication.
- In what context will it be viewed? The design might change depending on its home.
- Is the message clear and concise? Clarity is king.
- Is there a balance between visuals and text? Aim for harmony to keep viewers engaged.
- What's the hierarchy of information? Plan the order in which the viewer's eye should travel.

With these in your tool kit, you're shaping up to craft graphics that not only pop, but also pack a punch!

Make it a game. With every image, you create, be sure you can answer each question.

When you create designs, add your logo and website address to your images. Adding this extra bit of flair helps people know it's yours, builds your brand recognition, and hopefully deters others from using it without permission. This is what your brand kit looks like inside Canva:

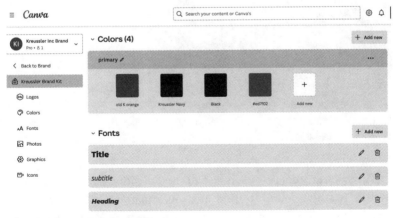

FIGURE 21.1. Canva Brand Kit.
Source: Canva.

Again, I'm not going to share a step-by-step guide for creating designs, because this is something you can Google yourself to find the most current how-to guides. I recommend learning from YouTube or free Canva's Design School.

Here are a few examples of social media posts for small businesses that can help their customers, reinforce their brand, and help grow their community:

This graphic is on brand with color, and the logo is included. They are sharing a pro tip for their customers, which is helpful, and they created a carousel with multiple tips. The message is clear and easy to follow.

FIGURE 21.2. Crouse's Cleaners social post.
Source: Crouse's Cleaners.

This social media graphic is also on-brand with color and logo. The website is at the bottom to find more information. The colors in the image fit with the brand colors. SYSTEMK4 is a product and the text supports this with more information.

FIGURE 21.3. Kreussler Inc. product post for SYSTEMK4.
Source: Kreussler Inc.

Creating a strong visual brand is crucial for small business owners to establish brand recognition and awareness. Consistency is vital; investing in a professional designer to create a logo and brand style guide can be a great way to achieve this.

MAXIMIZING VISUAL IMPACT: CREATIVE CROPPING TECHNIQUES

Selecting the right images to match your brand is a delicate process that calls for a keen eye and a deep understanding of your brand's core identity. Each image serves as a visual ambassador for your brand, carrying the weight of first impressions and the power to forge lasting connections. To ensure coherence, review your brand's values, color scheme, and the emotions you wish to evoke. These elements should be the cornerstone of every image you choose. For instance, a brand that stands for sustainability might opt for images with earth tones and natural settings. At the same time, a tech company might lean toward sleek, modern visuals with blue tones that evoke a sense of innovation.

Beyond aesthetics, consider the story each image tells. A well-chosen photograph goes beyond surface appeal to narrate a part of your brand's story, whether it's the craftsmanship behind a product, the warmth of your team, or the satisfaction of customers. The goal is to select images that will resonate personally with your audience, making them feel an integral part of the brand's journey. It's not simply what your brand looks like; it's also what it feels like. When your audience sees an image, they should instantly recognize it as a piece of your brand's narrative that aligns seamlessly with the messages you deliver through other channels. This consistency is the key to building a memorable brand that stands out in a crowded marketplace.

Repurposing images by cropping them in various ways and sizes is a clever strategy to maximize your visual content's potential while keeping your feed fresh and engaging. By altering the dimensions and focus of an image, you can highlight different elements, adapt the image to suit various platforms, or give a new perspective to your content. Take a high-resolution, well-composed photo, for example, and crop it tightly to draw attention to specific details for a powerful impact on platforms like Instagram. Conversely, a wider crop can set the scene on Facebook or LinkedIn, with more space for storytelling. This method stretches your content library and maintains visual consistency across your brand's touchpoints. It's efficient and sustainable, as one image can yield several unique assets, each perfectly tailored to various contexts and formats.

Remember to maintain high image quality and ensure each crop aligns with your brand's aesthetic and message. This approach keeps your visual branding cohesive and versatile, ensuring that your audience continues to engage with familiar, yet refreshing content.

With visual branding, every choice matters. The careful blend of color, shape, and text forms your brand's visual identity, which resonates with your audience. Consistency in these elements is the backbone of your brand's image, ensuring it stands out and stays memorable. As you fine-tune the details, from how you crop an image to the shades you select, you're not merely filling a space, but setting a stage. Through these choices, your brand's character shines through, distinguishing you from the competition. Embrace this process with intention and a clear vision, and you'll create a brand that looks great and communicates your business' unique narrative.

TO-DO-NOTES

1. Find videos to learn about Canva's Brand Kit.
2. Create five graphics using the guidelines.
3. Crop photos in different ways to reuse images.

22

Blogging Brilliance to Boost Your Business

If you want to lift yourself up, lift up someone else.

—Booker T. Washington

*D*o you need a blog or a website for your business? Both help customers find you on search engines. Blogging was once the gold standard for growing your brand and gaining views from search engines, but videos on YouTube and TikTok have partially replaced that. On the other hand, a website is your home on the internet. We'll go into the difference in a bit.

Here's how small businesses will benefit from a website and blog.

Why should you have a website? Here are just a few reasons. You can:

1. Be found when people are searching online.
2. Share your hours and location.
3. Create a hub for your community.
4. Gather email addresses.
5. Become the go-to local business in your niche.

IS IT A WEBSITE OR BLOG?

What is the difference between a website and a blog? Websites are static and organized into pages that aren't changed, whereas a blog has frequently updated content. You start by building a website, to which you can later add a blog. The terms are different, but they are used almost interchangeably today.

A website is the only property you can *own and control online*. If you build your business on a YouTube channel or TikTok account, you don't own everything you create.

It's scary, but you could spend years building a massive following on someone else's domain (TikTok or Instagram), and it could be shut down at any time. You'd lose all your followers and content. That very thing happened to the people who used Vine and Google+. Yikes!

Setting up a website is the way to go if writing and updating a blog are too much for you. Even creating a splash page, which is only one page people can scroll through, is helpful for potential customers.

A splash page is like the cover of a book for your website. It's the first thing visitors see when they land on your site. Think of it as a welcome mat that introduces them to what you're all about. It's typically a full-screen page showcasing the most essential bits—like your brand, current promotions, or must-know info. Splash pages are great because they're not just about looks; they're strategic, too. They can guide visitors to take a specific action, like signing up for a newsletter or announcing something big, like a grand opening or a special event. Plus, they're quick to load and easy to navigate, precisely what you want in a world where folks have the patience of a TikTok video. A well-designed splash page sets the stage for your business story and gives a taste of what's to come, encouraging visitors to step inside and see what you offer.

Let's face it; consumers immediately grab their phones when looking for something these days, so you want to have your website, aka your home base, set up for anyone searching for your services or your location and hours. This is where you tell your story and build your business reputation.

According to data from Salesforce,[1] *71 percent of growing small businesses say they survived the pandemic through digitization.* A website isn't a choice; it is necessary for today's small businesses.

Either Wix or Squarespace can provide easy options for getting started with templated websites. Canva has also created an easy way to create a website; if it's hosted on Canva's domain, you won't have a custom domain name. There is an option to buy the domain name within Canva; it's about twenty dollars per year, at the time of this writing.

When you start your website, you pick your domain name and own and control all the content forever. Well, if you pay your annual fees. No one else can use your website name. This helps you build authority for Google and other search engines, so your website pops up when, for example, people search for florists in your town.

Google authority is like your website's reputation in the eyes of Google. Like in high school, where popular kids get noticed more, websites with higher authority are likelier to appear at the top of search results. The more Google trusts your website as a go-to source for information on a particular topic, like flowers in your town if you're a florist, the higher your site will rank when people search for that topic.

FIGURE 22.1. Canva website.
Source: Canva.

You boost your website's Google authority by consistently publishing great content and getting other reputable sites to link back to yours. Think of it as a vote of confidence—every time a credible site links to you, it's like saying, "Hey, this site knows its roses and tulips!" The more votes you get, the more Google thinks, "Alright, this site is legit and knows its stuff," and the higher you climb the search results ladder. So, when someone types "best florist in [Your Town]," Google thinks of you and says, "I've got just the place," and up you pop. Remember, this takes time and effort, but it's like planting seeds for a thriving garden. Take care of it, and it'll bloom beautifully.

Pick a domain name close to your business name to make it easy for people to find and remember. Picking a domain name that's a mismatch for your business name is like giving someone directions to your house but leaving out the street number—they might end up somewhere close, but not quite at your doorstep. A bad URL can confuse customers and make it hard for them to find you; even worse, they might land on a competitor's site by mistake.

Also, if your URL is a tongue twister, too long, or stuffed with random numbers and characters, it's like handing out a business card with a typo. People won't remember it, and they might not bother to type it out. On top of that, if your URL isn't clear about who you are, it could end up buried on the fifth or sixth page of Google's search results, where no one really looks. It's like opening a shop in a back alley instead of the main street.

In the world of the internet, your domain name is your address, your sign, and part of your brand's first impression, all rolled into one. It's super important to make it count and keep it relevant, simple, and memorable. This way, you're not just another needle in the digital haystack.

Your small business website should include information on who you are, what you do, and how people can contact you. Your products and services should also be listed, as well as a mission statement and reviews. Photos from your business are preferable to stock photos to show people exactly who you are. I especially love seeing pictures of the owners and learning their personal stories.

Here's a website checklist:

Home Page
- Clear business name and logo
- A succinct, engaging tagline or welcome message
- A call to action (e.g., Shop Now, Learn More, Contact Us)

About Us Page
- Who you are (the owner's story and team introductions)
- What you do (the nature of your business)
- Company history and values (personal stories, business journey)

Products/Services Page
- Detailed list of products and/or services
- High-quality images of products or services in action
- Pricing, if applicable
- Special offers or discounts

Contact Information
- Phone number
- Email address
- Physical location with a map, if applicable
- Contact form for easy inquiries

Customer Testimonials and Reviews
- Real customer feedback
- Success stories or case studies
- Ratings, if available

Mission Statement
- Your business's purpose and goals
- What makes you different from competitors

Photo Gallery
- Authentic photos of your business and products
- Pictures of the team or the owner
- Behind-the-scenes snapshots

FAQ Section
- Answers to common customer inquiries
- Information about shipping, returns, and order processing

Blog or News Section
- Educational content related to your products/services
- Industry news or updates about your business

Social Media Links
- Icons linking to your business's social media profiles
- Social media feed integration, if possible

SEO Basics
- Keywords related to your business in page titles and content
- Meta descriptions for each page
- Alt text for images

Technical Essentials
- Mobile-responsive design
- Fast loading times
- Secure socket layer (SSL) certificate for security

Legal Pages
- Privacy policy
- Terms and conditions

Supporting a local small business is essential to many people. I am crushed when I see a small business in my community close, and many have closed due to not being online or adapting during the pandemic. One of my favorite local florists was not online at all pre-pandemic and was closed for long periods. They had a handwritten note on their door saying they were closed, but it wasn't enough for people to support their business. No one wants to drive to a business to see if they are open.

In a post-pandemic landscape, the florist shop is now under new ownership. The new owners have set up a website and created accounts on Instagram and Facebook. Now I can see their hours, get their phone number, and place an order online! They aren't near the top of Google search results yet, but they have only been online for over six months. All the other independent florists have closed. For reference, my town has about twenty-three thousand residents.

The top-sponsored spots in the Google search for florists near me were all national companies that ship orders, like 1-800-Flowers, which makes it even more critical for my local florist to have a website and social accounts. It would be best if you were found in local searches to grow as a local business.

Keywords are essential when you're writing content for your website. Keywords are the search terms typed by internet users into search engines. They help search engines know what your website is about. When you know what your target audience is looking for, you can leverage that information to attract them to your website. You'll want to find three to five keywords to focus on. For a local florist, they might be

- Flowers delivered (town name)
- Florist near me
- Local flower shop

Seventy-one percent of marketers say using strategic keywords was their number-one strategy for search engine optimization (HubSpot State of Marketing Report, 2021[2]).

Identifying the ideal keywords for your small business involves some strategic groundwork. Here's how to kick-start the process:

1. *Brainstorming*: Begin by jotting down keywords relevant to your business, products, or services. Consider terms your potential customers might use when seeking what you offer.
2. *Competitor Analysis*: Take a peek at the keywords your competitors are leveraging. Tools like SEMrush or Ahrefs can unveil the keywords they're ranking for.
3. *Keyword Research Tools*: Tap in to resources like Google Keyword Planner, Ubersuggest, or KeywordTool.io. These platforms offer insights into search volume, competition, and related keywords.
4. *Long-Tail Keywords*: Explore long-tail keywords—lengthier and more specific phrases. Despite potentially lower search volumes, they often boast higher conversion rates by targeting a more focused audience.
5. *Google Autocomplete and Related Searches*: Make use of Google Autocomplete and related searches. Type your main keywords into the search bar to unveil suggestions. Additionally, scroll to the bottom of the results page for related searches.
6. *Customer Feedback and FAQs*: Dive into customer feedback, questions, and comments. Pay attention to the language they use, as it may unveil valuable keywords.
7. *Content Analysis*: Scrutinize your existing content to spot keywords already driving traffic to your site. Tools like Google Search Console or Google Analytics can aid in this endeavor.
8. *Location-Based Keywords*: If your business caters to a specific geographic area, integrate location-based keywords to target local clientele. For instance, "best coffee shop in [city]."
9. *Regular Review and Optimization*: Remember, keyword research is an ongoing endeavor. Regularly reassess and tweak your strategy based on industry shifts, trends, and evolving customer behavior.

With these strategies in tow, you can identify prime keywords to optimize your website, bolster your search engine rankings, and entice potential customers to your small business. Once you've zeroed in on your target keywords, strategically embedding them throughout your website is key to maximizing their impact on search engine optimization. Here's where they should go:

1. *Page Titles*: Infuse your primary keywords into the titles of your web pages. This helps search engines grasp your page content's essence and boosts relevance for relevant searches.
2. *Meta Descriptions*: Craft compelling meta descriptions for each page, incorporating pertinent keywords. While they don't directly influence rankings, they can sway click-through rates from search engine results pages (SERPs).
3. *Headings and Subheadings (H1, H2, H3, etc.)*: Employ keywords in your headings and subheadings to enhance content accessibility for users and search engines alike. This aids in structuring your content logically and cohesively.
4. *Body Content*: Seamlessly weave your keywords throughout the body of your content. However, steer clear of unnatural keyword stuffing, which can deter user experience and incur penalties from search engines. Strive for a fluid and readable content flow.
5. *URLs*: Whenever possible, integrate keywords into your page URLs. Concise, descriptive URLs featuring relevant keywords can enhance search engine optimization (SEO) and the user experience.
6. *Image Alt Text*: Optimize your image alt text with descriptive keywords to bolster accessibility and furnish search engines with additional context about your image content.
7. *Anchor Text*: Incorporate relevant keywords into your anchor text when internally linking within your website or externally to other sites. This aids search engines in comprehending the linked pages' context.
8. *Page Footer*: Contemplate incorporating a footer section featuring keyword-rich links to pivotal pages on your website. This facilitates navigation and provides supplementary context to search engines.

9. *Navigation Menus and Bread Crumbs*: Infuse keywords into your navigation menus and bread crumb trails to bolster both user experience and SEO.

By strategically positioning your keywords across your website in these critical areas, you heighten your chances of ascending the search engine results ladder and attracting a greater influx of organic traffic to your site.

Using long-tail keywords (versus a single-word keyword) in your website text helps search engines know to populate your website in a search. When a search engine populates your website in a search, it means your site shows up as one of the results when someone looks for something online. It's like your website getting a spot on the list of suggestions when someone types a question or topic into Google or another search engine. So, if you've optimized your website well, it's more likely to show up and attract visitors who are searching for what you offer. You can type your keywords into Google to find related search terms.

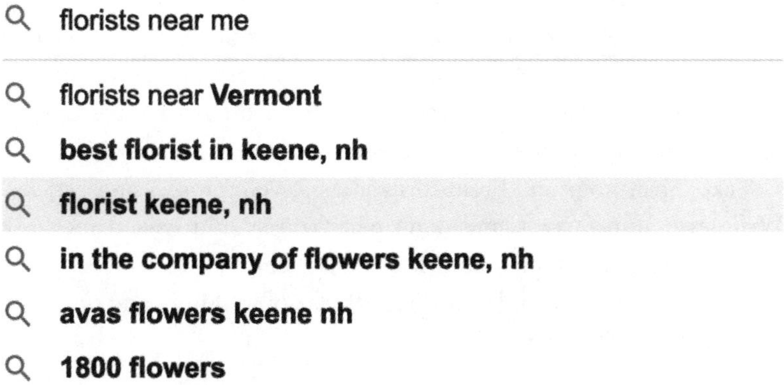

Q   florists near me
_____

Q   florists near **Vermont**

Q   **best florist in keene, nh**

Q   **florist keene, nh**

Q   **in the company of flowers keene, nh**

Q   **avas flowers keene nh**

Q   **1800 flowers**

FIGURE 22.2. Google search for "florists near me."

SHOULD YOU ADD A BLOG TO YOUR WEBSITE?

Here are a few reasons you might want to blog:

1. To bring people to your website
2. To create valuable content to share on social media
3. To help grow your email list
4. To answer questions to develop your expertise
5. Because search engines like fresh content

After deciding to add a blog to your website, you must consider what content you want to post. Will you write articles? Share personal stories? Develop recipes and take photos to show the step-by-step process?

I like to use Answer the Public, found at answerthepublic.com, a search listening tool. It collates, tracks, and alerts you to essential questions on Google. This can help you develop ideas on what to write about on your blog.

Create an Editorial Calendar

Having a plan will ensure that you'll create content for your blog. Having two or three posts drafted on your blog before launching it would be helpful so you can work ahead and not be pressured to come up with ideas at the last minute. While first learning, try to publish something new every other week. Then post on a schedule once a month. Pick a day of the week that works for you and stick with it.

Take a half hour and brainstorm ideas for blog topics and articles. Write everything down, and don't edit. You should have a monthly theme, or pick four topics and write about them.

For example, you could have a June theme of weddings and post four articles, one each week:

1. What to wear when attending a wedding
2. Wedding makeup ideas
3. Ten pairs of shoes for dancing the night away
4. How to Instagram your BFF's wedding

Or you could have four topics to rotate each month:

1. Spotlight a product.
2. Review a favorite book.
3. Post a how-to article.
4. Compose a round up article featuring ten items in a category or theme.

Planning will help keep you on schedule, organized, and on topic. Think about keywords related to your business that customers would use when searching on Google.

Share the love

Of course, you need to promote your new blog post to drive traffic back to your website. Distribute your post across various channels, like email, social networks, and forums. Here are some pointers to cross-promote effectively:

- *Use the top social media networks*: Share on Facebook, X, LinkedIn, Instagram, and Pinterest to promote your post.
- *Optimize your post for each social network*: For maximum engagement, create a unique title, write a short but relevant description, use high-resolution images, and mention people in your post, if applicable. For example, LinkedIn posts currently favor a post with a hook at the beginning, a short story, and a call to action at the end. The headline is the prominent title of your content, which sits at the top of an article or piece of writing. It is usually the first thing a reader will see when encountering your content online.

  A hook, however, is an intriguing word or phrase that captures the reader's attention and can be found in your content's headline and opening sentences. It's the bait that entices the reader to keep reading.
- *Use active groups on Facebook or LinkedIn*: Be sure to add relevant descriptions and attractive images to get more engagement.

- *Include your post's link on Pinterest in the "source" and the "description."*
- *Reshare your post every few days (or weeks)*: Use social media scheduling tools such as SmarterQueue or Agorapulse. Remember, not everyone will see your update the first time around.
- *Take advantage of your email newsletter*: You should include your blog post links if you regularly send newsletters to your subscribers. We'll talk more about building your email list later.

Applying these strategies every time you post a blog will excite your readers and even push them to bookmark your blog.

I hope this chapter inspires you to get your website set up or updated. Being found by Google or other search engines will help your business grow. Bonus points for you if you add a blog component to your website.

TO-DO NOTES

1. Will you blog?
2. Do you have a website set up?
3. Get your domain name and work on it!

III

MASTERING SOCIAL MEDIA SUCCESS

23

Setting the Bar

Defining and Achieving Your Social Media Milestones

Daring ideas are like chessmen moved forward; they may be beaten, but they may start a winning game.

—Johann Wolfgang von Goethe

THE POWER OF GOAL-SETTING IN SOCIAL MEDIA

*I*n the ever-evolving landscape of social media, where every post, tweet, and update can turn the tide of your business, setting precise goals isn't just helpful—it's essential. This chapter will be your compass in the vast sea of digital interaction. This chapter teaches us not to cast a wide net and hope for the best, but to craft a sharp, targeted spear designed to pierce through the noise and hit your mark every time.

For small business owners, the path to social media success is both a sprint and a marathon—it requires quick action and long-term endurance. Here, we lay the foundation for that journey, ensuring you start out on the right foot with clear objectives and continue with a steady pace, assessing and adjusting as you go. We're not just setting goals but charting a course for sustainable growth and meaningful engagement.

WHY GOALS MATTER IN SOCIAL MEDIA

Setting goals is like plotting points on a map for your small business journey on social media. Without these points, you're just wandering through the wilderness. Goals give you direction, purpose, and a clear-cut destination. They turn the wild frontier of likes and shares into a path toward real growth. By setting solid goals, your efforts become like a laser—focused, efficient, and powerful. This isn't busywork, but making every post and tweet work hard for your business, making sure you're not spinning your wheels, but driving your business forward toward a better return on every ounce of effort you put in.

Setting clear goals provides direction and focus, transforming your social media efforts from scattered actions into a coherent strategy for growth.

CRAFTING SMART GOALS FOR ONLINE SUCCESS

Steering your social media ship with precision requires more than just good intentions; it calls for SMART navigation. The SMART method—setting goals that are Specific, Measurable, Achievable, Relevant, and Time-Bound—is your compass for charting a successful course on social media waters.

SMART goals bring structure and measurability to your social media plans, ensuring that your objectives are clear, trackable, and aligned with your business' needs.

Here are five examples of social media goals that small businesses could set:

1. *Growing Your Online Community*: Let's boost your digital presence by ramping up those follower numbers and sparking more chatter on your posts. Imagine setting a goal to welcome a flurry of new followers or ignite a buzz of likes, shares, and comments. You'll be making your brand the new favorite talk of the online town.
2. *Turning Clicks into Visits*: Think of social media as your personal tour guide, leading curious clickers straight to your website's door-

step. How about setting a goal to see those click-through numbers
soar, drawing a crowd from your social pages right to your website?
Picture each post as a signpost, guiding potential customers to explore what you offer.

3. *Building Bonds with Your Audience*: Here's to transforming customers into a vibrant community. Set your sights on nurturing a space
   where conversations flow freely and loyalty blossoms. Regular heart-
   to-hearts through comments, direct messages, and engaging posts
   can create a sense of belonging and community around your brand.

4. *Converting Posts into Profits*: For those rocking an online store, how
   about turning your social media into a bustling marketplace? Track
   the journey from engaging posts to ringing cash registers. Set a goal
   to measure the leads or sales sprouting directly from your social media efforts—every campaign could be a seed for new growth.

5. *Ace Your Customer Service Game*: Let's redefine quick responses and
   make your social media the go-to spot for top-notch customer service. How about aiming to answer queries in record time? Set a goal
   for lightning-fast responses and watch customer satisfaction soar.
   It's all about showing your customers that behind every post, there's
   a team who cares and listens.

With these goals, you're not just playing the social media game;
you're setting the rules. Tailor them to fit your business like a glove,
and let's turn your social media presence into a beacon of success and
engagement.

IDENTIFYING KEY SOCIAL MEDIA OBJECTIVES

Let's dive into the heart of what makes social media tick for small businesses. We're looking at goals that are the bread and butter of your
online presence. Think of boosting brand awareness so your business
becomes the talk of the town, funneling a stream of curious clickers
right to your digital doorstep, transforming those online hellos into
solid leads, and nurturing a vibrant community that feels more like

a family reunion than a customer base. These are the milestones that mark the journey of a small business stepping into the spotlight of social media.

In essence, common social media goals, such as increasing brand awareness and building community, are vital milestones in your digital journey.

CONDUCTING EFFECTIVE SOCIAL MEDIA STRATEGY WORKSHOPS

Goal-setting workshops are your powerhouse in the realm of social media strategy. Imagine these not just as meetings, but as creative huddles where the magic of goal-setting unfolds. In this dynamic space, vague ideas transform into sharp, actionable objectives.

Imagine an environment, whether physical or virtual, buzzing with energy and ideas. This is where the brainstorming kicks off—a place where every thought, big or small, finds a voice. Here, you're encouraged to dream big, jotting down everything from skyrocketing your online engagement to building a robust community of followers.

The next step is the art of prioritization. Sifting through the cascade of ideas and identifying those that align seamlessly with your brand's mission and vision. This stage is crucial—it's where you differentiate the "good to have" from the "essential to have."

You'll then learn how to morph these top-tier goals into a plan of action, a clear path forward in your social media journey. This process isn't only setting targets, but charting a course toward tangible growth and measurable success.

If you're working alone, consider partnering with another small business owner to bounce ideas off one another and share expertise. Engaging in a collaborative relationship extends beyond mere goal-setting. Together, you can exchange tips on crafting engaging content, devise strategies for audience interaction, and even explore opportunities for cross-promotion to benefit both your businesses. It's a mutually enriching relationship, fostering growth and learning for both parties involved.

Gather your team or take this time for some focused solo planning. It's time to dive into a workshop that's not just about setting goals, but about igniting a strategy that truly resonates with your brand's unique voice and vision. Let's transform aspiration into achievement in the world of social media.

Overall, these workshops are crucial for turning ideas into actionable goals, fostering a collaborative approach to your social media strategy.

HARMONIZING SOCIAL MEDIA AND BUSINESS GOALS

Let's make sure your social media goals aren't just floating around in the digital ether. They've got to be in lockstep with the big-picture dreams you have for your business. Weave your social strategy into the very fabric of your business objectives, ensuring every like, comment, and share is a step toward where you want your business to be. We'll walk through aligning your online moves with your ultimate business goals, so your social media doesn't just mirror your business' heart and soul; it helps it beat stronger.

Aligning your social media goals with your broader business objectives ensures that your online efforts contribute directly to your business' success.

MEASURING YOUR SOCIAL MEDIA IMPACT

In the realm of social media, flying blind is not an option. You've set your goals and crafted your strategy, but how do you know if it's working? That's where tracking and measuring success come into play. This crucial phase in your social media adventure is all about making sure that your efforts are more than random stabs in the dark; they must be strategic and well-informed steps moving you closer to your goals.

UNDERSTANDING THE TOOLS AND METRICS

First up, let's talk about the tools at your disposal. Social media platforms provide built-in analytics tools. These dashboards offer a wealth of data—from basic metrics, like follower growth and engagement rates, to more advanced insights, like audience demographics and peak activity times. For a more in-depth analysis, tools like Google Analytics and Agorapulse can help you track your website traffic originating from social media, campaign performances, and even the best times to post.

Key Metrics to Focus On

- *Engagement*: This includes likes, comments, shares, and saves. High engagement rates often indicate content relevancy and audience interest.
- *Reach and Impressions*: Reach is the number of unique users who see your content, while impressions are the total number of times your content is displayed. Together, they measure your content's spread.
- *Follower Growth*: The rate at which your follower count is increasing is a direct reflection of your growing audience base.
- *Click-Through Rates (CTR)*: Especially important for posts with links, a high CTR means your content effectively prompts action.
- *Conversion Rate*: For businesses aiming for sales through social media, tracking how many users took the desired action (like making a purchase) is crucial.

Using Data for Strategy Adjustment

We're not only collecting data; we're interpreting it to make informed decisions. Notice a spike in engagement when you post videos? Make them a regular feature. Is a blog post shared on LinkedIn bringing in substantial website traffic? Consider focusing more on LinkedIn for your content distribution. The idea is to continually refine your strategy based on what the data tells you.

Remember, these metrics should always be viewed in the context of your goals. If your objective is brand awareness, focus on reach and engagement. If it's sales, concentrate on conversion rates and CTR.

By consistently monitoring these metrics, you can get a clear picture of what works and what doesn't. This process is not about obsessing over numbers, but about understanding the story they tell. Leverage this narrative to continuously refine and adapt your social media strategy, crafting an engaging and flexible storyline that not only connects deeply with your audience, but also propels your business toward achieving its aspirations.

YOUR BLUEPRINT FOR SOCIAL MEDIA GOAL SETTING
Quarterly Goal-Setting Brainstorming Session Template
   Session Date:
   [Insert date.]

   Attendees:
   [List names of participants.]

1. Review of Previous Quarter:
   — Key Achievements:
   [List key achievements from the last quarter.]
   — Areas for Improvement:
   [List areas where improvements can be made.]
2. Current Social Media Performance Analysis:
   — Key Metrics Overview:
   [Include metrics like follower growth, engagement rates, website traffic from social media, etc.]
   — Insights and Learnings:
   [Discuss any insights or learnings from the data.]
3. Brainstorming New Goals:
   — Goal Ideas:
   [List potential goals.]
   — Discussion:
   [Discuss feasibility, impact, and alignment with overall business objectives.]
4. SMART Goal Setting:
   — Specific:
   [Define specific goals.]

— Measurable:
[Establish criteria for measuring progress.]
— Achievable:
[Ensure goals are realistic.]
— Relevant:
[Ensure goals align with broader business objectives.]
— Time-Bound:
[Set deadlines for each goal.]
5. Strategy Development:
   — Action Plan:
   [Outline steps to achieve each goal.]
   — Resources Needed:
   [List the resources required, including time, tools, and personnel.]
6. Assigning Responsibilities:
   [Assign tasks and responsibilities to team members.]
7. Milestones and Check-Ins:
   — Milestones:
   [Set important milestones for progress tracking.]
   — Scheduled Check-Ins:
   [Schedule dates for regular progress reviews.]
8. Closing Remarks and Next Steps:
   [Summarize the session and outline immediate next steps.]
   Next Session Date:
   [Set date for next brainstorming session.]

EMBRACING ADAPTABILITY IN YOUR SOCIAL MEDIA STRATEGY

In the dynamic and ever-evolving world of social media, flexibility and adaptation are not just beneficial—they're essential. As you navigate through the shifting landscapes of online trends and market demands, it's crucial to stay open to adjusting your goals.

The ability to pivot in response to new information, audience feedback, or changes in the digital environment is a superpower in the social media realm. Embracing this flexibility allows your strategy to remain relevant, effective, and aligned with the current state of the market and your audience's evolving needs. Remember, the most successful social media strategies are those that can fluidly evolve with the times.

Staying flexible and ready to adapt your goals ensures that your social media strategy will remain relevant in the ever-changing digital landscape.

BRINGING IT ALL TOGETHER

As we close this chapter, remember that your goals today are not set in stone. They are living, breathing targets that should grow as you grow, adapt as you learn, and pivot as you encounter the unpredictable waves of social media trends. Equipped with the insights from this chapter, you're now ready to transform your vision into action, your action into habits, and your habits into the kind of success that resonates with your brand's unique voice.

24

How to Create a Budget for Social Media

Beware of little expenses; a small leak will sink a great ship.

—*Benjamin Franklin*, Poor Richard's Almanac

---

*S*adly, there is a cost to marketing for your business, even when you do all the work yourself. It would be best if you had the tools to create and plan your social media content.

Creating your "marketing stack" (marketing speak for the tools you use to create your marketing) doesn't have to be overwhelming, but you should use the free trials most companies offer to test different tools to see if you like them.

Canva is my Swiss Army Knife for creating marketing materials. It has moved beyond being "just" the place to create social media graphics to being invaluable to small businesses. Within Canva, you can design traditional marketing materials like flyers, posters, and business cards and print them at excellent prices. You can create videos for promotions and share them directly on social media. They have a great library of photos you can legally use included with the Pro version. There are photos in the free plan, too, but not as many.

Here are the costs for a few tools I recommend (with prices at the time of writing):

- Canva Pro for design work: $12.99 per month or $119 billed annually
- Trello for organization: Has a free plan and plans with more features at a cost
- SmarterQueue for scheduling: $29.99 per month or $299.88 billed annually
- Plann for scheduling and organizing: $14 per month or $132 billed annually
- Domain name: $20 per year
- Web hosting: from $10 to $50 per month, depending on what you choose
- Flodesk email platform: $38 per month or $420 billed annually
- Squarespace to create a website: $23 per month or $193.20 billed annually
- Wix another website option: $22 per month

Here are a few different variations for your starter marketing stack:

Plan 1
- Free photos from Unsplash and Pixels
- Canva: free version, you have to pay for photos and videos with this plan
- Trello: free version
- Total: $0.00 monthly

Plan 2
- Canva Pro: $12.99 per month (using premium photos, videos, and elements, for a webpage, and creating social media content)
- Trello: free version
- Flodesk: $38 per month
- Squarespace: $23 per month
- Total: $73.99 per month

Plan 3
- Canva Pro: $12.99 per month
- Trello: free version
- Flodesk: $38 per month
- Squarespace: $23 per month
- Plann That: $14 per month
- Total: $87.99

Determine what you'd like to create and publish monthly if you desire printed marketing pieces. What could those be? Perhaps a poster for a new class, postcards with the monthly class schedule, or an invitation to your monthly event with the cost and how to register.

You could create great things with a $100 monthly budget for printed marketing materials.

Some examples of pricing for print materials in Canva include:

- 50 double-sided postcards: $24 plus shipping
- 2 18×24 posters: $22 plus shipping
- 50 business cards: $15 plus shipping

You could safely budget $200 per month for your marketing budget, covering your website, tools, and some print collateral.

Planning for all your costs will help you stay on track and be more successful with your online marketing.

TO-DO NOTES

1. What's your monthly marketing budget?
2. Will you create traditional items, such as posters, business cards, flyers, or postcards?
3. Create your budget.

25

How to Grow Your Email List

The only person you are destined to become is the person you decide to be.

—Ralph Waldo Emerson

---

*E*mail is an essential part of a marketing strategy. Email isn't social media, but growing an email list is another marketing asset you can control, like your website.

Growing your email list will increase the longevity of your business and, in turn, build a better relationship with your loyal customers.

WHAT IS EMAIL MARKETING?

Email marketing sends commercial messages to potential and current customers through email. It's a form of direct marketing that uses electronic mail to communicate. The main advantages of email marketing are that it's relatively inexpensive, it's fast, and it's easy to track results.

"According to OptinMonster, 99% of people check their inbox daily, with some checking multiple times throughout the day, up to twenty times per day! 58% of consumers check their email first thing in the morning."[1]

Email marketing can cultivate relationships with potential and current customers, grow your customer base, and increase sales. Regular communication informs customers about your product or service, special offers, or company news.

Research from Litmus says, "Email marketing makes money. For every dollar spent on email marketing, you can expect an average return of $36. That's a higher return than you can expect from any other form of marketing."[2]

To get started with email marketing, you'll need to build a list of subscribers. You can collect email addresses from your website, social media, or offline sources, such as a QR code at your front desk. Do not buy email lists because you cannot legally send email to people who did not request it.

WHAT ARE THE BENEFITS OF EMAIL MARKETING?

Email marketing stands out as a powerhouse for customer engagement and business growth. By cultivating a dedicated subscriber list and consistently delivering tailored email newsletters, you're not just remaining visible—you're actively nurturing customer relationships. Email marketing isn't just potent; it's cost-effective and straightforward to implement, too. With the right platform, you can access a suite of user-friendly templates and automation tools that streamline the process. And don't worry, this isn't about using personal email services like Gmail or Outlook; specialized email marketing software is designed to handle your business needs at scale.

The benefits of email marketing are numerous, but here are a few of the most important:

1. It's an excellent avenue for building relationships with your customers.
2. It allows you to target a specific audience. You can segment your email list to send more targeted, relevant messages to your subscribers, leading to higher conversion rates and ROI.

3. An email is a personal form of communication. When you send an email to someone, you are reaching out directly. This can help build relationships with customers and potential customers.

4. Send out coupons and specials. According to Invespcro, "68% of consumers believe coupons build brand awareness and generate loyalty."[3]

HOW TO USE EMAIL MARKETING TO ENGAGE CUSTOMERS

Here are some tips on how to use email marketing to engage customers and grow your business:

1. Keep your emails focused and relevant. Put your most important information above the fold, before people scroll down to read more.

2. Make sure your emails are mobile-friendly. Most email providers have a feature to check your email format on desktop and mobile view. This is the mobile view in Flodesk when you preview an email you've created.

Source: Flodesk.

3. Use an engaging subject line. Keep it short and to the point with a relevant emoji.

   Here are some examples of a florist's email subject line for a Mother's Day promotion:
   - 🌹 Celebrate Mom with Flowers! 🌸 Mother's Day Sale!
   - Show Mom Some Love 🌹 with Our Mother's Day Bouquets 🌹
   - A Bouquet of Savings 🌹 for Mom this Mother's Day 🌸
   - 🌸 Bloomin' Amazing Deals 🌸 for Mom on Mother's Day 🌹

4. Use a call to action to entice people to click through to your website. A CTA, or Call to Action, is a prompt that encourages your reader to take a specific action. In the context of an email, it's usually a button, link, or explicit instruction telling the recipient what you'd like them to do next, like visit a website, sign up for a service, or purchase a product. The CTA should be attention-grabbing and direct, often using actionable language like "Sign Up," "Learn More," or "Buy Now."

   Here are some examples of CTAs you might use in an email to get people to click through to a website:
   - "Discover our new collection—Click here to start shopping!"
   - "Ready to level up? Join our course today!"
   - "Get exclusive member benefits—Sign up for free!"
   - "Don't miss out on this deal—Shop the sale now!"
   - "Learn more about our services—Visit our site for more information."

   Each of these examples includes an imperative verb that invites action, providing a clear idea of what the recipient will find when they click through. The best CTAs are usually short, visually distinct from the rest of the email, and create a sense of urgency or benefit.

5. Personalize your emails. When you set up your email forms for people to sign up for your list, ask for their first name. In your email provider, they will have a section to personalize the email by adding their name in the greeting or the text. Make it extra special by personalizing the CTA. According to HubSpot, "Personalized calls to action convert 202% better than default calls to action."[4]

An email form, often referred to as a "sign-up form" or "subscription form," is an online form that visitors can complete to subscribe to email communications from a business, website, or individual.

Here's the lowdown on how email forms work and why they're essential:

- *Collection of Information*: Email forms typically collect at least the person's email address. They may also ask for more details, like a name, phone number, or preferences to help tailor communications. Don't ask for information you don't need, like a phone number, especially if you're never going to use it. People don't feel comfortable giving out too much personal information. Name and email address are usually sufficient.

- *Integration with Email Marketing Tools*: These forms are usually integrated with email marketing platforms like Mailchimp, Constant Contact, or my favorite, Flodesk. When someone fills out the form, their information is automatically added to your email list in the associated marketing tool.

- *Customization for Targeting*: You can customize forms to target different segments of your audience based on the content they're viewing, their behavior on your site, or their stage in the sales funnel.

- *Compliance with Regulations*: Email forms help ensure that you're complying with regulations like GDPR or CAN-SPAM, as they typically include consent checkboxes or information about what the subscriber will receive.

- *Placement on Your Website*: You can strategically place these forms on your website, such as the homepage, in blog posts, or as a pop-up that appears when visitors are about to leave the site.

- *Call to Action*: Good forms have a clear CTA, encouraging visitors to sign up for newsletters, offers, updates, or other email content.

After someone submits their information, it's highly recommended to employ a double opt-in procedure. This method involves sending a confirmation email to the new subscriber, which contains a link they must click to verify their email address. This step confirms the validity of the email address and affirms the subscriber's intent to receive emails from you.

In essence, an email form is your digital sign-up sheet that serves as the first step in building a relationship with your audience through email marketing. It's a crucial element for growing your subscriber base and for kicking off targeted marketing campaigns.

6. Personalization isn't the only key to success; timing is also crucial. Most email providers offer scheduling options, allowing you to send your emails at the optimal time. Scheduling ensures that your message lands in inboxes at a moment when recipients are most likely to engage, whether that's first thing in the morning, over lunch, or in the early evening. By combining the power of personalization with strategic scheduling, you can significantly increase the chances of your emails being opened, read, and acted upon.

This addition underscores the importance of not just customizing content to be relevant to each individual, but also delivering it at a time when they're most receptive.

7. Make it timely. Create a sense of urgency with phrases like "act now" and "limited time only," but don't overdo it or use them too often.

8. Monitor your results in your email software.

9. Get creative! Use a few emojis and tap in to a current trend or pop culture event.

ARE THERE ANY REGULATIONS REGARDING EMAIL MARKETING?

A variety of laws guide commercial email marketing practices. In the United States, it's the CAN-SPAM Act. In Canada, it's CASL; in the United Kingdom, it's known as the Privacy and Electronic Communications Regulations 2003. Email marketing should be taken seriously. You cannot add people to your email list without their permission. There are actual financial and legal consequences if you send out marketing emails without following the rules. While this may freak you out, using legitimate email marketing tools, like Flodesk or MailChimp, will help you comply with the rules.

These anti-spam laws are, in a nutshell, aimed at blocking spammers from obtaining people's addresses without their permission and spamming them with unwanted advertising materials.

WHY DOES EMAIL GET MARKED AS SPAM?

Emails get marked as spam for various reasons, usually because they have characteristics that email providers associate with unsolicited or harmful messages. Here are some common reasons emails might end up in the spam folder:

1. *Spammy Content*: Certain words or phrases can trigger spam filters. Overly promotional language, aggressive sales pitches, or content that sounds too good to be true can raise red flags.
2. *Suspicious Attachments or Links*: Attachments or links that seem potentially harmful or unrelated to the email content can be a big no-no.
3. *Sender Reputation*: If your email address or domain has been previously flagged for sending spam, your emails might automatically be considered suspicious.
4. *Lack of Personalization*: Generic, impersonal emails that don't use the recipient's name or relevant content can be marked as spam.
5. *Inconsistent Sending Behavior*: It can seem spammy if you send emails erratically (e.g., nothing for months and then hundreds in a day).
6. *No Unsubscribe Option*: Legitimate emails typically allow recipients to opt-out or unsubscribe. Not having this feature is a standard spam indicator.
7. *Poorly Formatted HTML*: Emails that need to be better coded or look broken can end up in spam, as it may be a sign of a rushed or malicious email.
8. *User Behavior*: If many recipients mark your emails as spam, this will affect your sender's reputation.

To avoid your emails being marked as spam, you can:

- *Personalize Your Emails*: Use the recipient's name and ensure the content is relevant to them.
- *Maintain a Consistent Sending Schedule*: Avoid sending large volumes of emails at once.
- *Craft a Clear, Professional Subject Line*: Avoid using all caps, excessive punctuation, or spammy phrases.
- *Include an Unsubscribe Link*: Make it easy for people to opt-out.
- *Test Your Emails Before Sending*: Check for broken links and formatting issues, and ensure they display well on different devices.
- *Build and Maintain a Good Sender Reputation*: Warm up your email address by gradually increasing the email volume.
- *Avoid Spammy Content*: Be cautious with the language you use and the promotions you include.
- *Use a Reputable Email Service Provider*: They often have tools to help you avoid spam filters.
- *Get Whitelisted*: Encourage subscribers to add your email address to their contact list.

Remember, a big part of avoiding the spam folder is building trust and providing value to your recipients. Keep your content relevant, respectful, and engaging, and you'll be on the right track!

To recap, here are the rules to follow:

- Make sure you have permission to email.
- Don't buy email lists. You don't have permission to email them, and you'll get marked for spam.
- Have a way to unsubscribe from every email.
- Include your business address at the bottom.

You'll need to sign up for an email service like Flodesk, Constant Contact, or MailChimp to maintain your list and simultaneously send out emails to the whole list. I have tried several options, and my current favorite is Flodesk because they make it easy to create gorgeous emails—and they have a fixed rate plan so you don't get charged more as your list grows, which is helpful for budgeting. I like the user interface in Flodesk too.

Flodesk and Gmail serve different purposes in the realm of email and communication, each with its own unique features and target users.

Flodesk is primarily an email marketing tool designed for creating and sending aesthetically pleasing, engaging email campaigns. It's often used by businesses, entrepreneurs, and creatives who want to maintain regular communication with many subscribers. Here's what Flodesk does:

1. *Email Design and Templates*: They offer a range of customizable templates for newsletters, marketing campaigns, and announcements.
2. *List Building and Segmentation*: This helps you manage your email list and segment it into different groups based on subscriber preferences or behavior.
3. *Automation*: You can set up automated email sequences, such as welcome emails, follow-ups, or triggered responses based on subscriber actions.
4. *Analytics*: Analytics provides insights into how your emails are performing, like open rates, click rates, and subscriber engagement.
5. *Subscription Forms*: This enables you to create forms to embed on your website or social media to gather new subscribers.

On the other hand, Gmail is a free email service provided by Google, widely used for personal and professional communication. Its features are more focused on individual email management and communication. Here's what Gmail offers:

1. *Email Management*: Sending and receiving emails, organizing your in-box with labels and filters, and searching through e-mails.
2. *Integration with Google Services*: Seamless integration with other Google services, like Google Drive, Calendar, and Meet, for a more comprehensive productivity suite.
3. *Spam Filtering*: Advanced spam filtering to keep unwanted emails out of your in-box.
4. *Storage*: Significant storage space for emails and attachments and the ability to send large files via Google Drive.
5. *Security*: Strong security features, like two-factor authentication and suspicious activity alerts.
6. *Customizable Settings*: Provisions to customize the look of your in-box, create signatures, and set up out-of-office replies.

In summary, Flodesk is tailored more toward email marketing and managing subscriber lists with a focus on design and automation. Gmail is a versatile email service suited for everyday personal and professional communication, offering robust management and integration features. The choice between them would depend on your specific needs—whether you're looking to market your brand or manage daily email communication.

When subscribers sign up to receive your updates, they welcome you into their home—their in-box. Take the time to nurture your relationship by sending out valuable information without selling it to them immediately.

- Send only helpful, relevant, and targeted content to your list.
- Ask your readers for their opinions. Ask them what they like, what they don't like, what they want to see, and more.
- Email your list when you host special events, change your hours, or send out occasional coupons or specials.

We have all signed up for emails from companies that send great emails. Gather inspiration from your favorite brands for your email campaigns.

The Google Promotions tab can be a bit of a challenge for market-ers and businesses trying to reach their audience's primary in-box in Gmail. Gmail's algorithms automatically sort incoming emails into different tabs like Primary, Social, and Promotions based on various factors. Here's what you can do to increase your chances of landing in the Primary tab:

1. *Encourage Engagement*: If recipients regularly open your emails, re-ply to them, or move them to the Primary tab, Gmail is more likely to categorize them as necessary. You can ask your subscribers to move your emails to the Primary tab.
2. *Personalize Your Emails*: Tailor your emails to each recipient. Use their name, reference past interactions, and make the content rel-evant to their interests.
3. *Limit Promotional Language and HTML*: Emails that look too much like mass marketing, with heavy use of sales language, multiple im-ages, or extensive HTML formatting, are more likely to end up in the Promotions tab. Try to make your emails look more like a personal letter.
4. *Avoid Excessive Links and Images*: Emails with many links and im-ages can trigger filters. Keep them to a minimum.
5. *Be Careful with Sender Information*: Use a recognizable sender name, ideally a person's name rather than a company name, and avoid fre-quently changing it.
6. *Test Your Emails*: Send your emails to accounts with different email providers to see where they land. You can then tweak your approach based on these tests.
7. *Request Safelisting*: Ask subscribers to add your email address to their contacts. Emails from contacts typically go to the Primary tab.

8. *Mind Your Subject Line*: Avoid overly promotional phrases and excessive use of caps or exclamation marks in the subject line.
9. *Keep a Clean Email List*: Regularly clean your email list to remove unengaged subscribers. High engagement rates can positively influence where your emails are placed.
10. *Segment Your List*: Send emails to smaller, more targeted segments of your list, as this can lead to higher engagement.
11. *Monitor Your Performance*: Keep an eye on your open rates and other metrics to understand how different strategies affect where your emails land.

Remember, there's no guaranteed way to avoid the Promotions tab entirely, as Gmail's algorithms are complex and constantly evolving. However, these strategies can help improve your chances of reaching the Primary in-box. The key is to create genuine, engaging content that resonates with your audience.

Here's how to get people to sign up for your email list:

1. Add an email sign-up button to your email.
2. Add a link to sign up on your social media bios.
3. Add a QR code to the back of your business cards or flyers.
4. Have a paper sign-up sheet on your counter.
5. Add sign-up buttons on your website.

HOW TO USE EMAIL MARKETING TO INCREASE SALES

Data from Constant Contact[5] shows that "sixty percent of consumers say they've purchased because of a marketing email. Compare that with the 12.5 percent of consumers who say they'd consider using the 'buy' button on social media, and it's not much of a contest."

Develop a plan to interest potential customers with helpful content, resources, and tools that support them from initial interest to becoming a customer.

Here are a few tips on how to use email marketing to engage customers and grow your business:

1. Spend time creating a solid subject line. It's the first thing customers will see when receiving your email, so make sure it's catchy and attention-grabbing.
2. Keep your message short and sweet. Customers are more likely to read and engage with a concise email that's to the point.
3. Use images and videos. Adding these to your email can help capture your customers' attention and increase their chances of reading your message.
4. When creating email copy, it's best to use a storytelling format. Your story will help you define a clear flow for the email, making content creation easier. Keep your paragraphs short and easy to read, and end with a CTA that supports your goals.

By following these simple rules, you can ensure that your email marketing campaigns will be successful.

This chapter should have helped open your eyes to the benefits of starting your email list and how to grow it. When change is the only constant in marketing, reaching your customers directly in their inboxes can be the surest route to success.

TO DO NOTES

1. Do you have an email list?
2. What email provider do you or will you use?
3. How often will you send email?

26

How to Define Your Goals

"Would you tell me, please, which way I ought to go from here?" asked Alice. "That depends a good deal on where you want to get to," said the Cheshire Cat.

—*Lewis Carroll,* Alice's Adventures in Wonderland

---

*G*oals for social media for small businesses reach beyond growing your follower count. Because there's a good chance you're a local business, acquiring a smaller number of local customers who will frequent and support your business is infinitely more important than having a thousand followers. One hundred local customers who like your posts and come to your business regularly add to your bottom line; one thousand followers scattered around the globe won't be your new local customers.

We'll use a yoga and wellness studio for the examples in this chapter. They hold local and online video classes, host workshops, and have notable events in their space.

GOALS

- Increase brand awareness (so more people know about your business)
- Generate leads (gather email addresses)

- Build your community (grow your following)
- Grow traffic to your website (so you have more eyes on your home base)
- Increase sales (track coupons and promo codes)

Brand Awareness

There are many ways to increase brand awareness for your business. Building trust is an important currency for your business. Trust reigns supreme. Consumers place immense value on the recommendations of their loved ones and meticulously research brands, products, and services before making decisions. Engaging in brand awareness campaigns is important to foster trust with consumers, demonstrating your commitment to transparency and reliability. Trust and credibility build your positive brand awareness positively and breed loyalty. Sharing customer reviews or testimonials shows your audience how people feel about your products and services.

Example: A new review is posted on Google. Take the text, create a branded graphic in Canva with it, and tag the customer who left the review if they're on the social platform.

FIGURE 26.1. Customer testimonial.
Source: Author created in Canva.

Lead generation

Another smart way to grow is to focus on lead generation, a fancy way to gather email addresses. This can be done by creating landing pages and lead magnets and offering free trials of your products or services.

Lead magnets are pieces of content your ideal customer will love, like a checklist, infographic, list of tools, or video. They're exchanging their email for the lead magnet, so you should create something valuable or helpful. You can create a PDF in Canva with clickable links, which they will sign up to receive. Then make a great landing page so people can receive your lead magnet and you can add them to your email list.

Lead magnets can live on your blog post or a landing page. Don't miss the opportunity to grab your social media followers by sharing your exclusive download on X, in a Facebook or Instagram post, or a Pinterest Pin.

The social opportunity to connect with your current audience's friends and network is a solid way to grow. Your followers love your content, and their community might love it too!

The benefit of the email lead is that you now have permission to email this person for your weekly classes, upcoming workshops, and monthly newsletter.

How to Promote Your Lead Magnet on Social Media

Create three unique social posts for each lead magnet. As they say, variety is the spice of life. It's also the spark that will fuel engagement with your social content.

1. A link post (link to the lead page) with the title as-is
2. A quote from your content
3. An image with the title of your lead magnet

Now share these on all of your social sites and repeat them occasionally. You can add these posts to your queue and set them in rotation using a scheduling tool. It's also a great idea to pin your lead magnet post to the top of your page feed on X or Facebook so it's the first thing people see.

Example: Create a seasonal wellness checklist as a lead magnet. Design the list in Canva with clickable links leading to your website. Add your lead magnet to your website or create your whole lead magnet sequence in Flodesk. When the customer signs up to receive the checklist, they get an email with the checklist to download, and they are added to your email list.

This is what it might look like for you in Flodesk:

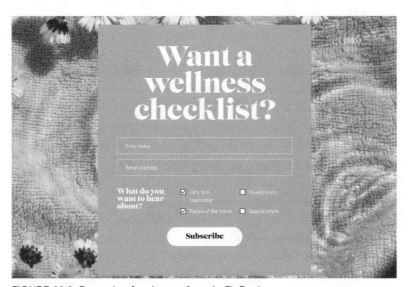

FIGURE 26.2. Example of a sign-up form in FloDesk.
Source: FloDesk.

Build Your Community

Building your community is part of growing your social media following. This can be done by engaging with your target audience on social media, creating informative blog content, and using hashtags and location tags.

As I mentioned, it's not about gaining significant numbers of random followers; it's about finding and connecting with the right people.

Start by letting people who visit your location know you're on social media, with minor signs saying, "Follow us on Instagram @WellnessToGo." You can buy custom window clings with your Instagram name and logo so your customers will know they can find and follow you there. It's subtle, and you don't need to ask them to follow you precisely, but all your customers on Instagram will recognize the logo and find you there.

Grow Traffic to Your website

Google Analytics will help you track your website traffic and growth. Most people have heard of Google Analytics as an essential tool for measuring website performance. This web-based software allows users to monitor key indicators, set goals, track conversions, and make decisions to improve business results.

You can make use of Google Analytics to:

- Use data to create strategies that work.
- Track your marketing campaign's performance.
- Learn what your audience likes.
- See how people behave on your website.
- Fix any bugs in your website.

In the audience tool, you can find the following:

- Location: Where your audience is located is helpful if you run a local business or if you're running a campaign that targets a specific area.

- Demographics: The gender and age of web visitors.
- Interests: Affinities, preferences, and the markets in which your audience is most active.
- Device and technology: Desktop, mobile, or tablet, as well as types of smartphones.
- Benchmarks: This compares your website performance with the average in your market.

Here are some of the most important metrics you should be watching regularly in Google Analytics:

- Number of page views, number of sessions, and new users
- Sources of traffic
- Bounce rate
- How many pages they visit on average
- How much it costs to convert
- How long they spend on the site
- What goals they achieve, and how much money they make

To grow traffic to your website, make sure you have your website URL in your bio on social media and add a link to your email signature. Small steps like this are what keep your website top-of-mind.

GROW YOUR SOCIAL ACCOUNTS

At the end of each month, take stock of your social account numbers and email sign-ups. It's helpful to have a spreadsheet so you can keep track of your progress. Refer back to chapter 12 if you want to review the steps to grow your social following.

Track Your Clicks

When you're getting ready for sales and promotions, you'll want a way to track clicks from social media to your website or landing page.

Enter Bit.ly, a popular tool used to create trackable links to see where people click on your content.

You can create tracking links to:

1. Measure the click-through rate of an email marketing campaign.
2. Monitor the traffic to a website from an online ad.
3. Determine which social media page is sending the most traffic to your website.
4. Track traffic to your site when it is featured in a media release, podcast, or another form of publicity.

Understanding what you want to get out of your social media campaigns can help establish what ROI will look like. Tracking the ROI of your social media campaign is no small feat, but it can be done. The majority of social media managers need to have everything under control.

Customizing your links looks professional and is only available in the paid version. Here's what it looks like when you track a link in Bit.ly:

5 Ideas for Small Businesses to Increase Sales with Social Media -...

📅 September 1, 2022 7:04 PM EDT by @PegFitzpatrick

ᐧᐧᐧ **8** Total engagements

FIGURE 26.3. Social post statistics.

If you are tracking and not getting any engagement on your links, it's time to change something, like taking more time with your social images or writing better copy. All the data you collect, whether positive or negative, will help you make more informed choices for the future.

Example: You're going to host a winter wellness workshop. You create a landing page with a link to sign up. Your next step is to take your link to Bit.ly and create a trackable link to share in your email, Facebook, and Instagram Stories.

If you use an email tool like Flodesk, you will get click stats within the platform. It could look like this:

29 clicks

29 subscribers clicked these
links a total of 57 times.

LINK	UNIQUE CLICKS	TOTAL CLICKS
https://pegfitzpatrick.com/	4	6
https://pegfitzpatrick.com/spinning-ideas-into-success-...	24	29
https://twitter.com/PegFitzpatrick	1	3
https://www.instagram.com/p/Cr3gxljgTlE/	1	2

FIGURE 26.4. Results of Flodesk clicks on email after campaign.
Source: Flodesk.

Decide what goals you want to focus on and use these tactics to help your social marketing boost your sales. Social media may be one of the drivers for sales growth, but tracking your efforts will help your small business stay in business and make informed decisions.

TO-DO-NOTES

1. Create a hashtag list for your business.
2. Create one week's worth of social captions.
3. Create a spot to capture all your ideas and inspiration, like a Trello Board or the Notion app.

Crafting Your Social Media Content

I have not failed. I've just found 10,000 ways that won't work.

—*Thomas A. Edison*

---

*W*e've reached a place where you can start creating social media content to help your small business achieve its goals. Hallelujah!

Based on a *New York Times* study called "The Psychology of Sharing,"[1] a few motivations inspire people to share content online. People want to share valuable content to enrich the lives of others and share entertaining content to make their friends and family smile. Seventy-eight percent of the study's participants felt that sharing content helped them stay connected with people, and sixty-nine percent of the people thought it helped them feel more involved with the world.

With these findings in mind , I'd like to share six guideposts to help you create social media posts that connect with your intended audience and help gain brand awareness. You can make a recipe for each post: guidepost, type of content, and caption. Choose a guidepost and apply it to your brand message and branding. Your goal is to have a purpose for social media posts and connect them with your goals to bring meaning to your online presence.

SIX GUIDEPOSTS FOR SOCIAL MEDIA POSTS

1. *Entertain*: Create content that captivates and delights your audience, keeping them engaged and amused with your unique style and personality.
2. *Inspire*: Share uplifting and motivational messages, images, or stories that ignite passion, spark creativity, and encourage your audience to pursue their dreams and aspirations.
3. *Educate*: Provide valuable and informative content that teaches your audience something new, helps them solve problems, or expands their knowledge in a particular area of interest.
4. *Converse*: Foster meaningful conversations and interactions with your audience by actively engaging with their comments, questions, and feedback, building a sense of community and connection.
5. *Connect*: Forge genuine connections with your audience by sharing personal stories, experiences, and insights that resonate with them on a deeper level, building trust and loyalty over time.
6. *Promote*: Strategically showcase your products, services, or offerings in a way that adds value to your audience members' lives and aligns with their interests and needs, encouraging them to act and become loyal customers or supporters.

Here are thirty examples of posts you can create as a video or photo post. Unleash *The Art of Social Media for Small Business* for your business with these creative post ideas:

1. Go behind the scenes with a production process video.
2. Showcase happy customers with testimonials.
3. Inspire your audience with motivational quotes or messages.
4. Teach and educate with tutorial videos.
5. Connect with your audience through a live Q&A with the founder or staff.
6. Increase engagement with a contest or giveaway.

7. Share the exciting news of new product or service launches.
8. Drive sales with promotions and special deals.
9. Showcase partnerships and collaborations.
10. Highlight your community involvement with charity or event support.
11. Get valuable feedback through polls or surveys.
12. Encourage website or store visits with a call-to-action post.
13. Show off customers using your products.
14. Introduce your team and the faces behind the business.
15. Give a tour of your office or store.
16. Highlight your customers.
17. Showcase your products or services.
18. Brag about your awards and certifications.
19. Keep your audience informed with industry news and updates.
20. Make it easy for followers to find you with easy-to-remember social media handles.
21. Promote events or workshops.
22. Share positive reviews and ratings.
23. Collaborate with partners and suppliers.
24. Address common questions with FAQ or Q&A posts.
25. Share valuable content with blogs or articles.
26. Showcase your success stories and case studies.
27. Display your portfolio and work.
28. Provide transparent information on services and pricing.
29. Make it easy for customers to reach you with contact information.
30. Boost your social media presence with campaigns and hashtags.

Now let's take one guidepost and create a post for a bakery. We'll choose "entertain" and "behind-the-scenes" video of production created for an Instagram Reel. You'll create a vertical video of a cupcake being frosted with sprinkles added to it.

Caption for the social post:

🧁 🎂 Sweeten up your day with our signature cupcake frosting! Watch as we sprinkle some love into every swirl. #BakeryLife #Cupcake-Craze #FrostedPerfection 👻

Some people dream of cupcakes; others bake it happen. #SprinkleLove

A piece of cake, right? I couldn't resist that joke. You'll find that sometimes happens when creating content; if it fits your brand, include humor.

Get creative with your content! Give your messages a monthly makeover by remixing this list to your heart's desire. There is no need to reinvent the wheel; have fun and make it your own by creating thirty individual posts.

You can generally use the exact text for your social media posts across different platforms—with a few caveats. A social media caption recipe is:

An intriguing opening sentence, a few sentences of context, an engaging question for people to answer, and a call to action at the end of the post, followed by three to five hashtags. Following this format, you can put your hashtags in a group at the bottom or add them contextually in the post, meaning work them into the sentences. Sprinkle in a few appropriate emojis. If you're not sure what an emoji means, look it up at https://emojipedia.org/.

Opening + emoji + purposeful text + engaging question + CTA + hashtags = a great social media caption

Here's an example:

🌟 Embrace the journey! 🌟

Life's adventures are full of twists and turns, but each step brings us closer to our dreams. Whether you're climbing mountains or navigating the bustling city streets, remember that every experience shapes who you are. 🏔️

What's the most memorable adventure you've embarked on? Share your stories in the comments below! 📷

Ready to embark on your next journey? Click the link in our bio to explore our latest collection of travel essentials and start planning your next adventure! 🎒 ✈️

#AdventureAwaits #ExploreMore #Wanderlust #TravelGoals #Journey OfDiscovery 🌍

This example incorporates all elements of the caption recipe:

- An intriguing opening sentence ("Embrace the journey!").
- Contextual text providing insight or setting the scene ("Life's adventures are full of twists and turns . . . ").
- An engaging question prompting audience interaction ("What's the most memorable adventure you've embarked on?").
- A call to action encouraging further engagement or action ("Click the link in our bio to explore our latest collection . . . ").
- And hashtags relevant to the post content and audience interests.

Once you put this into practice, you won't have to follow the recipe so closely, but this gives you a great place to start when creating your own social posts.

HASHTAG STRATEGIES

Let's create a hashtag strategy for your business.

Hashtags are words or phrases preceded by a pound or number sign (#) without spaces. Hashtags are essential on many of the most popular social platforms, regarding people being able to find you online and building brand awareness. When making a post, constantly research the hashtags you are using; you don't want your business to be associated with something that could turn away potential customers.

Two places where hashtags don't work are Pinterest and Facebook. On Pinterest, hashtags aren't clickable and don't work. On Facebook, they are clickable, but most people don't search for them on Facebook. If you use them on Facebook, only use a few and put them at the bottom of the text.

Taking the time to brainstorm your hashtags is incredibly beneficial and can separate you from your competitors. It will also help you gain traction with your target audience if you have a hashtag they cannot help but use after partaking in your services.

Take your hashtag game to the next level with a well-planned strategy that delivers results. Learn about the various types of hashtags and use them to boost your content's reach.

Location-based hashtags: #mydayinla #bigapple #NYC

Industry hashtags: #fashionista #fashionblogger

Holiday hashtags: #fourthofjuly #christmaseve

Calls to action: #pinitforlater #clicktoread #shareacoke

Branded hashtags: #thanksalatte is a hashtag I used for a Facebook Live series and all social media posts discussing the series. #MyBook Club is the first hashtag I created for my X chat. I started the #CanvaLove hashtag as the head of social strategy at Canva to help build the community and give Canva users a hashtag to share with their Canva designs. #CanvaLove is still being used today by the brand and Canva lovers on X, Linkedin, Facebook, and Pinterest.

McDonald's used #alldaybreakfast when they switched from breakfast ending at 10:30 to all-day breakfast. RIP, all-day breakfast.

High usage of a hashtag by many people can cause it to trend. This is an opportunity to check the hashtag and create a brand-relevant social post, not hashtag spam with irrelevant content. To check what the hashtag is, click on it and see what content is being shared.

Clicking on a hashtag can provide a wealth of information and potential connections. Here are a few ways that hashtags can be used:

- For real-time interaction with friends, fans, and influencers
- To reinforce your area of expertise
- To connect with other people interested in the same topic
- To create a social media campaign
- For brand awareness
- To catch the trends—daily, weekly, or holiday
- To find valuable UGC (user-generated content)
- To rock out live events such as conferences
- To build out a social contest

Hashtags should:

1. Be easy to spell.
2. Be easy to remember.
3. Not spell something awkward or potentially embarrassing.
4. Make other people want to join in, like #TeamOreo. If the hashtag is only about you, it limits other people's interest in using it.

Check hashtags to ensure they aren't used for another topic or reason. You don't want to hijack someone else's content or jump into something inappropriate accidentally.

Tools for Finding Hashtags

- TagDef—You can see the definitions of popular hashtags here.
- Allhashtag.com—Lots of great information here, including hashtags and a hashtag generator.

HOW OFTEN SHOULD YOU POST?

I would say:

- On *Instagram*, post between *3 to 5 times per week* and post Instagram Stories daily.

- On *Facebook*, post *once a day*.
- On *X*, post *1 or 2 Tweets a day*.
- On *LinkedIn*, post *once a day*.
- On *Pinterest*, create *one Pin per week*.

MAINTAIN YOUR SOCIAL MEDIA SUCCESS

Be Present

Being present is essential to maintaining your business's social media's identity. You must continue regular and consistent posts on whatever platforms you've committed to use. Walk before you run; choosing one platform and perfecting it is a perfect place to start. It might seem easy at first, but maintaining an active presence across multiple platforms takes more work than it looks.

A good rule of thumb is quality over quantity; ensuring each piece of material you publish meets your standards every time will only help you grow, even if it is just one post at a time.

FOSTER COMMUNICATION

Don't Post and Ghost

Communication is another critical aspect of marketing. It is reasonable to assume that after forming an online presence, your current and potential customers will try to reach out to you. Being active with your responses and helpful will only serve to grow your business in the best possible way. Proactive communication with your target audience is the perfect medium to obtain feedback and, more importantly, build the trust your business relies upon to survive.

Mix in Entertainment

Maintaining a specific entertainment value is an overlooked aspect of representing a business on social media. Constantly pushing your product or company can be highly off-putting. People will grow tired of self-serving content flooding their newsfeeds. Injecting a little humor into an otherwise-bland post, or even having some posts be unrelated to your business, is a great way to make people feel more comfortable with your brand.

An excellent way to add entertainment value is by incorporating GIFs instead of traditional images. GIFs always bring a smile, and with a vast selection available, you'll always find the perfect one to suit your content, even if you're not creating your own. However, it's essential to exercise caution and consider both the content of the GIF and the context in which you're using it. Ensure that the GIF aligns with your brand's tone and values and is appropriate for your audience. What's humorous to one group may be offensive to another, so always double-check to avoid any potential missteps. Additionally, be mindful of copyright issues when using GIFs from the internet, and whenever possible, opt for GIFs from reputable sources or create your own to maintain originality and authenticity.

Only Use Photos You Have Permission to Use

One of the biggest misconceptions is that just because the photo is online, you can post it anywhere. That is *not* true. Don't do it. You cannot legally take images from a Google search or anywhere online that you see a photo that you like.

Can you post a photo from Pinterest and put the link to Pinterest as the photo credit? No. From attorney Sara Hawkins[2]: "Attribution does not make it right." I should note, as Sara does, that she's an attorney, but she's not *your* attorney. Attorneys like to be thorough.

Sara further said, "Taking another person's image or graphic and giving them a "shout out," linkback or any other type of attribution does not negate copyright infringement. Common sense may say that an artist wants exposure for their work, but we're talking about the law here, and common sense doesn't always apply. Copyright law gives the copyright holder the right to decide where their work is published, and maybe they don't want their work on your site, in your book, included in your newsletter, or distributed to your social media network. It's not for us to question why they wouldn't want exposure."

If you use photos without permission, you can receive a DMCA (Digital Millennium Copyright Act) Takedown Notice and possibly be fined. Celebrities have been fined for posting photos of themselves from the Getty Images library. A DMCA takedown notice is a formal legal request from a copyright owner or representative to an online platform, such as a social media platform or website. This notice aims to eradicate copyrighted material uploaded without proper permission by service users. The DMCA acts as a protective framework for copyright holders, granting them the ability to demand the elimination of infringing content online. Platforms must swiftly remove or limit access to the specified content outlined in the takedown notice to evade potential repercussions for copyright infringement. Ignoring a legitimate DMCA takedown notice can lead to legal ramifications, potentially resulting in fines or other penalties.

The bottom line is that if you can't afford a stock photo, you can't afford the fine for stealing one.

Creative Commons is a great resource. Make sure that you check the box at the top if you will use the photo for commercial purposes or modify, adapt, or build upon it, like adding text or banners in Canva. If you have Canva Pro, they have millions of photos you can legally use. Other resources include Unsplash, Pexels, Pixabay, and FreeImages. com. If you have a budget and want more exclusive images, you can use Adobe Stock, Élevae Visuals, or Stocksy.

Only Use Music You Have Permission to Use

Legally using music follows a similar principle to using photos: you must obtain the appropriate permissions or licenses. Just because a song is available online doesn't mean it's free to use. Copyright laws protect musical works, and using music without proper authorization can result in legal consequences. Instead, consider using royalty-free music libraries or platforms that offer licensed music for commercial use. Some options include Epidemic Sound, Artlist, or Soundstripe, where you can find a wide selection of high-quality music tracks that you can legally use in your projects. Additionally, consider contacting musicians or composers directly to license their music for your specific needs. Remember, respecting copyright laws protects you from legal issues and supports artists and creators in their work.

Using music in the Instagram app requires adherence to copyright laws and platform guidelines. While Instagram offers a music library for users to incorporate into their posts and stories, it's essential to understand the terms of use and licensing agreements associated with each track. Instagram provides licensed music options from various artists and labels, allowing users to add popular songs to their content without worrying about copyright infringement. However, it's crucial to check the permissions and restrictions for each track before including it in your posts. By respecting copyright laws and platform guidelines, you can enjoy using music in your Instagram content while avoiding potential legal issues.

PRACTICE PATIENCE FOR SMALL BUSINESS SUCCESS
The most important lesson to learn is that you'll need to be patient. You can't expect to create an account and instantly be swarmed with followers and customers. It takes time to grow your small business through social media, but if you keep at it and remain consistent in your efforts, you will see the fruits of your labor.

TO-DO-NOTES

1. What's your location hashtag?
2. Create a list of five industry hashtags.
3. Create one week of content.

28

How to Create Short-Form Videos

Brevity is the soul of wit.

—*William Shakespeare,* Hamlet

*I*f you see people scrolling on their phones, there's a good chance that they're watching a short-form video. Short-form social videos are everywhere: Instagram Reels, TikTok, Idea Pins on Pinterest, and YouTube Shorts. The length of short-form videos varies by platform and, of course, constantly changes. Short-form videos can be from three seconds to two minutes in length.

For our short video discussion, I will discuss vertical, short-form videos. Short videos don't have to be vertical, but this is the most popular way they are consumed. Vertical videos are created in portrait mode and have an aspect ratio of 9:16. They are taller than they are wide, with the recommended dimensions being 1080 x 1920 pixels. Vertical videos can be shot or edited on cameras, but they are primarily shot and viewed on mobile phones. A vertical video fills the screen on a smartphone, so your audience isn't distracted by anything in the sidebar. It's all your video.

Think about it: how do you hold your phone most of the time? Vertically. We want to make it easy for people to enjoy (aka binge and watch over and over) our videos, and so shooting vertical for short-form videos helps optimize them for mobile devices.

There are many benefits of using short-form videos for social media marketing. Hubspot[1] research found that short-form video ranks number one for lead generation and engagement. Short videos are also the most shared content on social media.

Research from Animoto[2] found that *videos on social media helped 93 percent of brands acquire new customers.* You can create educational and entertaining videos to reach your target audience, build brand awareness, and cultivate your community.

UNDERSTANDING SHORT-FORM SOCIAL VIDEOS

Why are short videos essential for small businesses? Vertical video is important for small businesses because it is optimized for mobile devices, which are increasingly the primary way people consume video content. By using vertical video, small businesses can create more engaging content, and it is easier to watch on smartphones and tablets, which can help increase brand awareness and drive more traffic to their websites or social media pages. Additionally, vertical video can help small businesses stand out in crowded marketplaces and provide a more immersive viewing experience for their audiences.

Watching a short video is a small commitment of six to fifteen seconds. If it's entertaining or informative, people watch them over and over. Sometimes short videos share a lot of information or steps very quickly, and you must watch them more than once to learn everything. This is by design, to keep you watching. Everything on social media is about keeping you on the platform and paying attention to something. For example, a short video might show the steps to make a recipe in ten seconds, but you must watch it multiple times to catch the ingredients or process.

Have you noticed the last time you turned your phone sideways to watch a video, especially a short one? We usually don't change the orientation of our phones. Thanks to popular social media apps like

TikTok and Snapchat and other platforms joining the trend sooner or later, vertical videos have become the standard. *Ninety-four percent to of time spent on phones is in portrait mode.*[3]

Viewers are 90 percent more likely to watch a short vertical video until the end, making them more appealing to audiences. Data from Sprout Social[4] found that short-form video offers marketers the highest ROI of any social media marketing strategy. That's a compelling reason to give it a go.

Here are some examples of types of short-form videos for educating your audience:

Explainer videos are short videos that explain a concept, idea, or process. They are often animated or use simple graphics to make complex topics more accessible to viewers.

How-to videos demonstrate step-by-step instructions on how to perform a specific task or activity. They can be used to teach viewers new skills or provide helpful tips. Whether it's fixing a leaky faucet, learning a new dance move, or mastering the perfect pancake flip, how-to videos are there to show you the ropes.

Tutorial videos are like the wise sage of the internet. They dive deep into a particular topic or skill, providing comprehensive instruction and insight. If you're looking to really understand something or level up your expertise, tutorial videos are where it's at. They might unravel complex concepts, showcase advanced techniques, or offer a more thorough exploration of a subject.

In a nutshell: how-to videos are your quick guides for getting stuff done, while tutorial videos are your deep dives for becoming a true expert. Whether you need a quick fix or want to become a pro, there's a video out there ready to show you the way!

Whiteboard animations involve a hand-drawn animation on a whiteboard background. They can be used to explain complex concepts in a visually engaging way.

Infographic videos use animated infographics to present information in a visually appealing and easy-to-understand way. They can be used to showcase data or statistics or to explain complex ideas.

Q&A videos answer frequently asked questions or address common misconceptions about a topic. They can be used to provide clarity on complex issues or to help viewers better understand a subject.

Interview videos involve interviewing experts or professionals in a specific field. They can be used to provide insights or knowledge from people with expertise on a particular topic.

Documentary-style videos can dive deeply into a subject, such as history, science, or current events. They can be used to educate viewers on a particular topic in a more engaging and immersive way.

Here are some examples of types of short-form videos for entertainment:

Lip-syncing videos involve people lip-syncing to popular songs or movie dialogues. They are often performed in costumes or using props to add a fun element to the video.

Comedy skits are short, humorous sketches that often feature exaggerated situations, caricatures of people, or parodies of popular media. They are a popular form of entertainment on social media.

Dance videos involve people showcasing their dance moves to popular songs. They are often performed in choreographed routines or freestyle.

Reaction videos involve people watching and reacting to popular videos, memes, or events. They are often humorous and can be a way to provide commentary on current events or pop culture.

Vlogs are short, casual videos that feature people talking about their daily lives, sharing experiences, or providing commentary on various topics. They are often shot in a handheld style and can be a way to connect with viewers on a personal level.

Animations are short, often humorous videos that feature animated characters or objects. They can tell a story, deliver a message, or provide entertainment.

DIY videos involve people demonstrating how to make or create something. They are your creative allies, guiding you through the journey of making or crafting something unique. From building a birdhouse to sewing your own clothes, they're packed with inventive ideas and practical tips to inspire your inner maker.

Unlike how-to videos, which focus on specific tasks, DIY videos open the door to a world of creativity and innovation. They're not just guides; they're invitations to explore your imagination and express your unique style through hands-on projects.

Food videos showcase different recipes, cooking techniques, or food reviews. They are a popular form of entertainment on social media and can be a way to showcase culinary skills or inspire viewers to try new dishes.

Here are some examples of types of short-form videos for brand awareness:

Brand story videos share a company's history, mission, and values. They can showcase the brand's personality and connect with viewers emotionally.

Product showcase videos highlight the features and benefits of a specific product or service. They can be used to demonstrate how the product solves a problem or meets customers' needs.

Customer testimonial videos feature satisfied customers talking about their positive experiences with a brand or product. They can build trust with potential customers and provide social proof.

Behind-the-scenes videos offer a glimpse into the day-to-day operations of a company. They can be used to showcase the people and processes behind the brand, providing an authentic and relatable view.

Influencer collaboration videos: can help increase brand awareness and reach new audiences. Collaborating with influencers, on short-form videos, can showcase the brand's products or services in a way that resonates with their followers.

Social responsibility videos highlight a brand's commitment to social causes or environmental sustainability. They can be used to show that the brand is more than just a business and is actively working to impact the world positively.

Event videos can be used to showcase brand-sponsored events or participation in industry conferences or trade shows. They can be used to demonstrate the brand's involvement in the industry and build credibility with potential customers.

Humorous videos that align with a brand's values or personality can build awareness and increase engagement. They can help the brand stand out in a crowded social media landscape and make an emotional connection with viewers.

Here are some examples of types of short-form videos to build community:

User-generated content (UGC) involves featuring content created by the community, such as customer photos or videos. This can help foster a sense of community ownership and involvement.

Polls or surveys can engage the community and gather feedback on topics of interest. This can help the brand better understand the community's needs and preferences.

Collaborative challenges, such as fitness or cooking challenges, can be used to encourage community participation and build a sense of camaraderie.

Live videos can host Q&A sessions, product demonstrations, or other interactive events that allow the community to participate and engage in real-time.

Community spotlight videos showcase individual community members, highlighting their achievements or contributions. This can help build a sense of pride and recognition within the community.

Community events hosted, either in-person or virtually, can help build connections and foster a sense of community. Short-form videos can be used to promote these events and highlight key moments.

Educational videos can be used to share tips, tricks, and knowledge relevant to the community's interests. This can help establish the brand as a valuable resource within the community.

Emotional or inspiring videos can create shared experiences and emotions within the community. These videos can be particularly effective at fostering a sense of connection and belonging.

HOW CAN SHORT-FORM VIDEOS IMPROVE CUSTOMER ENGAGEMENT?

Humans connect with faces better than text or static images. We're drawn from birth to seek out faces, and neuroscience backs this up. Our brains light up with video, which engages more parts of our brains than photos or text. After we begin watching a video, the algorithm takes note of our preferences. Based on our engagement, meaning how long we watch the video, it suggests similar content, such as puppies, amusing lip-sync, or popular dance routines based upon your viewing habits. Once we start viewing, it becomes increasingly challenging to break away from the screen.

How does this improve customer engagement? It builds trust as viewers connect with the people in the video. Faces, voices, and video shot in your store or business build familiarity and the LKT factor. We've all seen the commercials on TV for local businesses featuring owners and family members. There's a reason those are successful; they promote the human connection by showing the same person representing the business—and who better to tell your story than you? You can create an emotional connection with your videos, and this builds trust and familiarity.

SETTING GOALS FOR EACH VIDEO

Back to our purpose: What is your goal for this video? You want to plan for eight to fifteen seconds with a hook in the first three seconds, then several examples or points, ending with a call to action, or CTA. A CTA is like the cherry on top of your favorite sundae—it's that final touch that makes everything come together. It's the friendly nudge at the end of a video or post that invites the viewer to take the next step, whether it's clicking a link, signing up for updates, or joining the conversation. CTAs add that extra value to your content, guiding your audience toward meaningful engagement and action.

A video call to action ends the video and asks the viewer to do something. Here are five examples of CTAs that you can use for videos:

1. *Follow me or us*: This CTA encourages viewers to follow your account for more content.
2. *Like and comment*: Encourage viewers to like and comment on your video to increase engagement and reach.

3. *Share with friends*: Ask viewers to share your video with friends and family to help your content reach a wider audience.
4. *Check out my website*: If you have a website or blog, encourage viewers to visit it for more information or resources related to the video.
5. *Shop now*: If you have a product or service that you're promoting, encourage viewers to shop or learn more by visiting your online store or website. You can provide a specific discount code or offer to incentivize viewers to act.

Facebook's video content data[5] reveals that 65 percent of viewers who watch past the initial three seconds are likely to continue to the ten-second mark, and 45 percent of those viewers will watch for at least thirty seconds. This statistic underscores the critical importance of creating a captivating hook in the first three seconds for the success of your video content.

In addition, incorporating an attention-grabbing hook in the first three seconds can have additional advantages. The more viewers who watch your video's initial seconds, the higher the performance of your video content will be. The performance in this context would be the watch time for the video and whether people engage with it by liking, commenting, or sharing. Social media algorithms recognize when viewers engage with your content, which results in more impressions and recommendations to other individuals interested in the same topic.

What is a *video hook*? A *hook* refers to the element that captures your audience's attention and sparks their interest in your video. It occurs in the initial moments and establishes the tone for the rest of the video. Your hook may take the form of a question, a promise, or a visual, and in some cases, it may involve highlighting a unique aspect of your product or service.

Here are three examples of video hooks that can capture viewers' attention in the first three seconds:

Shock factor: Begin with something unexpected or startling to immediately hook viewers' attention. For example, you could start with a loud noise, a sudden movement, or a striking visual.

Storytelling: Begin with a compelling narrative that piques viewers' curiosity and makes them want to learn more. This could involve opening up with a relatable situation, a problem that needs to be solved, or a question that needs answering.

Intrigue: Begin with a mysterious or thought-provoking scene that intrigues viewers and makes them want to learn more. For example, you could open with a cryptic message, an unusual visual, or a teaser of something exciting.

Creating a storyboard is a crucial step in planning a video. If you don't have a plan for your video, you'll end up taking a longer time to film and edit. Think of a storyboard as the blueprint for your short video—it's like sketching out the scenes before you hit *record*. It's a series of drawings or images arranged in sequence, representing each shot or scene in your video. A storyboard helps you visualize how your video will flow, plan out camera angles, and ensure that your message comes across clearly. It's your road map to creating a cohesive and compelling story in your short video. Here are some steps to follow when creating a storyboard for video:

Define your message: Identify the main message you want to convey in your video. This will help you determine the key scenes and visuals you want to include in your storyboard.

Determine the format: Decide the format you want for your videos, such as live-action or animation. This will impact the type of visuals you will use in your storyboard.

Sketch out scenes: Create a series of sketches to represent the various scenes in your video. Consider the timing and pacing of each scene, as well as any dialogue or voiceover that will be used.

Add details: Once you have a basic sketch for each scene, add details, such as camera angles, movement, and any special effects that will be used.

Consider the flow: Ensure that each scene flows smoothly into the next and there is a logical progression of events.

Refine and revise: Once you have a rough storyboard draft, review it and make any necessary revisions. Get feedback from others and adjust as needed.

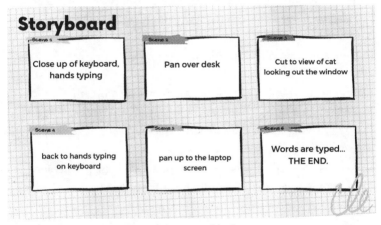

FIGURE 28.1. Storyboard example created in Canva.
Source: Canva.

Finalize: Once you are happy with your storyboard, finalize it and use it as a guide for filming and editing your video.

There are many tutorials on YouTube and TikTok for filming and editing your videos. I like to film on my phone or camera, edit in an app, and then add the finishing touches, like music or effects where I'm going to upload the video, so it fits in the native content on the app. This gives you the option to film it, edit it, load to different platforms, and tweak it a little bit in the music or text on the platform when you upload it.

For instance, if you're creating content for YouTube or TikTok, you'll want to ensure your videos align with the style and format that's popular and effective on those platforms. This might include filming and editing techniques that resonate with the audience, such as quick cuts, engaging visuals, and trendy effects. By filming on your phone or camera, editing in an app, and adding final touches, like music or effects that are native to the app, you're ensuring your content fits seamlessly into the platform's environment, maximizing its impact and engagement.

A few favorite video apps are Cap Cut, Adobe Rush Premiere, and Canva. You can also create animated videos in Canva. Find an app or two that you love and learn them. Again, there are many great tutorials out there.

Here are a few video tips for the road:

1. Whenever you don't know what to say, take a breath.
2. Talk loudly, quickly, and energetically. You aren't reading a book; you're trying to engage someone in a few seconds so they will stick around and watch your video.
3. Always look into the camera! If you're on your phone, look at the camera lens, you should not see yourself filming. If you look away, take a deep breath and repeat the sentence.
4. Smile.
5. Make sure you have good sound and lighting.
6. Move around in between sentences. It makes the video more visually intriguing.
7. Don't be afraid to redo words and sentences. If it isn't live, you can just edit it out.
8. Replay your video; if the footage isn't good, reshoot it.
9. Break the video into sections where you change the topics. This is where jump cuts can be edited in for transitions. This can allow you to review the footage and see if you need to retake anything or add footage. A jump cut is a film editing technique where two sequential shots of the same subject are taken from slightly different camera

angles or positions. When these shots are edited together, it creates a sudden jump in the continuity of the footage, often making the subject appear to "jump" or move abruptly within the frame. Jump cuts are commonly used in video editing to compress time, remove unwanted sections, or create a sense of urgency or pace in the footage. They're frequently seen in vlogs, interviews, and fast-paced content, where maintaining a continuous flow isn't necessary, and they can add a dynamic and energetic feel to the video.

10. Remember that you're going to want an end screen. Film this separately. This is where you put your thank-you and your call to action to like the video and subscribe or follow your account. Filming your end screen separately can be a smart move, especially if you want to craft a polished and professional final touch to your video. By filming it separately, you have more control over the content, layout, and timing of your end-screen elements. Plus, it allows you to focus solely on delivering a clear call to action or displaying important information without distractions from the main content of your video.

11. Filming your end screen separately gives you the flexibility to update or change it easily in future videos without needing to re-edit the entire video. This can be particularly useful if you have a consistent branding strategy or if you want to promote different content or links in each video.

12. Check out people who make video content in your area of expertise. What do you like? What don't you like? Take these things into consideration when you're filming.

13. Write a script and outline for your video. This will help with the "ummms" and fumbling.

14. Use the rule of thirds for being in the frame. You shouldn't be centered.

I hope you're inspired to add short-form, vertical videos to your content mix!

TO-DO-NOTES

1. Research Instagram Reels. What do you like?
2. Do you want to use TikTok?
3. Create a short six-to-eight-second vertical video and share it.

29

How to Create Long-Form Videos

I have the simplest taste. I am always satisfied with the best.

—*Oscar Wilde, from* Oscar Wilde: An Idler's Impression *by Saltus Edgar*

*L*ong-form social videos are an excellent way to showcase your brand's personality and build a strong connection with your audience. Unlike shorter social media videos, long-form videos provide a more comprehensive view of your product or service, allowing you to convey your message in greater detail and depth. Long-form videos are two minutes and longer, but they can be up to twenty minutes or more.

YouTube is the number-two website for global traffic after Google. The same parent company, Alphabet Inc. owns YouTube and Google. As a result, there are several similarities between the two platforms:

1. *Search Functionality*: Both YouTube and Google have powerful search engines that allow users to find relevant information quickly and easily. Keywords are important. Keywords are essential for optimizing content on platforms like YouTube and Google. By strategically incorporating relevant keywords into your video titles, descriptions, and tags, you can improve your content's visibility in

search results. This helps users find your content quickly and easily when searching for relevant topics.

2. *Advertising*: Both platforms offer advertising options for businesses and advertisers to reach their target audience.

3. *Data and Analytics*: YouTube and Google both provide detailed data and analytics to users and businesses, allowing them to track engagement, views, and other metrics.

4. *Integration*: Google owns YouTube, which means that the two platforms can integrate seamlessly with each other. For example, a user can log in to YouTube using their Google account, and videos from YouTube can appear in Google search results.

While there are some differences in how YouTube and Google operate, there are also many similarities between the two platforms. This makes it easier for users and businesses to use both platforms to reach their target audience and achieve their goals. Of course, you can only upload videos to YouTube, but they will be found in Google search.

The best place to learn the ins and outs of YouTube is, of course, through YouTube videos. There are endless videos on creating, editing, and growing your YouTube channel. If you decide to start making videos, you'll be able to learn everything down to the smallest detail.

One of the most significant benefits of long-form social videos is that they allow viewers to get to know your brand deeper. Showcasing your expertise and knowledge can help to establish your brand as an authority in your industry. By providing valuable content, you can build trust and loyalty among your audience, leading to increased sales and customer retention.

Small businesses, particularly, can benefit from long-form social videos, as they provide a cost-effective way to showcase their products or services to a broader audience. Creating engaging and informative videos can build a loyal following and increase brand awareness.

In addition to helping small businesses reach a larger audience, long-form social videos can also improve customer engagement. By providing in-depth information about your products or services, you can address common questions and concerns your customers may have, which can help to build trust and foster a stronger connection with your audience.

PLANNING YOUR LONG-FORM VIDEO

It is important to adopt a robust approach to increase the visibility of your video. This involves devising a targeted keyword, carefully crafting the title and description of your video, and implementing effective search optimization techniques. Additionally, using relevant keywords within your YouTube video content can help signal to viewers the topics your video covers.

Keywords on YouTube are crucial for optimizing your video's visibility. Here's how they count:

1. *Targeted Key Word Search*: Start by researching keywords relevant to your video's topic. Look for terms that your audience is likely to search for when looking for content like yours.
2. *Title and Description*: Once you've identified your target keywords, incorporate them strategically into your video's title and description. The title should be engaging and descriptive while including your primary keyword. The description provides more context about your video and offers another opportunity to include relevant keywords naturally.
3. *Tags*: Tags are another important element for YouTube SEO. Use relevant keywords as tags to help YouTube understand the content of your video and suggest it to users searching for similar topics.
4. *Video Content*: Incorporating keywords naturally into your video's content can also boost its visibility. This doesn't mean keyword stuffing; rather, seamlessly integrate relevant keywords into your dialogue or visual elements. This signals to both viewers and YouTube's algorithm what topics your video covers.

By following these steps and implementing effective search optimization techniques, you can increase the likelihood of your video being discovered by your target audience on YouTube. TubeBuddy is a great tool that can help you find keywords and optimize your YouTube content. This is a paid tool, but highly valuable for your video content optimization. They have a plan that's $3.75 per month.

Deciding on the concept and format is the first step when creating social media videos. This involves brainstorming ideas that align with your brand's messaging and goals and determining the most effective way to communicate that message through video.

To get started, consider what type of video would resonate most with your audience. Would a product demo be helpful? Could a behind-the-scenes look at your business be intriguing? A Q&A with your team or a customer testimonial would be a great way to showcase your brand.

Once you have your concept in mind, it's important to determine the most effective format for your video. Do you want to use animation, live-action footage, or a combination of both? Would a short, snappy video work best, or do you need a longer, more in-depth video to convey your message? You don't have to create something twenty minutes long; make sure to remember that attention spans are short, and you want your video to keep people's attention.

Once you've decided on your concept and format, it's time to create a storyboard or script. This involves planning out the structure and content of your video in advance, so you can ensure that your messaging is clear and concise.

A storyboard visualizes your video, with each panel depicting a different scene or shot. This can be a helpful way to plan out the visual elements of your video and ensure that everything flows smoothly. Alternatively, create a script that outlines your video's dialogue and narration. This can be especially helpful if your video involves interviews or voiceovers. You can record it in smaller pieces and edit them together.

When it comes to filming videos and reading scripts, you can use several tools and techniques to ensure a smooth and professional process. Here are a few options:

1. *Teleprompter Apps*: Teleprompter apps allow you to display your script on your smartphone or tablet, which can be placed near the camera lens. These apps often include adjustable scrolling speed and font size to match your reading pace and preferences.

2. *Traditional Teleprompter*: If you have a larger budget or need a more professional setup, you can invest in a teleprompter. This device uses a transparent screen positioned in front of the camera lens, allowing you to read the script while maintaining eye contact with the audience. You can also find affordable options on Amazon to use with your phone or tablet.

3. *Cue Cards or Prompt Cards*: For a low-tech option, you can write out your script on cue cards or prompt cards and hold them just out of sight of the camera. This method allows for a more natural delivery while providing a visual reference for your lines.

4. *Memorization*: Depending on the length and complexity of your script, you may choose to memorize it instead of reading from a prompter. This requires practice and rehearsal, but it can result in a more authentic and engaging performance.

5. *Voice Assistants*: Some voice assistant devices, like Amazon Echo or Google Home, have features that allow you to input and read scripts aloud. While not specifically designed for video production, they can still serve as helpful tools for practicing and rehearsing your lines.

Ultimately, the best tool for reading scripts while filming videos will depend on your budget, preferences, and the specific requirements of your project. Experiment with different options to find the one that works best for you.

Having a clear plan before shooting your video is important regardless of your chosen approach. This will help ensure that your final product is compelling, engaging, and aligned with your brand's messaging and goals.

CREATING YOUR LONG-FORM VIDEO

Creating a long-form social media video can be an exciting and reward-ing process. But before you get started, having the right equipment and software in place is essential to guarantee a polished final product.

Regarding equipment, you'll want to choose a camera capable of cap-turing high-quality video footage. This could be a DSLR camera or even your smartphone, if it has a good camera and video capabilities. Test your phone video and see if your video is clear. Make sure you clean your lens carefully before filming. Chances are that your phone can do the trick! You'll also want to invest in a tripod and lighting equipment to ensure your video is steady and well-lit. Sound is equally important. Many YouTubers like Rode shotgun mics.

Various video editing programs are available, from free options, like iMovie and Windows Movie Maker to Canva and Adobe Premiere Rush, to more advanced programs, like Adobe Premiere Pro and Final Cut Pro. Choose the software that best suits your needs and budget. Adobe Premiere Rush is easy to use and available on desktops, Mac apps, and smartphones.

Once you have your equipment and software, it's time to set up the shooting location. Choose a space that is well-lit and free from distrac-tions and be sure to test your equipment and lighting before you start shooting.

When capturing footage or recording screen captures, take multiple shots from different angles to ensure you have plenty of material to work with during the editing process. Consider adding elements like B-roll footage or product close-ups to keep your video engaging and visually attractive. B-roll refers to supplementary footage that is intercut with the main footage in a video production. It's used to provide addi-tional context, enhance storytelling, or simply make the video more vi-sually appealing. B-roll footage often includes shots of the environment, details, or actions related to the main subject of the video.

Incorporating B-roll footage can help keep your video engaging and visually attractive. By capturing multiple shots from different angles and including elements like product close-ups, you add variety and depth to your video. B-roll footage can break up the main content, provide visual interest, and help maintain the viewer's attention throughout the video. It's an effective technique for enhancing the overall quality and professionalism of your video production.

Once you have your footage, it's time to add any necessary elements, like music, voiceover, or text overlays. These can add context and personality to your video and help emphasize key points or calls to action.

When editing your video, be sure to focus on length and flow. Long-form videos can convey detailed information, but keeping your viewers engaged and interested is essential. Consider breaking up longer segments with B-roll footage or other visual elements, and be sure to edit out any unnecessary or repetitive content.

By following these tips, you can create a long-form social media video that is engaging and informative and showcases your brand's personality and expertise. With the right equipment, software, and attention to detail, you can create a video that resonates with your audience and helps you achieve your marketing goals.

OPTIMIZING YOUR LONG-FORM VIDEO FOR SOCIAL MEDIA

Once you've created your video, optimizing it for maximum engagement and reach is essential. This involves various techniques, from adding captions and subtitles to creating an eye-catching thumbnail image.

Adding captions or subtitles to your video can help to make it more accessible to a broader audience, including those who may be deaf or hard of hearing. It can also be helpful for viewers watching your video in a noisy environment or who prefer to watch videos with captions.

Creating a thumbnail image that grabs attention is also crucial for maximizing engagement with your video. Enter Canva (again). Choose a visually compelling image that accurately represents your video's content; this can be a still from your video. Add text overlays or other design elements to make your thumbnail stand out in crowded social media feeds. Match your thumbnails to your brand to create a cohesive, branded video experience. TubeBuddy has a tool to help analyze your thumbnail—and create them, too.

When choosing the right platform for your video, consider where your audience will most likely be active. Facebook, Instagram, and YouTube are popular options for sharing long-form videos, but each platform has its own unique audience and features.

Once you've chosen your platform, setting up video optimization for each medium is essential. This may involve customizing your video's aspect ratio, selecting the proper video resolution, and optimizing your video's description and tags for search.

Finally, when uploading and publishing your video, consider the details. Add a clear and concise description that accurately represents the content of your video, and be sure to include relevant tags and keywords. Also, promote your video through paid advertising or social media posts to reach a wider audience.

Following these tips, you can optimize your long-form social media video for maximum engagement and reach and ensure that your content resonates with your audience and achieves your marketing goals. With careful planning and attention to detail, you can create a video that genuinely showcases your brand's personality and expertise and helps you connect with your audience on a deeper level.

To help your video rank in YouTube and Google searches, it's essential to provide as much information as possible about your content, especially regarding the search terms you want to target. You can start by including your target keyword in the title and description of your video, but you can take things a step further by incorporating the keyword into the script of your video itself. Be sure to include the keyword in the first sentence of your video and a few more times throughout.

Once you've uploaded your video, you must check that the keywords are correctly included in the subtitles. If they're not, you can create your own subtitles and add the keywords to make it clear to Google that your video is optimized for those search terms. You can even rank for multiple keywords with one video. To do this, include all keywords in the video description and make sure they're prominent.

By giving algorithms as much information as possible about your video and optimizing it for your target keywords, you can help ensure that your video ranks well in search results and attracts the right audience. With careful attention to detail and a strategic approach, you can maximize your video content and achieve your marketing goals.

PROMOTING YOUR LONG-FORM VIDEO

Here are four ways to promote long-form videos:

1. *Share on Social Media*: Social media is an excellent platform for promoting long-form videos. Share your video on your business' social media accounts, including Facebook, X, LinkedIn, and Instagram. Be sure to include a catchy caption, relevant hashtags, and a link to the video. Also, consider promoting your video through paid social media advertising to reach a wider audience.
2. *Include in Email Marketing*: Email marketing is another effective way to promote your long-form video. Send your subscribers a video preview or GIF and a link to watch the full version. You can also include the video in your email signature to promote it in your communications.
3. *Embed on Your Website*: Embedding your long-form video on your business's website is a great way to drive traffic to your video and your website. Create a dedicated landing page for your video and embed it there, or include it on relevant product pages or blog posts. Optimize the page with relevant keywords and a clear call to action to encourage viewers to act after watching the video.
4. *Create Short Clips from Your Video*: Break down your long-form video into shorter, bite-sized clips that highlight key moments or insights. These clips can be shared across social media platforms, such as Instagram, X, or TikTok, to capture the attention of viewers who prefer shorter content. Make sure each clip is engaging, is

informative, and includes a call to action directing viewers to watch the full video for more. Additionally, repurpose these short clips for use in email newsletters, blog posts, or as part of your social media content calendar to extend the reach of your long-form video.

Long-form social videos are a powerful tool for businesses to showcase their brand's personality and connect with their audience on a deeper level. By planning and creating engaging and informative videos, companies can establish themselves as an authority in their industry and build trust and loyalty among their audience members. Optimizing and promoting these videos through captions, thumbnails, and targeted marketing strategies can maximize engagement and reach, increasing sales and customer retention. With careful attention to detail and a strategic approach, businesses can create impactful long-form social videos that achieve their marketing goals and resonate with their audience.

TO-DO-NOTES

1. Find and subscribe to three YouTube channels in your niche.
2. Write a script for a three-to-five-minute horizontal video.
3. Shoot, edit, and share it!

How to Create a Social Media Campaign

By failing to prepare, you are preparing to fail.

—*Benjamin Franklin*

*F*or our purposes, social media campaigns are different from simply creating social posts because they will all be on one topic with one goal.

For example, you're having a one-week anniversary sale. Within the framework of the social campaign for your anniversary sale, you'll create a series of social posts that make up a social campaign. It will have multiple pieces and formats to make it interesting and eye-catching. Your social media campaign will be the sole focus of your social media for the duration of your event.

HOW TO PLAN AND EXECUTE A SUCCESSFUL SOCIAL MEDIA CAMPAIGN

We'll start with setting the campaign goal. Do you want to drive online sales? Bring people into your physical location? Set your goal and decide where to lead people with your calls to action. Write a list of your goals.

Next, you can decide how to measure the success of the campaign. To align your goals with measurable metrics, consider the form of engagement you want to track. For instance, track likes, retweets, comments, replies, or clicks to *measure engagement*.

To *measure awareness*, use metrics like volume, reach, exposure, and amplification to assess how far your message is spreading.

To *drive traffic to your website*, track URL shares, clicks, and conversions to see if people are moving from social media to your site and what actions they are taking.

You can track these elements in social media management tools such as Agorapulse or SmarterQueue and gather data from the social platform analytics in your business accounts. I like to use Trello to create campaigns because you can add links to the social posts to track them later. Planning saves time if you need to track all the links for reporting purposes and have them all saved on a Trello board.

Here's an example of a post in SmarterQueue, which shares the social analytics for the post.

FIGURE 30.1. Social stats from a LinkedIn post in SmarterQueue.
Source: SmarterQueue

In a campaign collaboration with Mercedes for the L.A. Auto Show, organization was key. To ensure seamless execution across multiple social media platforms, I turned to my trusty organizational tool: Trello. Within the Trello board dedicated to the campaign, I meticulously structured each aspect. The initial list served as a repository for all campaign assets, such as Canva designs, relevant photos, graphics, or shared Google documents for team collaboration.

The heart of the board was where the real magic happened. Here, I crafted individual cards for each social post, detailing specific texts, hashtags, and platforms for distribution. As the campaign unfolded, these cards evolved, tracking progress from draft to publication.

Finally, in the "Published social media posts" list, I cataloged each completed post alongside its corresponding link. This served as both a record of accomplishment and a valuable resource for future reference. With Trello as my organizational backbone, executing a comprehensive and effective social media campaign became manageable and truly seamless.

CUSTOM URLS

Using a link shortener like Bit.ly can help, too. Link shortening is good for two reasons: tracking activity, and you can choose a custom URL. Bit.ly not only shortens long URLs but also provide analytics on link clicks, such as the number of clicks, geographic location of users, and referral sources. You can create a shortened version of your long link using one of these services and then track its performance through the analytics dashboard provided by the service. I use a WordPress plug-in called Pretty Links. Pretty Links is a comprehensive WordPress plug-in for custom link shortening, URL redirection, and branded link management. With Pretty Links, you can create redirected links from your website's domain.

For example, I made pegfitzpatrick.com/sign-up as a custom short link to my email sign-up page for my Flodesk email. The URL looks like it's part of my website versus sharing this link: https://view.flodesk.com

/pages/63d7e77ede520bd60dc34206, which is confusing. If you don't use a link shortener, you can track full links from your website using Google Analytics, but it's more complicated, and it doesn't give you the same information for social media traffic.

LANDING PAGES

When creating your social media campaign, create a landing page to send people your anniversary sale details. A landing page is a stand-alone web page designed for marketing or advertising campaigns. It serves as the destination where visitors "land" after clicking on a link or advertisement from an external source, such as social media or email. Landing pages focus on a single objective, such as promoting a product, gathering leads, or announcing an event. In the context of a social media campaign, creating a landing page allows you to provide targeted information about your anniversary sale and encourage visitors to take specific action, such as making a purchase or signing up for updates.

CALL TO ACTION

It's extra important during a social campaign to ensure you use a strong call to action and get people excited about your sale while letting them know it's time-sensitive. A strong CTA lets people know exactly what you action you want them to take to nudge them along. Here are some examples of calls to action:

- Take your chance to be a part of history! Our one-week anniversary promotion ends this Saturday, March 18th.
- Join the celebration before the moment passes! Time-sensitive opportunity ending March 18th.
- Be a part of something special! Our one-week anniversary celebration ends this Saturday, March 18th.
- This is your opportunity to join the fun! Time-limited promotion ending March 18th. Don't miss out!
- Get in on the excitement before it's too late! Limited-time promotion ending March 18th. Join us now!

You could also have a coupon code. According to the Sprout Social Index, 40 percent of people follow brands for coupons or deals. Give the people what they want! Each of these could work for a promo code:

- Save 20—20% off the entire purchase
- FlashSale—15% off for 24 hours only
- BigDeal—25% off orders over $100
- NewCustomer—10% off first purchase
- WinterWarmup—20% off select winter items.

DETERMINE CONTENT FOR EACH CHANNEL

Daily content for each social platform is great if you have a week long campaign. If you focus on Instagram, you'll want to keep Instagram Stories going the whole time the campaign runs so you stay top-of-mind when people are on Instagram.

Here's a brief explanation of Instagram Posts, Stories, and Reels, along with how you might use each in a social media campaign:

Instagram Posts are the foundation of your Instagram presence. They typically consist of photos or videos on your profile's grid, accompanied by captions, hashtags, and tags. They are ideal for sharing high-quality content, such as product photos, behind-the-scenes shots, or informative videos. In a social media campaign, you can use Instagram Posts to showcase your brand, highlight products or services, share user-generated content, and engage with your audience through likes, comments, and shares.

Instagram Stories, with their ephemeral nature, are your avenue for sharing casual, spontaneous content. They disappear after twenty-four hours, making them perfect for behind-the-scenes moments, quick updates, polls, quizzes, and interactive features like stickers and GIFs. In a social media campaign, Instagram Stories is your means for providing real-time updates, teasing upcoming launches or events, running limited-time promotions, and encouraging direct engagement with your audience through polls, questions, and swipe-up links (if you have over ten thousand followers). You can save a Story as a highlight if you want to show it at the top of your profile.

Instagram Reels, with their short-form videos up to ninety seconds long, are your canvas for creative and entertaining content. They play in a loop and appear on the Explore page, as well as in a dedicated Reels tab on your profile. In a social media campaign, Instagram Reels is your opportunity to showcase your brand's personality, participate in trending challenges, share educational content, and reach a wider audience through the Explore page.

Each Instagram feature serves a unique purpose in your social media campaign strategy. Posts and Reels offer a permanent showcase of your brand, Stories provide real-time updates and engagement opportunities, and Reels offer creative and entertaining content to engage your audience in new and exciting ways. Integrating all three into your campaign can help you effectively connect with your audience and achieve your marketing goals on Instagram.

Here's a sample social media campaign for a one-week anniversary sale on Instagram:

Posts—One per Day

- Create a visually appealing graphic or video for each post showcasing your products with a one-week anniversary sale tagline.
- Highlight popular products and offer special deals to encourage customers to purchase.
- Use relevant hashtags to increase visibility.

Reels—One on the First Day, One on the Last Day

- Create a fun and creative dance or lip-sync video with the anniversary sale message.
- Showcase your products in action, giving customers an idea of how to use them.
- Use music in the app so you have permission to use it and special effects to make the Reel more engaging.

Instagram Stories—Multiple Stories per Day

- Offer sneak peeks of new products or exclusive deals available during the sale.
- Share customer testimonials and showcase how your products have impacted their lives.
- Use countdown stickers to create excitement and urgency for sales. You can find the countdown sticker in the Stories tab. It adds a countdown that people share to their own Story, and they'll get a reminder of the event.

Instagram Live—The Day before the Sale Starts and the Middle of Your Campaign

- Remember to include calls to action in each post, encouraging customers to visit your page and purchase during the one-week anniversary sale. Your text could look like this:

  🎉 🛍️ Don't miss out on our one-week anniversary sale! 🛍️ 🎉
  It's been an incredible journey, and we're celebrating with a special treat just for you! 🎁 For the next week, enjoy exclusive discounts on all your favorite products. From stylish apparel to must-have accessories, there's something for everyone!
  But hurry, the clock is ticking! ⏰ This sale ends in just one week, so make sure to visit our page and stock up on your favorites before it's too late. Don't miss your chance to save big and treat yourself to something special!
  Click the link in our bio to shop now and join the celebration! 🎉 ✨
  #AnniversarySale #LimitedTimeOffer #ShopNow
  [Image: Stunning product photo showcasing our anniversary sale items]

- Choose what content to create for each social media platform.

Promoting on Different Platforms

If you're creating a special sale, you would want to promote this on all your available social platforms. I gave examples above for Instagram. Here's what campaigns could look like on other platforms:

TikTok: Create short videos. In the TikTok app, you can create fifteen-second, thirty-second, or three-minute videos with their templates. I like to make videos on my phone, edit in the CapCut app, then upload them to the TikTok app and add music and other elements. Many videos on YouTube and TikTok give you step-by-step instructions on how to create TikTok videos.

If you make a short, vertical video, you can repurpose this on Instagram and Pinterest as an Idea Pin. The CapCut app allows you to share the video without the TikTok logo on other platforms.

Facebook: Consider creating engaging posts highlighting the critical features of your sale. You can share longer-form content, such as carousel posts showcasing different products, video demonstrations of your products in action, or live streams where you announce the sale details and interact with your audience in real-time. To generate excitement among your followers, encourage engagement by asking questions, running polls, or hosting giveaways.

LinkedIn: Focus on creating professional and informative content related to your sale. Share posts that highlight the value proposition of your products or services, industry insights or trends, or success stories from satisfied customers. You can also write longer-form articles or LinkedIn Stories to provide more in-depth information about the sale and its benefits for your audience. Utilize LinkedIn's business-focused audience to network with industry professionals, share thought leadership content, and generate leads for your business, showing your audience that you value their professional engagement.

X, formerly Twitter: X is ideal for sharing quick updates and engaging with your audience in real-time. Create short and punchy tweets that announce the details of your special sale, highlight specific products or discounts, and encourage followers to act. Use hashtags related to your sale or industry to increase visibility and reach a wider audience.

By tailoring your content to each platform's unique features and audience preferences, you can effectively promote your special sale across multiple social media platforms and maximize its impact.

PLAN THE CONTENT CALENDAR

Create a schedule for the week or month of the campaign. I like to start with a physical calendar, write out my dates, and plan my social channels. After deciding what messaging and creative copy to use daily, putting these all on a Trello Board or in a Google document is helpful. Give yourself plenty of time to create your content in advance so you can work on other aspects of your sale during the event.

Create Visual Content

While maintaining brand consistency with cohesive imagery across platforms, create your visual content.

As a time-saver, you can visit CreativeMarket.com and find Canva templates for your social campaign. Templates are included in the Canva library, but finding one and customizing it will help your content stay fresh, unique, and on-brand.

I searched in Creative Market for "Instagram templates for Canva." These come to you as a digital download, like a link on a PDF with instructions, and when you click the link, the template will go into your Canva account. You can then add your images, change the colors to your brand colors, and change the text. There are hundreds of choices, and it is easy to customize something and make it 100 percent your brand.

Schedule Posts

Use a social media scheduling tool like SmarterQueue, Agorapulse, or Plann to plan and schedule posts.

This is an example of scheduling a new post in SmarterQueue.

I love Plann for its ease of use and the visual aspects of the platform for content creation. You can plan and schedule content for Instagram, Facebook, LinkedIn, Pinterest, and TikTok in Plann. I also love the Collections feature, where you can create all your graphics and images and load them into a folder for the month and use this to create your social posts. You can also generate hashtag groups stored in the program and get help with strategy, and they have social caption starters as well.

FIGURE 30.2. The post composer box in SmarterQueue when you add a new post with AI caption writer.
Source: SmarterQueue.

Monitor and Respond

Don't post and ghost. Stay active on your profiles and respond to comments and messages during your sales campaign. Turning on your notifications during your open hours for the campaign could be helpful if it doesn't cause you anxiety. Alternatively, be present when your social posts go live, and check in for comments and messages later in the day.

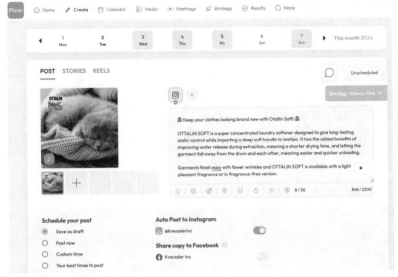

FIGURE 30.3. Post composer box in Plann.
Source: Plann.

Document Your Event

Share updates, photos, and a recap of the event or promotion.

Analyze and Adjust

If one type of post does well, adjust your game plan to get the most out of your campaign. This could be getting interaction from your location tag, checking which hashtags perform well, or noticing your videos are on-point. Evaluate the campaign's success and adjust future campaigns based on the results.

These steps serve as guidelines, but each campaign may have different goals. Align your social media strategy with your overall marketing plan to achieve the desired results. You are taking baby steps as you learn how to create and manage a social campaign. Be kind to yourself, and don't compare yourself to others. It's a lot harder than it looks to pull off an extensive social media campaign. But it's doable if you plan and make it as workable for you as you can!

TO-DO-NOTES

1. Create a social campaign.
2. Track social posts.
3. Evaluate success of campaign. How can you improve on it for next time?

How to Create an Editorial Calendar

Plan for the future because that's where you are going to spend the rest of your life.

—*Mark Twain*

*I*n writing, there are two types of writers: planners and pantsers. Pantsers don't outline or plan; they float by the seat of their pants. While you might have pantser tendencies, I will share a simple plan to create a monthlong editorial calendar to help you become a planner.

As a small business owner, you likely have so much to do that you can't afford the time to do your social media last minute in what I call "random acts of marketing or RAM," and haphazard marketing won't help. RAM won't get your goals; your editorial calendar will become your social media marketing bible and help you reach your goals.

An *editorial calendar* is a marketing plan that links your social media content strategy to your broader business goals, scheduling campaigns and initiatives to be integrated into the social media content.

Your content strategy will be a mix of targeted campaigns, which we covered in the last chapter; posts featuring your product or services; user-generated content, or UGC, content created by your customers or brand fans; holiday posts; and any other helpful or entertaining posts.

We have about thirty days each month to cover. Creating a strategy that covers those posts will help you stay on target for reaching your goals.

Your content strategy plan could look like this:

1. Social sales campaign/promotional content—5 days
2. Highlighting of a product or servi—4 days
3. UGC—3 days
4. Behind-the-scenes entries—4 days
5. Holiday or social media holidays—4 days
6. Customer education on your products or services—4 days
7. Blog promotion—1 for each new blog post

This plan gives you plenty of room to post a wide variety of content while staying on target with your goals. Choosing an organizational planning tool helps a lot. I start with paper and pen while plotting out my days based on a plan like the one I shared, and then I move to Plann to create my content plan using their strategy tool. This allows me to put together the graphics and text, as well as schedule them.

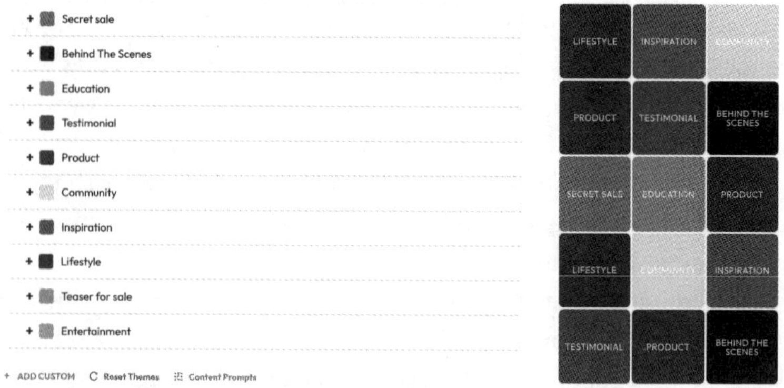

FIGURE 31.1. Plann strategy themes.
Source: Plann.

In the above image of Plann, the categories on the left are customizable by color and topic: you customize them to match your days in the content strategy, then you can create your graphics, gather photos, and write your copy. Plann has social prompts and starters if you get stuck.

Once you've got your categories down, you can create a hashtag group for each and store them in the app to make adding hashtags to your posts easy. Again, Plann has some hashtag groups to get you started, or you can fully customize them. You will create one hashtag group, with three to five hashtags, to use for your social campaign.

Here's an example of a hashtag group for Small Business Saturday: #smallbusinesssaturday #beyourownboss #smallbusinesssaturdaysale #smallbusinesssaturdays #smallbiz.

FIGURE 31.2. Hashtag sets in Plann.
Source: Plann.

Alternatively, you can save hashtag groups in the Notes app on your phone or Trello, but I've found that using a social media scheduling tool with hashtags included is extremely helpful.

Here are a few tools you can research to choose what you like best. You'll need one tool for posting and one for organization.

Plann: Desktop and phone apps, $21 per month charged annually, currently my favorite tool. This is my Instagram-first tool, and I schedule for Facebook and LinkedIn based on what I plan for Instagram. I love that you can see things planned out in Instagram's smartphone view, and Plann creates fantastic educational materials.

SmarterQueue: $20 per month, an excellent tool for planning desktop social campaigns for Twitter, Facebook, and LinkedIn.

Trello: You can't post from Trello, but it's a fantastic planning tool for keeping all your assets together. Trello is great for planning content and holding ideas if you have a blog.

Notion: Like Trello, great for planning and organizing, but not for scheduling content.

Other tools: These include Agorapulse, Buffer, Hootsuite, and Sprout Social. Most of these robust social media scheduling tools are expensive and are geared more towards enterprise brands with entire teams working on social media. You get more analytics, but they cost $75 per month and up, except Buffer, which is $5 per social media channel per month.

Your first step will be to get a calendar or planner and map your days based on your content plan (sales, four products, four holidays, etc.). Then you can figure out what type of content you want to post, write the social captions, add hashtags, and schedule in your content scheduling tool.

The content planning calendar in Plann has prompts and holidays built in. You could skip the paper and work entirely within Plann. As I mentioned, I like to start on paper to map out my most important content, then fill in with the lighter content, and finally, I move things to Plann, my digital planner; you might not need the paper step. I'm sharing my entire process to give you a jumping-off point so you can build your own system. This process helps me plan a month of content without getting brain freeze or writer's block.

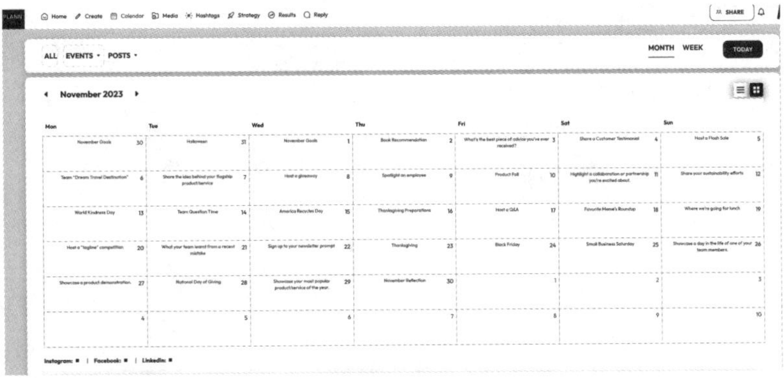

FIGURE 31.3. Content calendar in Plann.
Source: Plann.

Your creativity will flow better when you're more organized, and your content creation skills will soar. Don't worry about using different tools or trying too many simultaneously. Pick one organizational tool and one scheduling tool. Try getting the bones of the month mapped out on a calendar and work on creating content. If you can't make all the content for the month, start your monthly calendar, bang out a week's worth of content at a time, and work up to a month if you can. If you have one week's content created and scheduled ahead of time, you'll be in great shape.

An editorial calendar is crucial for effective content planning as it helps ensure a consistent, well-thought-out strategy, rather than a haphazard approach. Quick fixes may seem more manageable in the short term, but they are unlikely to yield meaningful results. Successful content requires a focused, long-term approach, as immediate results are not guaranteed. Investing in a comprehensive strategy demonstrated through an editorial calendar will yield higher returns and a better return on investment in the long run. You can work this plan successfully and be a planner, not a pantser.

TO-DO-NOTES

1. Create an editorial calendar.
2. Set up themes and strategy in Plann.
3. Create five hashtag groups and save in Plann.

32

How Much Time Does It Take?

It is better to fail in originality than to succeed in imitation.

—*Herman Melville, "Hawthorne and His Mosses" (1850)*

---

*A*s we're getting toward the end of the book, I'm going to assume you're all in-on creating a social media plan, and you're going to batch-create your content by the week or month using the editorial calendar. If not, you'll need more time daily to create content.

Although you've already put in much work in creating and scheduling your content for the week, you must make time daily to ensure your content is doing well and reply to comments and messages. Suppose you need to block time on your calendar, so you have a schedule to stick to. If you're scheduling your content, add your daily time block to your calendar simultaneously to help build engagement and check to make sure your post went out as planned. A half hour a day will go a long way for targeted social communications.

Consider this sample daily checklist:

- Respond to all messages.
- Reciprocate follows from others, relevant accounts for your business.

- Review and reply to mentions.
- Track relevant keywords and phrases on social media.
- Explore other social media profiles in your community.
- Select and prepare content to share.
- Interact with customers and other accounts.
- Build new connections daily by commenting on other posts.
- Create and share Instagram Stories.

Here is a sample weekly checklist:

- Check weekly stats on the social media platforms.
- Tweak scheduled content if you spot a trend that you want to try.
- Check out the competition's social media.

And here is a sample monthly checklist:

- Run analytics reports.
- Check Google analytics for monthly trends.
- Work on your content ideas for next month.

Consistency with your social media is essential for brand awareness, growing trust with your customers, and growing your social media. Adding time into your schedule each day to check in and check off your daily checklist will help you stay connected with your social media audience and what's happening around your brand when you're posting.

TIME MANAGEMENT

To effectively manage your time, try something like the Pomodoro technique, where you block off your time and set a timer to stay on track. The recommended time is twenty-five minutes; then take a five-minute break.

Here's how it works with social media:

1. Choose the social networks you will visit.
2. Determine your goals for each network, and have content ready to share.
3. Set the timer for twenty-five minutes.
4. Focus on your task(s) for twenty-five minutes, then shut down your social networks.
5. Give yourself a five-minute break.
6. Move on to your next moneymaking activity.

You can spend a lot of time on social media and get nothing out of it. The key is to be efficient and productive with your time to not waste it on things that don't help you make money.

Here's an example of an engagement plan for Instagram:

- Before posting, respond to comments and direct messages.
- After you post, check your feed and comment on five posts, leaving a meaningful comment that relates to their post and opens communication.
- Interact with five to ten accounts in the same niche as your account.
- Share your recent post to Stories and use an interactive sticker to build engagement.
- Go back to your post and respond to questions and comments.

A similar plan works for LinkedIn, except for sharing to Stories, which is only on Instagram. Naturally, engagement brings more engagement and activity to a post.

Social media will work, but only if you put in the work!

TO-DO-NOTES

1. Create a daily checklist.
2. Create a weekly checklist.
3. Create a monthly checklist.

What Metrics Should You Measure?

It was the best of times, it was the worst of times, it was the age of wisdom, it was the age of foolishness. . . . we had everything before us, we had nothing before us.

—*Charles Dickens*, A Tale of Two Cities

*M*easuring is essential because you need to know what works, but most social media goodness isn't trackable without a little behind-the-scenes magic.

I keep an eye on my stats, but I'm not fixated on the numbers. Gary Vaynerchuk once asked, "What's the ROI of your mother?" to push back against the obsession with metrics in a customer meeting.[1] He's right—it's not just about the tools. ROI on social media isn't about throwing money at it; it's about investing time and effort into mastering the platforms. Let's focus on understanding social media and blending creativity, copy, and strategy for the best results.

You can track these metrics using a combination of tools and platforms tailored to each specific metric:

- *Reach and audience engagement*: Social media platforms, like Instagram Insights, Facebook Insights, and LinkedIn Analytics, provide detailed data on reach, impressions, engagement, and audience demographics.

- *Site traffic*: Google Analytics is a powerful tool for tracking website traffic, including traffic sources, referral sources, and user behavior.
- *Leads generated*: Customer relationship management (CRM) systems like HubSpot, Salesforce, or Mailchimp can track leads generated from social media campaigns and interactions.
- *Sign-ups and conversions*: CRM systems are often used to track sign-ups and conversions, but social media advertising platforms, like Facebook Ads Manager and Google Ads, also provide conversion-tracking capabilities. You can also track email sign-ups in your email software.
- *Revenue generated*: Revenue tracking can be more complex and may involve integrating sales data from e-commerce platforms with social media and website analytics tools.

Here's an example of a simple Google Sheets document to track your stats. It doesn't have to be fancy, just something you can use to track your monthly stats. I have a spreadsheet in Google Drive with my own stats.

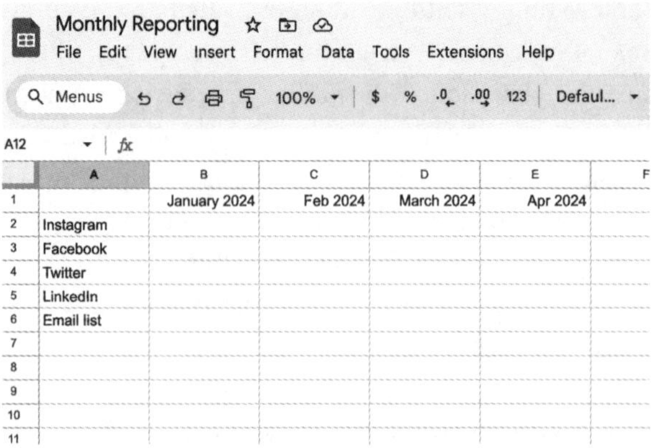

FIGURE 33.1. Google spreadsheet for monthly tracking.

Within your monthly tasks, update the stats you want to track, and track where you're getting the most traction. While doing this, remember that many people lurk on social media and never like or comment, but that doesn't mean they're not looking and listening.

Sign your website up to Google Analytics and get a monthly report of your Google traffic. You can customize the reports. Like Meta, Google has free training tools for you at: marketingplatform.google.com/about /small-business/.

Andy Crestodina of Orbit Media is my go-to expert on Google Analytics. On the Orbit Media blog and in YouTube Videos, Andy shares valuable information on setting up your Google Analytics. Andy created a very useful custom Google Analytics report[2] that will compile your traffic from social media.

Some insights I gained from loading this report and checking out my traffic from social media include:

1. I was testing a social media planning tool called MissingLttr to see if I liked it, and links from this service brought 17.04 percent of my social traffic for these thirty days. This tells me that I could get more traffic to my website by creating more content to share from Missing Lttr. This tool uses AI to help you create content from your blog content, but in the end, it wasn't my favorite tool to use.

2. I can click on my number-one referral, Pinterest, to see what drove the traffic, and I learn it was my Inspirational Quotes page on my website. So I spent time this month fixing the page and updating it with a new WordPress plug-in for a better mobile experience and easier pinning. This work paid off.

3. Clicking on each link on Google Analytics shows me what content performs the best, so I know what to tweak in my content plan for next month.

Click the Custom Report tab in the left sidebar to find your custom reports. Andy says, "Measuring social media marketing is challenging.

It takes a bit of skill to set up the dimensions, filters, and segments. Even then, your data won't be 100% accurate when everything is tracking correctly." Remember that Google Analytics may have accuracy issues. Our objective isn't to achieve flawless data; that's unattainable. Instead, our aim is to gather sufficient data to make informed marketing decisions. You can never get it perfect; good enough must do.

CUSTOM URLS

The key to measurement is custom URLs. Anything you want to track, you need to make it trackable. Tracking down links you've posted from social media posts individually is a huge time suck. Many social media scheduling tools have trackable links baked into their services, which is extremely helpful.

It's crucial to clearly understand what's working and what's not in your campaigns and social postings. With proper measurement and analysis, making informed decisions and optimizing your strategies for success can be easy. This is where custom URLs come in.

Custom URLs allow you to easily track specific actions and conversions from your social media posts. Using a unique URL for each campaign, you can easily see which posts drive the most traffic, leads, or conversions. This information is critical in helping you understand the effectiveness of your campaigns and make data-driven decisions. With custom URLs, you can have all the data you need at your fingertips. This saves time, streamlines your measurement process, and helps you get the most out of your social media efforts.

In short (pun intended), custom URLs are the key to unlocking the full potential of your social media measurement. Custom URLs are a must-have tool to track your campaign's success and make informed decisions. You will save time trying to piece together the impact of your social media efforts.

Here are four popular tools for tracking links:

1. *Google Analytics*: Google Analytics is a free web analytics service that provides insights into website traffic, audience behavior, and conversions. It also provides a UTM builder tool to create custom links and track their performance. A UTM builder, short for Urchin Tracking Module, is a tool that generates unique tracking URLs for your marketing campaigns. It appends specific parameters to your URLs, enabling you to track campaign performance in platforms like Google Analytics. With UTM parameters, you can measure metrics, such as clicks, conversions, and revenue generated from each campaign.

2. Bit.ly: Bit.ly is a link management platform that provides real-time link tracking and analytics. It allows you to create custom links, track clicks, and measure the performance of your campaigns across multiple channels.

3. UTM.io: UTM.io is a link-tracking and analytics platform that provides detailed insights into the performance of your campaigns. It allows you to create custom links, track clicks, and monitor conversions from your social media posts, email campaigns, and other marketing efforts.

4. Pretty Links: Pretty Links is a link tracking and management plug-in for WordPress that allows you to create custom links and track their performance. It provides detailed click analytics and can shorten and brand your links.

Each tool provides different features and benefits, so choosing the best fit for your needs is essential. Whether you're looking for a simple link-shortening tool or a comprehensive analytics platform, these tools can help you track the success of your campaigns and make data-driven decisions.

WORK SMARTER, NOT HARDER!
When you're beginning the process, using the reporting in your social media tools and setting up Google Analytics to prepare custom reports is the best place to start. Choose what you want to track, and create a

quick spreadsheet that you can use monthly to track your metrics and make data-driven decisions.

As a small business owner, it's essential to clearly understand what's working and what's not to make informed decisions and optimize your strategies for success.

The key to measurement is custom URLs. Custom URLs allow you to easily track specific actions and conversions from your social media posts. Using a unique URL for each campaign, you can easily see which posts drive the most traffic, leads, or conversions.

In the end, it's about working smarter, not harder. By using the reporting in your social media tools and setting up custom reports in Google Analytics, you can track the metrics that matter and make informed decisions about your social media strategies.

Remember, the goal of tracking metrics is not to get perfect data, but to get good enough data to make intelligent marketing decisions.

TO-DO NOTES

1. Create a Google Sheet or Excel doc to track stats.
2. Set up Google Analytics reports.
3. Choose how you will track URLs

34

To Pay or Not to Pay

Navigating Paid Promotions

Advertising is to a genuine article what manure is to land—it largely increases the product.

—*P.T. Barnum,* The Humbugs of the World

---

*A*s a small business, every dollar counts, so deciding to do paid promotions is big. Whether you're just starting with social media advertising or looking to improve the results of your current campaigns, let's look at the landscape as it fits within social media marketing.

MAXIMIZING YOUR SOCIAL MEDIA ADVERTISING BUDGET

Targeting: One of the most significant benefits of social media advertising is the ability to target specific audiences. By understanding your ideal customer, you can tailor your targets using demographics, interests, behaviors, and more to ensure that your ads reach the right people. When it comes to targeting, it's essential to test different audience segments to see what works best for your business.

Budgeting: Setting a budget for your social media advertising is crucial to getting the results you want. Regarding budgeting, consider your overall marketing budget, your goals, and your target audience's cost per click or impression. It's also a good idea to start small and gradually increase your budget as you see positive results. There's no guarantee that ads will work, and it will take some trial and error to see what your audience responds to. Ads are a gamble, but they can pay off.

Creative: The creative elements of your social media advertising, such as images, videos, and text, are what will capture the attention of your target audience. Regarding creative assets, it's essential to use high-quality photos and videos and keep your message clear, concise, and attention-grabbing. It's also a good idea to test different creative elements to see what resonates best with your audience.

By following these best practices for targeting, budgeting, and creative, you can maximize the ROI of your social media advertising budget and achieve your marketing goals. Whether you're looking to increase brand awareness, drive website traffic, or generate leads, social media advertising can be a powerful tool for small businesses.

To answer the chapter's titular question, you should use paid promotion if you have extra funds in your marketing budget. A brilliant place to start would be running advertisements in coordination with announcements or social media campaigns.

USING META

Meta is the giant in the social advertising space, covering Facebook and Instagram. If you want to tackle social advertising, I recommend heading to Meta Blueprint to learn how to create and manage it step by step. Meta Blueprint is their global education platform with free online classes. You'll find the latest specs for the length of text and image sizes. Who better to learn from than the makers of the platforms?

Here's an overview of paid promotions within the Meta-sphere, specifically Facebook and Instagram. You'll need a personal Facebook profile to verify who you are, and a Facebook Business Page set up to do any promotions within Meta. Then you can set up your Business Manager account.

To create a Business Manager account, follow these steps:

1. Go to business.facebook.com/overview.
2. Click Create an account.
3. Enter a name for your business, your name, and your work email address, then click *Next*.
4. Enter your business details and click *Submit*.

Once you are set up in Meta Business Manager, it will walk you through step by step how to do ads. It's worth the time to set up Business Manager because there are lots of additional tools to help you manage your account better, including scheduling "away messages" in Messenger and Instagram and responding to comments from your desktop. They've greatly improved their scheduling and calendar.

Within the Ads tab of Meta Business Manager, you will have three options: Automated Ads, Choose a Goal, and Boost Existing Content. Once you choose one, you have more options to drill down upon, or you can create a custom audience based on demographics, interests, and keywords. Based on the data that Meta has been collecting on users, the audience can be very targeted and will reach the right people. There's no harm in clicking around the Ads section, seeing the options, and creating a few drafts while contemplating your strategy.

These steps might change periodically, but Meta continually improves, walking you through each step and decision as you go.

Ad Creative is the images or graphics plus the text: the look and feel of your ad are critical to its success. Make sure your ad is visually appealing and easy to understand. Use high-quality images and persuasive language to grab the attention of your target audience. Also, consider the format of your ad and whether it will be a video, image, or carousel ad.

A great ad headline should be attention-grabbing, concise, and relevant to the target audience. Here are some tips for creating a compelling headline:

1. *Keep it short and sweet*: Facebook headlines are limited to twenty-five characters, so make sure your headline is brief and to the point.
2. *Make it relevant*: Your headline should communicate what the ad is about and why the target audience should care.
3. *Create a sense of urgency*: Use language that conveys a sense of urgency or scarcity, such as "limited time offer" or "last chance."
4. *Use strong action verbs*: Verbs such as "Get," "Discover," and "Unlock" can help entice users to click on your ad.
5. *Ask a question*: A question headline can effectively engage the target audience and encourage them to click.
6. *Be clear and concise*: Avoid puns, jokes, or overly clever language. The headline should be easy to understand and communicate the message.

Remember, the headline is one of the first things a user sees, so making a solid impression is essential. By following these tips, you can create a headline that effectively communicates the value of your ad and encourages users to act.

Here are some tips for writing great ad captions:

1. Ask people to do something, like send a message, including times when you'll be live to answer.
2. Share essential information, like prices and details about services.
3. Keep it simple. Shorter captions perform better than longer ones.

You could use an automated message to reply with a coupon code or a link to a custom landing page.

IS THERE AN EASY BUTTON?

The gateway drug to paid promotions is boosting an Instagram post using the "boost post" button. This option uses previously posted content for your promotion, and the steps are simplified. Once you click the "boost post" button, you have three choices: "more profile visits," "website visits," and "more messages." Next are options to define your audience, and then you choose your budget and duration of the ad. When you're on mobile, you have help with editing your caption.

If you're overwhelmed with getting started with social ads, this could be a place to hire a consultant or social advertising specialist. You could find an assistant to set up your Meta Blueprint account and advertising campaigns. Again, Meta would like to help, with a free Meta Marketing Pro program. This resource can help you with questions if you're figuring it out yourself.

Social advertising is a powerful tool for businesses looking to reach and engage with their target audience. Companies can create highly personalized and effective campaigns that drive actual results by leveraging the vast data and targeting capabilities of platforms such as Facebook and Instagram. Whether your goal is to increase brand awareness, drive website traffic, or generate leads, social advertising provides a cost-effective and scalable solution. With the right strategy and execution, social advertising can help businesses achieve their marketing objectives and grow.

Social advertising will play a critical role in marketing as the world becomes increasingly digital. Stay ahead of the curve by embracing the power of social advertising and using it to drive tangible business outcomes.

TO-DO NOTES

1. Do you have money for ads?
2. Where do you want to run ads?
3. Create graphics and videos for ads in Canva. Research the ad specs and best practices of different social media platforms.

35

How to Give CPR to a Dead Account

Isn't it nice to think that tomorrow is a new day with no mistakes in it yet?

—*Lucy Maud Montgomery,* Anne of Green Gables

---

*T*he good news is that you have an account set up. The bad news is that business and life got busy, and you haven't posted in so long you can't remember the last time it was. What can you do?

Let's ditch the term *dead account* and just call it a *sleeping account.* It's not deceased; it just needs a wake-up call. Start by checking to see if anything needs updating in your bio or profile photo. No need to start from scratch; let's revive this account.

Don't start with a "sorry I haven't posted" post. You need to come in strong with a solid post and plan out your content for a good stretch—a week or two—to get back into the groove then *be consistent.* If you were overwhelmed by posting daily, creating Reels, and running Stories, cut back to a workable plan *for you*—and plan time for engagement and conversation. Plann[1] says, "While you're warming up your account, consistency is the next step in your comeback tour (and will help you gain all the followers). That begins with creating a content strategy you can execute for longer than a week." I love that Plann calls it the "Comeback Tour"! Reframing this process as a positive experience instead of making you feel like a failure is super-helpful.

Here are three ideas for posts that can help boost engagement and restart a "sleeping" Instagram account:

1. *Introduce Yourself*: Introduce yourself or your brand to your followers. Share your story, what you stand for, and what your followers can expect to see on your page. This can help establish a personal connection with your audience and make them feel more invested in your content. You could include a photo dump to show what you've been up to. A photo dump refers to a compilation of images and videos consolidated into a single post on platforms like Instagram or occasionally TikTok. Unlike meticulously edited content, a photo dump typically is comprised of casually assembled visuals aimed at narrating a story or capturing a particular vibe with minimal effort.

2. *"This or that" Post to Boost Engagement*: Create a graphic that showcases two different options related to your business or industry and ask your followers to choose their preferences in the comments. For example, if you own a bakery, you could create a graphic that shows two different cupcakes, one with vanilla frosting and one with chocolate, and ask your followers which one they prefer. This post encourages engagement by prompting followers to share their opinions and start conversations in the comments section.

3. *Behind the Scenes*: Share behind-the-scenes content to give your followers a peek into your life or brand. This could be anything from a day in your life to a look at your creative process. People love feeling like they're part of an exclusive club; behind-the-scenes content can help foster that feeling of inclusion.

Agorapulse[2] researched reviving a dead account, tested restarting, and found, "If you've neglected your Instagram account for months, you can revive it. Just start posting! Instagram will still show your content to your followers; they will continue to see and engage with it." There's no optimal time to wake up your account.

There is hope for your account; but you must commit and be consistent again.

TO-DO NOTES

1. Do you need to apply CPR to your account? If so, what is your plan?
2. Refresh your bios and header images.
3. Write a post to introduce yourself.

36

Unlocking the Power of AI for Small Business Social Media

The mind is its own place, and in itself can make a heaven of hell, a hell of heaven.

—*John Milton, "Paradise Lost"*

Artificial Intelligence (AI) has the potential to benefit humanity significantly, touching many aspects of our lives, including search algorithms, voice assistants, autonomous vehicles, and facial-recognition technology.

Despite its many potential uses, AI is still in its early stages, and there are concerns about its impact as it continues to advance and potentially surpass human intelligence. As renowned physicist Stephen Hawking[1] once said, "The immediate impact of AI will depend on who controls it, but its long-term impact is uncertain and may be beyond our control." Hawking's thoughts highlight the importance of responsible development and deployment of AI technologies and their impact, both positive and negative, on society.

AI IN THE CONTEXT OF SMALL BUSINESS SOCIAL MEDIA

Time is always of the essence for small business owners, and guaranteed, AI can help with some shortcuts for content creation and ideas. It's all a matter of using it to help your business; it can't replace your attention to your social media platforms, but it can assist you in improving speed for content creation and automation.

How AI Can Help Small Businesses with Social Media

While the limit probably doesn't exist for possibilities, AI can help automate repetitive tasks, improve targeting and audience analysis, assist with content creation and ideas, and create chatbots for customer service.

Here are a few terms to know for AI:

Chat: A chat refers to a conversation or exchange of messages between two or more individuals in a digital platform. It typically involves sending and receiving text-based messages in real-time. You can type messages or prompts to the AI, and it will respond with generated content or suggestions based on the input it receives.

Prompt: AI prompts are messages or requests that you send to an AI tool to get it to generate content for you. It's like giving the AI a task or a starting point for it to create something. For example, you could ask the AI to write a blog post introduction or come up with social media captions.

AI uses advanced algorithms and models to understand the prompt and generate content. It learns from vast amounts of data to provide accurate and relevant responses. You can refine and iterate the prompts to get the desired content output from the AI.

AI prompts make content creation faster and more efficient, especially when you're dealing with large volumes of content. They take the burden off you by letting the AI do the heavy lifting and assisting you in generating creative and engaging content.

Automation of repetitive tasks: AI can automate many time-consuming tasks, such as scheduling and publishing posts, monitoring social media mentions, and analyzing user behavior. Small businesses can focus on more strategic tasks, such as creating engaging content and building relationships with their community.

Improved targeting and audience analysis: AI can provide deep insights into your audience and help you understand what types of content resonate with them. This information can create more effective social media campaigns and improve targeting, helping to reach the right people with the right message at the right time.

Content creation and suggestion: AI can help small businesses generate new ideas for content, suggest the best times to post, and even create content for them. Faster planning allows you to produce high-quality, engaging content at scale, helping to reach and engage your audience more effectively.

Chatbots and customer service: AI-powered chatbots can provide fast and efficient customer service, answering common questions, resolving issues, and directing customers to the right resources. Chatbots can assist small businesses in delivering a better customer experience and building stronger customer relationships.

AI can help small businesses save time, improve their targeting, and create engaging content, which can positively impact their social media efforts. By embracing AI, small businesses can stay ahead of the curve and remain competitive in an increasingly crowded online landscape.

TOP-FOUR AI TOOLS I USE MOST

1. *Grammarly*: Powered by an advanced system, Grammarly combines rules, patterns, and artificial intelligence techniques like machine learning, deep learning, and natural language processing to improve

your writing. It integrates with many products like Google Docs, email clients such as Outlook and Gmail, and a Chrome Extension and Mac app. Grammarly is a must-have for anyone writing anything to sound better and be as error-free as possible.

2. *ChatGPT*: ChatGPT is a language-generation model developed by OpenAI. It is a pre-trained AI model that can generate human-like text based on a given prompt or input. The model is trained on a massive amount of text data, including web pages, books, and other sources, and can generate text in various styles, from formal writing to casual conversation.

   ChatGPT is often used in natural language processing (NLP) applications, such as chatbots and virtual assistants, to generate human-like responses to user input. Someone can create creative writing, summarize text, translate languages, and perform other NLP tasks.

   ChatGPT is a powerful tool that can help businesses and organizations automate and improve their language-related tasks and interactions.

3. *Canva Magic Write*: I'm in Canva all day creating graphics and using it for design work, and adding AI into the workflow is a snap. Go from idea to your first draft in seconds with Magic Write, an AI-powered content generation tool within Canva Docs. Use it to write anything from social media captions and profile bios to brainstorming and seeking inspiration for presentation outlines.

4. *Magai*: Magai is an AI tool that makes content creation easier for small business owners. It uses advanced AI models and a chat interface to help you create and refine content quickly. A standout feature of this technology is that it can analyze the content of a webpage from its URL and then craft new content that aligns with the theme and subject matter of that page. Magai also offers chat folders, a prompt library, and secure chat history storage. It seamlessly integrates with GPT-4, allows document collaboration, and provides AI image tools.

   Having AI read a URL can be helpful for several reasons:

- AI can automatically extract relevant information from a URL, saving time and effort for business owners who need to gather data from websites. This can include extracting product details, contact information, pricing, or any other pertinent information.
- AI's role in competitive analysis is not to be underestimated. By analyzing competitors' websites, it can provide small business owners with valuable insights into their strategies, product offerings, pricing, and customer reviews. Armed with this information, business owners can make informed decisions, adjust their strategies, and stay competitive in the market.
- AI's ability to scan URLs of industry-related websites, forums, or social media platforms is a powerful tool for market research. It can gather insights into market trends, customer preferences, and emerging topics. This data is invaluable for small business owners, as it helps them understand their target audience better and tailor their products or services to meet customer needs, ultimately enhancing customer satisfaction and loyalty.
- AI can analyze URL content to curate relevant articles, blog posts, or social media content for small business owners to share with their audience. This helps businesses stay active on social media and engage their audience with valuable content.
- By scanning the URLs of relevant websites or social media profiles, AI can identify potential leads for small business owners. This could include identifying individuals or businesses interested in similar products or services, allowing business owners to target their marketing efforts more effectively.

Having AI read URLs can provide you with valuable insights, automate tedious tasks, and support decision-making processes, ultimately helping you save time, reduce costs, and grow your business more efficiently.

Here are three AI tools that can help small businesses improve their targeting and audience analysis:

1. *Hootsuite Insights*: Hootsuite Insights uses AI to analyze social media data and provide insights into audience behavior and preferences, allowing small businesses to create more effective social media campaigns.
2. *Brand24*: Brand24 uses AI to monitor social media and the web, providing insights into audience sentiment, competitors, and emerging trends, allowing small businesses to understand their audience better and stay ahead of the curve. They have great automatic reports.
3. *Emplifi*: Emplifi offers an AI image-recognition software that allows you to identify trends, logos, or objects in millions of social media posts. It's easy to customize social listening using their queries.

Each tool provides unique features and benefits, so small businesses must research and choose the right one for their needs. By using AI to improve their targeting and audience analysis, small businesses can reach the right people with the right message, ultimately leading to better results and a more substantial social media presence.

AI TOOLS FOR CHATBOTS AND CUSTOMER SERVICE

Here are four tools that can help small businesses improve their customer service using AI-powered no-code chatbots. A no-code chatbot builder is a platform or tool that allows users to create chatbots without needing to write any code. These platforms typically provide a user-friendly interface where you can design, configure, and deploy chatbots for various purposes, such as customer support, lead generation, or sales assistance.

With a no-code chatbot builder, you can customize the bot's conversation flow, set up responses to user inquiries, integrate with other systems or platforms, and deploy the chatbot on your website or messaging apps. The advantage of using a no-code chatbot builder is that it eliminates the need for technical expertise or programming skills. Anyone with basic computer skills can use these platforms to create powerful and interactive chatbots quickly and easily.

Here are a few you might try for your own small business:

Tars: Tars is a no-code chatbot builder that uses AI to provide fast and efficient customer service, answering common questions, resolving issues, and directing customers to the right resources.

ManyChat: ManyChat helps you automate interactive conversations in Instagram Direct Messages, Facebook Messenger, and SMS to grow your brand. You can set up workflows to respond to comments and direct messages.

SnatchBot: SnatchBot is a chatbot builder. You can create an automated (bot) or human (human hybrid) chatbot. No coding or technical skills are required.

Genesys: Genesys is a customer engagement platform that uses AI to provide fast and efficient customer service, answering common questions, resolving issues, and directing customers to the right resources.

With AI-powered chatbots, small businesses can provide a better customer experience and build stronger customer relationships. As I've stressed throughout the book, creating original, quality content is key for your social media success, and incorporating AI into your strategy can help—but it cannot replace you and your passion for your business.

POTENTIAL PITFALLS WHEN USING AI IN MARKETING

Lack of personalization: While AI can automate many tasks, it can also lead to a lack of personalization in your marketing efforts. Small businesses often have a unique brand voice and personality that can get lost in automation. Your passion for your business is a super-power.

Dependence on technology: Small businesses may become too dependent on AI technology, leading to a lack of creativity and original thinking. More reliance on technology can also lead to errors and issues that could harm your brand reputation. For example, if you set up a chatbot incorrectly and don't monitor it, you could turn off your customers.

Data privacy concerns: AI relies on collecting and analyzing large amounts of data, which can raise privacy concerns for your customers and employees. Small businesses must ensure they have appropriate data privacy policies and are transparent about their data collection practices.

High cost: Implementing AI technology can be expensive, and small businesses may need more resources to invest in it. Additionally, the cost of maintenance and upgrades can add up over time.

Lack of control: AI technology can sometimes make decisions that are outside the line with a small business' goals and values. Small business owners need to be aware of the limitations of AI technology and maintain control over their decisions.

While AI can be a valuable tool for small businesses in marketing, it's essential to be aware of these pitfalls and make informed decisions.

Here are a few ways that you can incorporate AI, using ChatGPT or Magai, into your weekly or monthly content creation. Ask your AI tool to:

1. Create hashtag lists for your business.
2. Create an outline for a long-form post.
3. Write calls to action for better click-throughs.
4. Break a blog post into social media posts.
5. Generate email subject lines.
6. Write an outline for a video script using a product description.

As you improve with using ChatGPT, you'll learn to customize your questions and be more specific, which will help generate better responses. For example, asking ChatGPT to create a hashtag list for a dry cleaner will give good results, but asking ChatGPT to create a hashtag list for the best dry cleaner in Boston using environmentally safe products will create great results. Be as clear as possible to get the best results.

Here are some examples of AI-generated prompts for your social media posts:

1. See why [product name] stands out from the crowd! Compare our product to similar products on the market and discover the benefits of choosing [Brand Name]. #[BrandName] #[ProductName]
2. Hear it from our satisfied customers! Check out these testimonials for [product name] and see why it's the [benefit of product/service]. #[BrandName] #[ProductName]
3. How can [product name] make a difference in your life? Check out these real-life scenarios and see the potential of [Brand Name]'s [product/service]. #[BrandName] #[ProductName]
4. Are you part of [specific audience]? Discover how [Brand Name]'s [product name] can help you [benefit of product/service]. Learn more now! #[BrandName] #[ProductName]

Take these results and be more specific; ask AI to redo these prompts with your company name and the service or service you want to promote this week. When you have great results, save your prompts in your Notes or on a Trello board for future use.

To train the AI model, ChatGPT, to mimic your writing style and use your brand voice, follow these steps:

1. *Introduce Yourself:* Clearly explain the purpose of the training and what you expect from ChatGPT. For example, tell it: "I'm a small-town florist, and I use a positive, funny brand voice. I want to create a prompt to help write future content."
2. *Provide Writing Examples:* Share samples of your writing that reflect your style, including sentence length, vocabulary, tone, and format.

3. *Name Your Style*: Assign a name to your writing style and brand for easy reference. Ask ChatGPT to summarize the style in bullet points to ensure accuracy.
4. *Give Clear Instructions*: Once ChatGPT understands your brand and style, provide specific instructions on what you want it to write. Give context and specify your requirements.
5. *Review and Edit*: Carefully review the first draft produced by ChatGPT and request any necessary edits. Provide clear instructions on desired changes.

Deliberate and strategic prompting is essential to achieve the desired output from ChatGPT. With the right approach, you can train ChatGPT to generate content that matches your writing style and fits your brand voice seamlessly. You will cut and paste this into ChatGPT so it learns your brand and so the outputs will match your needs. If you use Magai, you can create these personas in the app and save them, as well, which is very helpful.

AI can provide small business owners with a wealth of information, help with brainstorming, and insights to help them create compelling and engaging social media content. By leveraging AI technology, you can stay ahead of the curve and make informed decisions about your social media strategies.

TO-DO NOTES

1. Create three AI prompts to help with your social media.
2. Check out Grammarly for editing.
3. Create an outline for a blog post using Canva Write.

Putting It All into Practice

A Case Study Approach

The secret of getting ahead is to get started.

—*Mark Twain*

---

*L*et's look at some fictional case studies to showcase what we've discussed and what they look like in practical application. I'm dreaming these up and hoping they inspire your choices. I made up the names and the stats; they're purely examples.

BOOSTING BRAND AWARENESS AND ENGAGEMENT THROUGH INSTAGRAM: A CASE STUDY OF SWEET TREATS BAKERY

Sweet Treats Bakery is a small, family-owned bakery in the heart of downtown. With increasing competition from larger chain bakeries, the owner sought ways to stand out and reach new customers. The bakery already had a Facebook page, but the owner wanted to expand their social media presence to Instagram, which was popular among younger generations.

Objectives

- Increase brand awareness among potential customers.
- Boost engagement with existing followers.
- Drive more traffic to the bakery's physical location.

Strategy

The bakery focused on visually appealing content, showcasing their baked goods and the bakery's atmosphere. They also used relevant hashtags, tagged their location on posts, and interacted with other users in their niche.

Results

- Within six months of launching its Instagram account, Sweet Treats Bakery had gained over two thousand followers.
- Engagement on their posts (likes, comments, and shares) increased by over 50 percent.
- The bakery noticed a significant increase in foot traffic, with many customers mentioning they had learned about the bakery through their Instagram accounts.

Conclusion

By focusing on visually appealing content and interacting with its audience on Instagram, Sweet Treats Bakery increased brand awareness and engagement and drove more traffic to its physical location. This case study shows the importance of having a solid social media presence for small businesses and the positive impact it can have on their success.

PROMOTING COZY SEASON WITH A SOCIAL MEDIA CAMPAIGN: A CASE STUDY OF GREEN CLEAN DRY CLEANERS

Green Clean Dry Cleaners is a chain of environmentally friendly dry cleaners with multiple drop-off store locations. They wanted to create a social media campaign to promote a weeklong discount on dry-cleaning sweaters for the "cozy season." The goal was to attract new customers and engage with their existing customers on social media.

Objectives

- Attract new customers with the discount on dry-cleaning sweaters.
- Engage with customers and build brand loyalty.
- Raise awareness of the environmentally friendly practices of Green Clean Dry Cleaners.

Strategy

Green Clean Dry Cleaners created a social media campaign centered around the "cozy season." They used eye-catching graphics and promotional language to highlight their weeklong discount on dry-cleaning sweaters. They also utilized user-generated content by encouraging their followers to share photos of themselves in their favorite sweaters and tag the dry cleaners.

Results

- The discount on dry-cleaning sweaters attracted many new customers to Green Clean Dry Cleaners.
- The social media campaign generated over one thousand new followers for the dry cleaners.
- Customer engagement on social media increased by over 40 percent, with many customers sharing positive comments about the dry cleaners' promotion and environmentally friendly practices.

Conclusion

By creating a social media campaign centered around the "cozy season" theme, Green Clean Dry Cleaners successfully attracted new customers and engaged with their existing customers. The promotion also raised awareness of the company's environmentally friendly practices, further solidifying its commitment to sustainability, and building brand loyalty among its customers. This case study demonstrates using a theme while promoting a business' services and values.

EXPANDING REACH AND CONVENIENCE WITH SOCIAL MEDIA: A CASE STUDY OF DOT'S CAFÉ

Dot's Café is a local eatery that serves daily specials and has a strong following. The restaurant recently introduced a new online reservation system and wanted to promote it through its social media channels. They decided to use Instagram and Facebook and incorporate their positive Yelp reviews as testimonials into their social posts.

Objectives

- Promote the new online reservation system to increase bookings.
- Engage with customers and build brand loyalty.
- Showcase the positive feedback from customers through Yelp reviews.

Strategy

Dot's Café created visually appealing posts on Instagram and Facebook, highlighting their daily specials, the new online reservation system, and positive Yelp reviews. They also utilized user-generated content by encouraging their followers to share photos of their meals and tag the Café with tent cards on the tables with instructions for social media posting.

Results

- The new online reservation system saw a 20 percent increase in bookings within the first month of the social media campaign.
- Dot's Café's social media following grew by over 15 percent.
- Customer engagement on social media increased by over 30 percent, with many customers sharing positive comments and photos of their meals.

Conclusion

By incorporating their positive Yelp reviews into their social media posts and promoting their new online reservation system, Dot's Café increased bookings and engaged with their customers. This case study shows the importance of incorporating customer feedback into social media campaigns and its positive impact on a business' success.

LEVERAGING SOCIAL MEDIA FOR LOCATION MARKETING AND E-COMMERCE: A CASE STUDY OF PEACH STREET BOUTIQUE

Peach Street Boutique is a specialty clothing store in a small town that sells unique and handmade goods. The store has a brick-and-mortar location downtown, but it also sells goods online. To increase sales and reach new customers, the store decided to leverage social media for location marketing and e-commerce. They used Instagram Stories and Reels to showcase their products and create a robust online presence.

Objectives

- Drive more foot traffic to the brick-and-mortar location.
- Increase online sales through e-commerce.
- Build brand awareness and engage with customers on social media.

Strategy

Peach Street Boutique created visually appealing videos showcasing its products and the store's unique atmosphere. They used Instagram Stories and Reels to share these videos and promote their online store. They also incorporated location tags and hashtags relevant to their target audience to increase visibility.

Results

- Foot traffic to the brick-and-mortar location increased by 10 percent within the first month of the social media campaign.
- Online sales increased by 15 percent due to increased visibility and promotion on social media.
- The store gained over five hundred new followers on Instagram, with a high engagement rate on their posts.

Conclusion

By leveraging social media for location marketing and e-commerce, Peach Street Boutique was able to drive more foot traffic to its brick-and-mortar location and increase online sales. The visually appealing videos and strong online presence helped the store build brand awareness and engage with customers on social media. This case study shows the importance of a robust online presence for small businesses and its impact on their success.

BUILDING ONLINE PRESENCE THROUGH SOCIAL MEDIA: A CASE STUDY OF WICKSON FAMILY DEALERSHIPS

Wickson Family Dealerships is a family-owned and-operated car dealership with a long history of traditional marketing through radio ads and commercials. However, they wanted to expand their reach and build their online presence by starting an Instagram account. They want to showcase their family business on social media and tell the story of their dealership through location marketing, brand photo shoots, and videos.

Objectives

- Increase brand awareness and reach a wider audience.
- Build a solid online presence for the dealership.
- Showcase the family aspect of the business and the multiple generations involved.

Strategy

Wickson Family Dealerships created a brand photo-shoot featuring three generations of the family, showcasing their family heritage and commitment to their customers. They also made videos at the dealership showcasing their cars and the business atmosphere. They utilized location tags and hashtags to increase visibility and engage with customers on social media by responding to comments and messages.

Results

- The dealership's Instagram following grew by over 20 percent within the first month of the social media campaign.
- Brand awareness increased, with many new customers mentioning the dealership's online presence when visiting the dealership.
- Customer engagement on social media increased by over 30 percent, with many customers sharing positive comments and photos of their experience at Wickson Family Dealerships.

Conclusion

By utilizing social media to showcase the family aspect of the business and its commitment to its customers, Wickson Family Dealerships was able to build a solid online presence and reach a wider audience. The brand photo shoot and dealership videos helped increase brand awareness and customer engagement, demonstrating social media's impact on a family-owned business. This case study shows the importance of incorporating the story of a company into a social media strategy for increased success.

BUILDING TRUST AND GROWING A DENTAL PRACTICE THROUGH SOCIAL MEDIA: A CASE STUDY OF DAZZLING SMILES

Dr. Phil McCavity recently took over the Dazzling Smiles dental practice from a retiring dentist. He wanted to grow the practice and reassure patients that they would continue to receive excellent care in an updated, modern dental practice. He used social media to introduce online booking, location marketing, and educational videos to achieve this.

Objectives

- Increase patient trust in the new practice and the new dentist.
- Grow the practice through location marketing and online booking.
- Educate patients on the importance of oral hygiene and dental care.

Strategy

Dr. Phil McCavity created educational videos showcasing the benefits of caring for your teeth and flossing. He used Instagram and Facebook to promote the videos and the new online booking system, incorporating location tags and hashtags to increase visibility. He also engaged with patients by responding to comments and messages and showcasing patient testimonials.

Results

- The number of online bookings increased by 25 percent within the first month of the social media campaign.
- The practice's social media following grew by over 15 percent.
- Patient trust in the new practice and the new dentist increased, with many patients mentioning their positive experience with the educational videos and online booking system.

Conclusion

By using social media to educate patients and showcase the benefits of oral hygiene and dental care, Dr. Phil McCavity increased patient trust and grew the practice. The online booking system and location marketing also helped reach new patients and increase patient engagement. This case study shows the importance of incorporating educational content into a social media strategy for health-care practices and its positive impact on patient trust and growth.

BUILDING TRUST AND GROWING A REAL ESTATE BUSINESS THROUGH SOCIAL MEDIA: A CASE STUDY OF DIAMOND REAL ESTATE

Diamond Real Estate is a business located in a booming suburban location. The Realtor wanted to use social media to share new bookings, showcase recent sales, and highlight her positive attitude and personal side. She also wanted to educate potential customers on how to get their homes ready to sell and connect with the community through location marketing and tasteful humor.

Objectives

- Increase trust and engagement with potential customers.
- Showcase recent sales and new bookings.
- Educate potential customers on how to get their homes ready to sell.
- Connect with the community through location marketing and a personal touch.

Strategy

The realtor at Diamond Real Estate created videos showcasing recent sales, new bookings, and tips on how to get your home ready to sell. She also included video outtakes to show her personal side and sense of humor. She used Instagram and Facebook to share these videos and engage with potential customers, incorporating location tags and relevant hashtags to increase visibility.

Results

- The Realtor's social media following grew by over 20 percent within the first month of the social media campaign.
- Engagement with potential customers increased by over 30 percent, with many customers mentioning the helpful tips and personal touches in the videos.
- The Realtor received several new bookings and closed several sales due to the increased visibility and engagement on social media.

Conclusion

By using social media to educate potential customers and showcase her positive attitude and personal side, the Realtor at Diamond Real Estate increased trust and engagement with potential customers. The videos and location marketing helped reach new customers and increase visibility, leading to several new bookings and closed sales. This case study shows the importance of incorporating a personal touch and educational content into a social media strategy for real estate businesses and its positive impact on building trust and growing the business.

BUILDING TRUST AND GROWING A SPEAKING CONSULTANCY THROUGH SOCIAL MEDIA: A CASE STUDY OF MARIANNE WITH SPEAK WITH CONFIDENCE CO.

Marianne, with Speak with Confidence Co., is a speaking consultant who helps customers become better speakers and build their speaking careers. The consultant wanted to work with local and online customers and use social media to establish their expertise in the field and build trust. They used a website, online booking, and short-and long-form videos to achieve these objectives.

Objectives

- Establish expertise in the field of speaking consultancy.
- Build trust with potential customers through an online presence.
- Reach both local and online customers through location marketing and online booking.

Strategy

Marianne with Speak with Confidence Co. created short-and long-form videos showcasing her expertise in speaking consultancy and her services. She used their website and social media platforms, including Instagram and Facebook, to promote the videos and reach potential customers. She also incorporated location tags and relevant hashtags to increase visibility and engagement with potential customers through online booking and messaging.

Results

- Marianne's social media following grew by over 20 percent within the first month of the social media campaign.
- Engagement with potential customers increased by over 30 percent, with many reaching out for consultations after viewing the videos and learning more about the services offered.
- Marianne received several new bookings and customers due to her increased visibility and engagement on social media.

Conclusion

Using social media to establish expertise and build trust with potential customers, Marianne with Speak with Confidence Co. reached local and online customers and grew her speaking consultancy business. The videos and online booking system helped increase visibility and engagement, leading to several new bookings and customers. This case study shows the importance of incorporating expertise and a personal touch into a consultant's social media strategy and its positive impact on building trust and growing the business.

CASE STUDY: BOOKSHOP UNDER NEW OWNERSHIP

I want to share a final case study with you. This scenario involves a bookshop under new ownership, which is planning a grand reopening. The bookshop seeks to use social media, particularly Instagram and Tiktok, to spread the word about the reopening and engage with its customers.

Establishing a Strong Foundation

To get started, the bookshop must refresh its online profiles and ensure they're all consistent in appearance and information. This includes updating the avatars, email signatures, and service hours on their website and social bios. The bookshop should set up Google Alerts to keep track of any mentions of the book or its authors.

Gathering Digital Assets

The bookshop should create a three-to four-second intro/outro clip with the store's logo or image for all other videos. A thirty-second video about the grand reopening and two-minute videos showcasing different store sections or highlighting featured books should also be created.

In addition to the videos, the bookshop should write a five-hundred-word blog post about the grand reopening and any special events or promotions they have planned. A one-thousand-word LinkedIn long-form post that summarizes the reopening can also be created. Graphics with book or author quotes would be inspirational content.

Finally, the bookshop should provide a copy of a popular book to anyone who promises to visit the store and review it on social media.

Going to Market

To promote the grand reopening, the bookshop should create a weeklong social media campaign, including posting daily to Instagram and TikTok. A series of Instagram Stories should run through the entire week to keep their account at the top of their followers' Instagram apps. The posts should be in various styles, highlighting the store's events, educating customers on what you have in store, entertaining with videos, and inspiring people to be a part of the community with engaging questions and conversational tones.

Tapping into BookTok on TikTok

BookTok is a popular trend on TikTok that's all about books and reading. To tap in to this trend, the bookshop can:

- Create short, vertical videos for TikTok that showcase their store, the books they offer, or book-related content, such as book reviews or author interviews.
- Use popular hashtags related to BookTok and reading, such as #book stagram, #booknerd, or #booklover, to reach a wider audience.

- Participate in trending book-related challenges, such as lip-synch challenges with famous book quotes or dance challenges set to book-themed music.
- Collaborate with book-tubers, authors, and other bookstores to reach a wider audience and drive engagement.
- Host a monthly book club on TikTok, where the bookshop can engage with customers and promote their store, books, and events.

By tapping in to the BookTok trend on TikTok, the bookshop can reach a new and engaged audience, drive engagement, and promote its store and offerings.

Utilizing Location Marketing

Location marketing is a way to reach customers near your business and engage with them meaningfully. To use location marketing, the bookshop can:

- Use geolocation targeting on social media platforms such as Instagram and TikTok to reach customers in the store's vicinity.
- Offer location-based promotions, such as a discount for customers who check in at the store on Facebook or a special offer for customers who use the store's loyalty app.
- Use augmented reality (AR) filters to create a fun and interactive customer experience. For example, the bookshop could create an AR filter allowing customers to browse the store's shelves virtually.
- Collaborate with local businesses and organizations to reach a wider audience and drive foot traffic to the store.

Using location marketing, the bookshop can engage with nearby customers and create a fun and interactive experience that encourages them to visit the store.

Developing a Hashtag Strategy

Hashtags play an important role in social media marketing, as they help to categorize content and make it more discoverable. To develop a hashtag strategy, the bookshop can:

- Use popular hashtags related to the book industry and reading, such as #BookTok, #Bookstagram, #BookLovers, and #ReadingIsFun.
- Create unique hashtags for the bookshop, such as #[Bookshop Name] Books or #[Bookshop Name]Readers, to build brand recognition and drive engagement.
- Encourage customers to use the bookshop's hashtags when sharing photos or reviews of the store or books they've purchased.
- Monitor the bookshop's hashtags and engage with customers who use them by liking or commenting on their posts.
- By developing a solid hashtag strategy, the bookshop can increase the visibility of its content, build brand recognition, and engage with customers meaningfully.

With hard work and dedication, the bookshop can effectively use social media to promote its grand reopening and engage with its customers. This might seem like much work, but a grand reopening is a big deal!

REAL-LIFE CASE STUDY ON TIKTOK

Clancy's Auto Body,[1] a local auto shop based out of Fort Lauderdale, Florida, was relatively unknown when it hugely impacted TikTok. Their viral video generated 21.2 million views, 4.1 million likes, 13.7 thousand comments, and 34.4 thousand shares. The response was so overwhelming that their TikTok community named itself "Clancy's Cult."

It was not a well-produced showpiece; this was a homegrown TikTok using trending music from the app, and they added a trending TikTok effect called "Maxwell In The Sky," which is a black-and-white tuxedo cat floating up in the air.

This success wasn't a one-hit wonder. Clancy's Auto Body's social media manager continued and produced more viral videos with 11.9, 3.1, and 2.3 million views, and several others crossed the one million mark.

What made their social media strategy so effective? Here are three methods their social media manager executed well:

1. *Platform-specific humor*: Clancy's Auto Body leaned into meme templates and the type of humor TikTok loves. This unhinged humor is optional for social media success, but it sure does help on TikTok.
2. *Characters and storylines*: The social media manager worked with other employees at the auto shop to create characters and storylines for the brand. This created a "reality show" for the brand and entertained its audience.
3. *Capitalizing on a viral hit*: While they may have yet to hit twenty-one million views again, Clancy's Auto Body made the most of their viral success by continuing to produce engaging videos that racked up millions of views. They found an angle that crushed and ran with it.

Where they went wrong:

1. They used music that wasn't cleared for commercial usage, and they didn't have the rights to it.
2. Maxwell the cat is a meme[2]; they didn't own the commercial rights to use it. You can find the history of "Maxwell the Spinning Cat" on KnowYourMeme.com. People came back to the account and wanted more of the cat, which didn't relate to their business.

Understanding the guidelines set by TikTok and any social platform you will use as a business is essential. In terms of music, the platform's Commercial Music Library is exclusively available for users who use TikTok for marketing, advertising, sponsorships, endorsements, or publicity—this includes *official brand accounts*. Therefore, businesses must adhere to TikTok's *pre-approved* audio and cannot use any other music outside the library. Companies must follow these guidelines to ensure their content complies with TikTok's policies and avoids potential penalties.

Clancy's Auto Body was flooded with positive Google reviews, which Google flagged. And while their TikTok community continues to grow, that social media manager is gone.

Here's what they need to do next: move some viewers over to Instagram, where it will be easier for people to book appointments. They need to update their website with links to Instagram and TikTok and have a designated spot to share their funny TikTok videos.

I hope these case studies show you that social media is not a one-size-fits-all endeavor and that there isn't just one way to succeed. It's more like a free-form painting than paint by number. Your business is unique, and your creative ideas will bring the spark to your social media marketing.

As Glinda the Good Witch told Dorothy in *The Wizard of Oz*, "You've had the power all along, my dear."

TO-DO NOTES

1. Which case study inspired you the most?
2. How will you use objectives and strategy to reach your goals?
3. Review any Terms of Service for business accounts you plan to use.

The End

Everything has to come to an end, sometime.

—*L. Frank Baum*, The Marvelous Land of Oz

You made it! I hope you've been taking notes, and that your mind is crammed with ideas.

The next step is to dive in. Create your strategy and get ready to watch your social media flourish. My goal was to give you all the tactics, tips, and strategies and for you to take them and create a recipe that will work for you. I hope this book is helpful and a resource you can return to when you need it.

Use the resource list in the back to find what you need, and don't get overwhelmed with options.

The most important lesson to learn is that you'll need to be patient. You can't expect to create an account and instantly be swarmed with followers and customers. It takes time to grow your small business through social media, but if you keep at it and remain consistent in your efforts, you will see the fruits of your labor.

Thank you for reading every bit of this book. If you liked it, please take a moment to *add it to your Goodreads* and *write a review for the book*. Take a photo with you and the book, post it on social media, and please tag me. It would mean a lot to me and help more people decide to purchase the book.

Here's to your success!

TO-DO NOTES

1. Take a breath.
2. Make a plan.
3. Work for your social media success.
4. Tag me on a post you create on social media @pegfitzpatrick. Email me at hello@pegfitzpatrick.com to tell me your favorite part of the book.

Resources

List of Apps and Services

A

Adobe Premiere Rush. Easy-to-use video editing tool.

Adobe Stock. Images by Adobe.

Agorapulse. Agorapulse is a social media management platform designed to help businesses manage their social media accounts more efficiently. It offers a range of features, including social media scheduling, content publishing, social media monitoring, and social media analytics.

Answer the Public. A search listening tool.

B

Brand24. A social listening tool.

C

Canva. *A* free-to-use online graphic design tool. Canva provides users with a user-friendly drag-and-drop interface, a library of pre-designed templates, stock photos, icons, illustrations, and various customization tools to create high-quality designs without requiring advanced design skills. Canva offers a free version and a paid sub-scription service with additional features and benefits. It has become a valuable resource for businesses of all sizes to create professional-looking designs for their marketing materials, social media, and other visual content.

ChatGPT. A large language model developed by OpenAI based on the GPT architecture. Designed to understand and generate human-like language, enabling it to respond to a wide range of prompts and questions.

Chrome. Google's Web browser.

ClickToTweet. Service to add clickable links to send tweets.

Color Splash. Mobile photo-editing app.

Creative Commons. A nonprofit organization that enables sharing of creative works, it maintains a front end to search other sharing websites.

E

Élevae Visuals. Styled stock photo and video membership site.

Emplifi. AI image recognition.

F

Facebook. Social-media platform owned by Meta.

Flickr Creative Commons. Flickr collection of Creative Commons photos.

Flodesk. A popular email marketing software designed to help busi-nesses and creators create and send beautiful, branded emails to their subscribers. Flodesk allows users to create custom email templates using a drag-and-drop editor, which can be customized to match their branding. The platform also offers advanced automation features, segmentation tools, and detailed analytics to help businesses improve email marketing campaigns.

G

Genesis. Automated customer engagement platform.

Google. A search engine.

Google Scholar. Specialty search engine to find scholarly research.

Grammarly. AI-powered writing assistant that helps with grammar, spelling, and tone. Apps for phone, Mac, and there's a desktop version.

H

Hootsuite. Social media monitoring and scheduling platform.

I

Instagram. Instagram is a popular visual social media platform that allows users to share photos and videos, as well as connect with other users and brands. Owned by Meta.

L

LinkedIn. Professional social networking platform owned by Microsoft.

M

Magai: An AI assistant that works with ChatGPT and helps you organize using folders and a prompt library.

MailChimp. Service for e-mail lists.

ManyChat. A customizable no-code chat automation or chatbot.

Meta. Meta Platforms, Inc., doing business as Meta and formerly named Facebook, Inc., and TheFacebook, Inc., is an American multinational technology conglomerate based in Menlo Park, California. The company owns Facebook, Instagram, and WhatsApp, among other products and services.

N

Notion. Productivity and note-taking website used to organize and save things.

P

Pexels. Royalty-free images owned by Canva.

Pixabay. Royalty-free images owned by Canva.

Pinterest. A social media platform and visual search engine that allows users to discover, share, and save images and videos, known as "pins," to virtual pinboards. Pinterest is a valuable platform for businesses, allowing them to showcase products and services through visually appealing pins and reach a highly engaged audience. Businesses can create a business account, share their own content, and participate in various advertising and promotional opportunities, including paid advertising, sponsored content, and promoted pins.

Plann. An effortless Instagram Scheduler and Social Media Suite. Visualize, plan, auto-post, and schedule your entire Instagram in advance, right from your smartphone. Also works with Linkedin, Facebook, Pinterest, and TikTok with a slick Canva integration.

R

Reddit. User-generated and user-rated Internet news service.

S

SmarterQueue. A social media management tool that allows businesses and individuals to schedule, post, and analyze their social media content across various platforms. It allows users to create content categories and schedule posts to be published at specific times on multiple platforms, including Facebook, Twitter, LinkedIn, Instagram, and Pinterest.

SnatchBott: A chatbot builder.

Sprout Social. Social media management and measurement service.

Square Space. A customizable website builder.

Stocksy. Stock-photography website.

StumbleUpon. Website for discovering and rating content.

T

Tars. A no-code chatbot builder.

Threads. A conversational social media platform tied to Instagram created by Meta.

TikTok. Short-form video platform.

Trello. My favorite place to organize projects and materials.

Tumblr. Blogging platform.

Twitter. Now called X. Social-media platform.

U

Unsplash. Free stock photos.

W

What's App. WhatsApp is a popular messaging app that allows users to send text messages, send voice messages, make voice and video calls, and share files with other WhatsApp users over the internet—owned by Meta.

Wikimedia Commons. Collection of public-domain and freely licensed images, sound clips, and video clips.

Wikiquote. A free online compendium of quotations and their sources.

Wix. Website builder.

WordPress. A web content management system used to make websites and blogs.

X

X. Formerly Twitter. A social media platform.

Y

YouTube. A popular video-sharing website that allows users to upload, share, and view videos. YouTube is also used for social networking, with users able to subscribe to channels, like, comment, and share videos with their friends and followers. Google owns it, and it is a powerful tool for businesses to reach and engage with their audience through video content.

Notes

CHAPTER 1

1. "History of Facebook" (2023), Wikipedia, April 17, https://en.wikipedia
.org/wiki/History_of_Facebook.

2. "Demographics of Social Media Users and Adoption in the United States"
(2023), Pew Research Center: Internet, Science & Tech, May 11, 2023, https://
www.pewresearch.org/internet/fact-sheet/social-media/.

3. "Demographics of Social Media Users and Adoption in the United States"
(2023), Pew Research Center: Internet, Science & Tech, May 11, 2023, https://
www.pewresearch.org/internet/fact-sheet/social-media/.

4. "About X Blue" (n.d.), https://help.X.com/en/using-X/X-blue.

5. "Demographics of Social Media Users and Adoption in the United States"
(2023), Pew Research Center: Internet, Science & Tech, May 11, 2023, https://
www.pewresearch.org/internet/fact-sheet/social-media/.

6. "Instagram Reels—Help" (n.d.) Instagram Help, accessed May 31, 2023,
https://about.instagram.com/features/reels.

7. "A more positive internet? It's possible" (2023), Pinterest blog, February
22, https://business.pinterest.com/en-ca/blog/a-better-internet-is-possible.

8. "———" (2023b), Pew Research Center: Internet, Science & Tech, May 11, https://www.pewresearch.org/internet/fact-sheet/social-media/?tabId=tabb14b718d-7ab6-46f4-b447-0abd510f4180.

9. "———" (2023b), Pew Research Center: Internet, Science & Tech, May 11, https://www.pewresearch.org/internet/fact-sheet/social-media/?tabId=tabb14b718d-7ab6-46f4-b447-0abd510f4180.

10. S. Maheshwari, and A. Holpuch, (2023), "Why Countries Are Trying to Ban TikTok," *New York Times*, April 12, https://www.nytimes.com/article/tiktok-ban.html.

11. Elizabeth Minkel (2023), "The End of the Tumblr Era," *Wired*, November 14, https://www.wired.com/story/end-of-the-tumblr-era/.

CHAPTER 2

1. Wikipedia (2023), "Walter Cronkite," Wikipedia, The Free Encyclopedia, accessed April 17, 2023, 17:26 UTC Permanent link: https://en.wikipedia.org/w/index.php?title=Walter_Cronkite&oldid=1143994593.

2. B. Kramer, "There is no more B2B or B2C: It's Human to Human, H2H," accessed April 17, 2023, http://www.bryankramer.com/there-is-no-more-b2b-or-b2c-its-human-to-human-h2.

3. Adweek, "Branded Content Leads to 59% Better Recall Than Other Digital Ads," http://www.adweek.com/digital/branded-content-leads-59-better-recall-other-digital-ads-173671/.

4. IPG Media Lab (2016), "IPG Media Lab + Forbes Evaluate The Current State of Branded Content," September 23, accessed April 18, 2023, https://ipglab.com/2016/09/23/ipg-medialab-forbes-evaluate-the-current-state-of-branded-content/.

CHAPTER 3

1. Anyware Dominos, accessed April 17, 2023, https://anyware.dominos.com/.

CHAPTER 4

1. Rieva Lesonsky. "How to Get the Most from Your Marketing Budget," SBA: United States Small Business Association, July 9, accessed April 18, 2023, https://www.sba.gov/blog/how-get-most-your-marketing-budget.

2. Meta Business Learn (n.d.), Meta Blueprint, accessed April 18, 2023, https://www.facebook.com/business/learn.

CHAPTER 5

1. Create a mood board in Canva (n.d.), Canva, accessed April 18, 2023, https://www.canva.com/create/mood-boards/.

2. Ryan created such a great brand he sold his gin company, Aviation Gin, for $610 million in 2020.

CHAPTER 7

1. D. Farnworth, (2020), An Introduction to the 4 Essential Types of Content Every Marketing Strategy Needs—Copyblogger. Copyblogger, March 28, accessed April 18, 2023, https://copyblogger.com/essential-content-types/.

2. A. Kohli, (2022), Why the FBI Is Concerned About TikTok, *Time*, December 3, https://time.com/6238540/tiktok-fbi-security-concerns/.

CHAPTER 10

1. L. Kannenberg (2022), Social Spotlight: REI's #OptOutside and how a campaign becomes a movement, Sprout Social, https://sproutsocial.com/insights/social-spotlight-rei/.

CHAPTER 11

1. Sprout Social (2023), Social Media Trends for 2022 and Beyond, Sprout Social, March 9, https://sproutsocial.com/insights/index/#get-us-report.

2. Effortless Experience Is Key to Customer Loyalty (n.d.), Gartner, https://www.gartner.com/smarterwithgartner/effortless-experience-explained.

CHAPTER 12

1. See https://copyblogger.com/seth-godin-marketing/.

2. M. Silcoff (2022), Dove's Latest Stand in the Virtue Wars. *New York Times,* July 20, accessed April 18, 2023, https://www.nytimes.com/2022/07/20 /magazine/doveadvertising-beauty.html.

CHAPTER 14

1. Jay Baer, *Youtility: Why Smart Marketing Is About Help Not Hype.* New York: Portfolio, 2013.

2. A. Crestodina (2018), The Ideal Length for Blog Posts, Tweets, and Everything Else in Your Marketing, Orbit Media Studios, https://www .orbitmedia.com/blog/ideal-blog-postlength/.

3. K. Oberthaler (2022), 52 content marketing statistics (with key takeaways), Ziflow, August 25, accessed April 18, 2023, https://www.ziflow.com/blog /content-marketing-statistics.

CHAPTER 15

1. I. Wigmore (2019), "attention economy," WhatIs.com, https://www .techtarget.com/whatis/definition/attention-economy#.

2. Sandee LaMotte "Your Attention Span Is Shrinking, Studies Say. Here's How to Stay Focused," CNN, January 11, 2023, https://www.cnn .com/2023/01/11/health/short-attention-span-wellness/index.html.

3. P. Engineering (2022), How Pinterest Leverages Realtime User Actions in Recommendation to Boost Homefeed Engagement Volume, Medium November 12, accessed April 18, 2023, https://medium.com/pinterest -engineering/how-pinterest-leverages-realtimeuser-actions-in-recom mendation-to-boost-homefeed-engagement-volume-165ae2e8cde8.

CHAPTER 17

1. *The Stones of Venice,* 1851–1853.

2. K. Komiya (2020), A Majority of Consumers Expect Brands to Take a Stand on Issues Before Purchasing, Survey Finds, Barrons, July 7, accessed April 18, 2023 https://www.barrons.com/articles/a-majority-of-consumers -expect-brands-to-take-astand-on-issues-before-purchasing-survey-finds -51594143666.

3. A. Sonnenberg (2022), When to Pause Your Social Media Channels, Agorapulse, https://www.agorapulse.com/blog/pause-social-media-channels/.

4. R. Broderick (2013), This Is the Most Epic Brand Meltdown on Facebook Ever, BuzzFeed, accessed April 18, 2023, https://www.buzzfeed.com /ryanhatesthis/thisis-the-most-epic-brand-meltdown-on-facebook-ever//.

CHAPTER 18

1. Nielsen, (2022), The Reviews Are In: Yelp Users Are Four-Star Consumers, Nielsen, July 21, https://www.nielsen.com/insights/2013/the-reviews-are-in -yelp-users-are-four-starconsumers/.

2. S. R. U. Today (2017), Massachusetts man has to pay more than $30K for negative Yelp review. *Usa Today,* April 16, accessed April 18, 2023, https:// www.usatoday.com/story/news/nation-now/2017/04/06/mass-man-has-pay -morethan-30k-negative-yelp-review/100113022/.

CHAPTER 19

1. https://developers.google.com/search/blog/2022/08/helpful-content -update.

CHAPTER 20

1. G. Conn (2020), Episode #7: The Secret Story Behind McDonalds' All Day Breakfast, Sprinklr, https://www.sprinklr.com/blog/episode-7-secret-story -behind-mcdonalds-day-breakfast/.

CHAPTER 21

1. "How Brands Can Win in Today's Visual Economy" (2023). Newsroom—Latest Canva News Announcements, Brand Guidelines and Media Kit, April 18, https://www.canva.com/newsroom/news/visual-economy-report/.

CHAPTER 22

1. "Digital Transformation for Small Businesses: 4 Tips to Enable SMBs to Embrace a Digital-First Future" (n.d.), Salesforce, https://www.salesforce.com/in/blog/2022/03/smb-digital-transformation-4-tips.html#:~:text=Running%20an%20SMB%20has%20always,%2C%20and%20future%2Dproof%20manner.

2. HubSpot. (n.d.), "2022 Marketing Statistics, Trends & Data—The Ultimate List of Digital Marketing Stats," https://www.hubspot.com/marketing-statistics.

CHAPTER 25

1. A. Hott (2023), 40+ Email Marketing Statistics You Need to Know for 2023, OptinMonster. https://optinmonster.com/email-marketing-statistics/.

2. See https://www.litmus.com/blog/infographic-the-roi-of-email-marketing.

3. Khalid Saleh (2022), "Digital Coupon Marketing—Statistics and Trends [Infographic]," Invesp, May 16, https://www.invespcro.com/blog/digital-coupon-marketing/.

4. J. Vocell (2022), Personalized Calls to Action Perform 202% Better Than Basic CTAs [New Data], Hubspot, May 6, accessed April 18, 2023, https://blog.hubspot.com/marketing/personalized-calls-to-action-convert-betterdata#sm.000awoxgniktcoi11jl2et1nit4os.

5. Constant Contact (2023), "2023 Email Marketing Statistics: Facts & Figures," *Constant Contact*, May, https://www.constantcontact.com/blog/email-marketing-research-and-statistics/.

CHAPTER 27

1. *New York Times* (n.d.), "The Psychology of Sharing," https:// foundationinc.co/wp-content/uploads/2018/12/NYT-Psychology-Of -Sharing.pdf.

2. Peg, (2021), "The Insider's Guide to Proper Photo Usage," *Https:// Pegfitzpatrick.Com/*, June. https://pegfitzpatrick.com/insiders-guide-proper -photo-usage/.

CHAPTER 28

1. Martina Bretous (2022), "6 Short-Form Video Trends Marketers Should Watch in 2022 [New Data]," *Hubspot*, July 18, https://blog.hubspot.com /marketing/short-form-video-trends#:~:text=Short%2Dform%20ranks%20 %231%20for,companies%20leverage%20short%2Dform%20videos.

2. "Emerging Video Marketing Trends for 2022" (n.d.), Animoto Video Maker—Stand Out on Social Media. Easily, https://animoto.com/video -marketing-trends.

3. ScientiaMobile (2019), "How Do Mobile Video Viewers Hold Their Phone? | ScientiaMobile," February 5, https://www.scientiamobile.com/how -do-mobile-video-viewers-hold-their-phone/.

4. Tracey Witt (2023), "Social Media Video Statistics Marketers Need to Know for 2023," *Sprout Social*, May, https://sproutsocial.com/insights/social -media-video-statistics/.

5. See https://www.facebook.com/business/news/updated-features-for -video-ads.

CHAPTER 33

1. Gary Vaynerchuk (2015), "What's the ROI of Your Mother?" December 21, https://garyvaynerchuk.com/social-media-roi-calculate-metrics/.

2. Andy Crestodina (2023), "How to Use GA4 to Track Social Media Traffic: 6 Questions, Answers and Insights [VIDEO]," *Orbit Media Studios*, March, https://www.orbitmedia.com/blog/google-analytics-social-media/.

CHAPTER 35

1. L. Melnick (2023), How to revive a Dead Instagram Account—Fast, Plann, accessed April 18, 2023, https://www.plannthat.com/revive-a-dead-instagram -account/.

2. S. Ayres (2021), Resuscitating Dead Instagram Accounts! Social Media Lab Powered by Agorapulse, https://www.agorapulse.com/social-media-lab /resuscitating-dead-instagramaccounts/.

CHAPTER 36

1. Stephen Hawking (2016), "The Best or Worst Thing to Happen to Humanity," October 19, https://www.cam.ac.uk/research/news/the-best-or -worst-thing-to-happen-to-humanity-stephen-hawking-launches-centre-for -the-future-of.

CHAPTER 37

1. Clancy's Auto Body (@clancysautobody) | TikTok (n.d.), TikTok, https:// www.tiktok.com/@clancysautobody.

2. #maxwellthecat | TikTok, (n.d.), TikTok, https://www.tiktok.com/tag /maxwellthecat.

References

Ask Wonder. Consuming Information Research | Wonder. (n.d.). Retrieved April 18, 2023, from https://askwonder.com/research/consuming-informa tion-research-gngr6owc2?h=c2ea0077b81b60170524893115bbc6b9942f9ca6 75882d97751358022ed812cf.

Ayres, S. (2021). Resuscitating Dead Instagram Accounts! *Social Media Lab Powered by Agorapulse.* https://www.agorapulse.com/social-media-lab /resuscitating-dead-instagram-accounts/.

Barnhart, B. (2023). Reputation management: How to stay in good standing with your audience. *Sprout Social.* https://sproutsocial.com/insights/social -media-reputation-management/.

Broderick, R. (2013, May 14). This Is the Most Epic Brand Meltdown on Facebook Ever. *BuzzFeed.* Retrieved April 18, 2023, from https://www .buzzfeed.com/ryanhatesthis/this-is-the-most-epic-brand-meltdown -on-facebook-ever//.

Canva. Create a mood board in Canva. (n.d.). Canva. Retrieved April 18, 2023, from https://www.canva.com/create/mood-boards/.

Canva. (2023). *The Visual Economy Report* (1st ed.). https://canvavisual economy.com/.

Clancy's Auto Body (@clancysautobody) | TikTok. (n.d.). TikTok. https://www
.tiktok.com/@clancysautobody.

Community—New World Encyclopedia. (n.d.). https://www.newworld
encyclopedia.org/entry/Community.

Conn, G. (2020). Episode #7: The Secret Story Behind McDonalds' All Day
Breakfast. *Sprinklr.* https://www.sprinklr.com/blog/episode-7-secret-story
-behind-mcdonalds-day-breakfast/.

Crestodina, A. (2018). The Ideal Length for Blog Posts, Tweets, and
Everything Else in Your Marketing. *Orbit Media Studios.* https://www
.orbitmedia.com/blog/ideal-blog-post-length/.

Design Seeds website. (n.d.). Design Seeds. Retrieved April 18, 2023, from
https://www.design-seeds.com/.

Distraction Blocker for Mac—Focus. (n.d.). Focus. https://heyfocus.com/.

Engineering, P. (2022, November 12). How Pinterest Leverages Realtime
User Actions in Recommendation to Boost Homefeed Engagement
Volume. *Medium.* Retrieved April 18, 2023, from https://medium.com
/pinterest-engineering/how-pinterest-leverages-realtime-user-actions-in
-recommendation-to-boost-homefeed-engagement-volume-165ae2e8cde8.

Farnworth, D. (2020, March 28). *An Introduction to the 4 Essential Types
of Content Every Marketing Strategy Needs—Copyblogger.* Copyblogger.
Retrieved April 18, 2023, from https://copyblogger.com/essential-content
-types/.

Gartner. Effortless Experience Is Key to Customer Loyalty. (n.d.). Gartner.
https://www.gartner.com/smarterwithgartner/effortless-experience
-explained.

Hott, A. (2023). 40+ Email Marketing Statistics You Need to Know for 2023.
OptinMonster. https://optinmonster.com/email-marketing-statistics/.

Howarth, J. (2023a, April 3). Internet Traffic from Mobile Devices. (April
2023). *Exploding Topics.* https://explodingtopics.com/blog/mobile-internet
-traffic.

Howarth, J. (2023b, April 3). Internet Traffic from Mobile Devices (April 2023). *Exploding Topics*. https://explodingtopics.com/blog/mobile-internet-traffic.

Huang, K. (2022, September 17). For Gen Z, TikTok Is the New Search Engine. *New York Times*. https://www.nytimes.com/2022/09/16/technology/gen-z-tiktok-search-engine.html.

Iskiev, M. (2022, February 16). The HubSpot Blog's 2023 Social Media Marketing Report: Data from 1200+ Global Marketers. *Hubspot*. Retrieved April 18, 2023, from https://blog.hubspot.com/marketing/hubspot-blog-social-media-marketing-report?hubs_content=blog.hubspot.com%2Fmarketing%2Fshort-form-video-trends&hubs_content-cta=social%20media%20trends%20report%20.

Kannenberg, L. (2022). Social Spotlight: REI's #OptOutside and how a campaign becomes a movement. *Sprout Social*. https://sproutsocial.com/insights/social-spotlight-rei/.

Kohli, A. (2022, December 3). Why the FBI Is Concerned about TikTok. *Time*. https://time.com/6238540/tiktok-fbi-security-concerns/.

Komiya, K. (2020, July 7). A Majority of Consumers Expect Brands to Take a Stand on Issues Before Purchasing, Survey Finds. *Barrons*. Retrieved April 18, 2023, from https://www.barrons.com/articles/a-majority-of-consumers-expect-brands-to-take-a-stand-on-issues-before-purchasing-survey-finds-51594143666.

Log in or sign up to view. (n.d.). https://www.facebook.com/business/news/updated-features-for-video-ads.

#maxwellthecat | TikTok. (n.d.). TikTok. https://www.tiktok.com/tag/maxwellthecat.

Manychat. *How To Resources | Manychat.* (n.d.). manychat.com. Retrieved April 18, 2023, from https://manychat.com/resources/how-to.

Melnick, L. (2023). *How to Revive a Dead Instagram Account—Fast.* Plann. Retrieved April 18, 2023, from https://www.plannthat.com/revive-a-dead-instagram-account/.

Meta.com. Updated Features for Video Ads. (n.d.). Meta.com. Retrieved April 18, 2023, from https://www.facebook.com/business/news/updated-features-for-video-ads.

Meta Business Learn. (n.d.). Meta Blueprint. Retrieved April 18, 2023, from https://www.facebook.com/business/learn.

MOVR. (Mobile Overview Report) Quarterly Report. (October–December 2014). (n.d.). [PDF]. ScientiaMobile. https://data.wurfl.io/MOVR/pdf/2014_q4/MOVR_2014_q4.pdf.

Nielsen. (2022, July 21). *The Reviews Are In: Yelp Users Are Four-Star Consumers | Nielsen.* https://www.nielsen.com/insights/2013/the-reviews-are-in-yelp-users-are-four-star-consumers/.

Oberthaler, K. (2022, August 25). 52 content marketing statistics (with key takeaways). *Ziflow.* Retrieved April 18, 2023, from https://www.ziflow.com/blog/content-marketing-statistics.

Patterson, B. (2022, December 1). 5 Yelp facts business owners should know (but most don't). *MarTech.* Retrieved April 18, 2023, from https://martech.org/5-yelp-facts-business-owners-should-know/.

Philipp. (2023). Maxwell the Cat / Spinning Cat. *Know Your Meme.* https://knowyourmeme.com/memes/maxwell-the-cat-spinning-cat#fn5.

Rainmaker.FM. Seth Godin on When You Should Start Marketing Your Product, Service, or Idea. (2020, March 30). Rainmaker.FM. Retrieved April 18, 2023, from https://rainmaker.fm/audio/lede/seth-godin-marketing/.

Rozario-Ospino, J. (2019, October 22). Social Video Trends: Marketer Insights for 2020. *Animoto video maker—Stand out on social media. Easily.* https://animoto.com/blog/news/social-video-trends-marketers-2020.

SEM Rush. Top Websites. (n.d.). SEM Rush. Retrieved April 18, 2023, from https://www.semrush.com/website/top/global/all/.

Silcoff, M. (2022, July 20). Dove's Latest Stand in the Virtue Wars. *New York Times.* Retrieved April 18, 2023, from https://www.nytimes.com/2022/07/20/magazine/dove-advertising-beauty.html.

Sonnenberg, A. (2022). When to Pause Your Social Media Channels. *Agorapulse*. https://www.agorapulse.com/blog/pause-social-media -channels/.

Sprout Social. (2023, March 9). *Social Media Trends for 2022 and Beyond | Sprout Social*. https://sproutsocial.com/insights/index/#get-us-report.

Today, S. R. U. (2017, April 6). Massachusetts man has to pay more than $30K for negative Yelp review. *USA TODAY*. Retrieved April 18, 2023, from https://www.usatoday.com/story/news/nation-now/2017/04/06/mass -man-has-pay-more-than-30k-negative-yelp-review/100113022/.

Vaughan, P. (2022, October 14). *How to Create Detailed Buyer Personas for Your Business*. Hubspot. Retrieved April 18, 2023, from https://blog .hubspot.com/marketing/buyer-persona-research.

Vocell, J. (2022, May 6). Personalized Calls to Action Perform 202% Better Than Basic CTAs [New Data]. *Hubspot*. Retrieved April 18, 2023, from https://blog.hubspot.com/marketing/personalized-calls-to-action-convert -better-data#sm.000awoxgniktcoi11jl2et1nit4os.

Ward, M., and Akhtar, A. (2023, January 18). How to write an email subject line that catches a hiring manager's attention. *Business Insider*. Retrieved April 18, 2023, from https://www.businessinsider.com/how-to-write-an -email-subject-line-2015-1.

Wigmore, I. (2019). attention economy. *WhatIs.com*. https://www.techtarget .com/whatis/definition/attention-economy#.

Witt, T. (2023). Social media video statistics marketers need to know for 2023. *Sprout Social*. https://sproutsocial.com/insights/social-media-video -statistics/.

Index

About the Author

Social media is **Peg Fitzpatrick**'s passion. She works with global brands and leaders spearheading successful social media campaigns for companies like Motorola, Audi, Google, and Virgin. She was the first Head of Social Strategy for Canva. She's been a brand ambassador for McDonald's, Kimpton Hotels, and Adobe Spark.

Peg is the co-author of *The Art of Social Media: Power Tips for Power Users* with Guy Kawasaki. She's contributed to two other books, *What the Plus! Google+ for the Rest of Us* and *APE: Author, Publisher, Entrepreneur: How to Publish a Book.*

Peg is a sought-after social media speaker. She's presented at Hubspot's INBOUND conference, Alt Summit, BlogHer, BlogHer Pro, and Social Media Examiner's Social Media Marketing World, as well as been a keynote speaker at SXSW with Guy Kawasaki.